"*Reaching People under 40 w*
a contemporary classic. Eddi(
and their leaders, clergy and lu,, ، ، ، ، ، their approach to ministry and
outreach. This new *Reaching People under 30* edition retains the meat of
the original, but provides new material for the rapidly changing times in
which we live and minister. The added voices of Cornell Thomas and Paul
Anderson provide a much-needed perspective. Churches must shift from
monocultural to multicultural in order to thrive in the future and engage
people of every generation."

　　　—Larry Hovis, Executive Coordinator, Cooperative Baptist
　　　Fellowship of North Carolina

"Major shifts are being experienced in church life today and with them
come the usual tensions between the old and young. Through this book,
Eddie Hammett guides a church and its leadership through this foreign
territory of change and transition, and he does it with a pastor's heart
and the expertise of a congregational coach. Every church will face this
challenge sooner or later. Eddie's book offers you the opportunity to have
a 'Coach in Residence'."

　　　—Scott Wagoner, Deep River Friends Meeting, High Point,
　　　North Carolina

"Once again Eddie Hammett has written a book that is relevant to the
everyday issues facing the church. This book should be required reading
for every church leader and pastor."

　　　—Kent Rogers, First United Methodist Church, Wichita, Kansas

"Whether you prefer research and statistics, opinion polls, or anecdotal
narrative, you will appreciate this book. Eddie has written a thorough,
thought-provoking, enlightening, and practical text for all congregational
leaders facing the challenges of ministry in this century. He has done the
research for us, and he adds his own wisdom from years of experience
working with congregational leadership as a coach, educator, and
mentor. As a Presbyterian who works in an ecumenical setting, I know
how important it is that Christian leaders listen to the stories and ideas
of people from different faith traditions. Although most of Eddie's stories
and theological perspective comes out of the Baptist tradition, his writing
permeates denominational boundaries. This book covers it all! Eddie gives
congregational leaders a blueprint for transforming their churches while
keeping every generation included, nurtured, and engaged. Though there
is no miracle fix-it for ministry today, this book is a powerful tool."

　　　—Peggy Hinds, Executive Director of the Kentucky Council
　　　of Churches

"This is such a great and needed tool for churches today. What makes this work a necessary tool for churches is first found in the fact that it is very practical, with examples that can assist churches in being effective for members of any age. I personally appreciated the coaching questions throughout the book. For me the questions took this from just being good information to causing me to critically think about the concepts I just read and how they can be implemented in my own context. I also appreciate the fact that this book isn't written from the standpoint of someone who has only studied this subject from the outside. This book is written from the trenches by someone who is doing the work of restoring hope in our churches and is sharing his wisdom and insight so more churches can be healthy and impact the world for the kingdom of God. If you are considering reading this book, then go for it. You will be glad that you did."

—Jason Lumpkin, Collaboration Church, Atlanta

"Being church today is as complex and dynamic as ever. Eddie Hammett provides profound insights that offer practical guidance to congregations committed to doing the work of Christ's church across generations. This book is a must-read for anyone desiring to make deep investments in the people of God of every age. Timeless truths are brought to light in a timely manner with an eye toward the health and well-being of congregations. I wish everyone in our church would read this book, absorb its wisdom, and live into its challenges!"

—Stephen Cook, Pastor, Second Baptist Church, Memphis

"What I appreciated most about this book is how Eddie Hammett gives voice to the tension and issues that frequently divide congregations today and embroils them in conflict. There are some in the church who more or less recommend choosing either those under 30 or those over 60 to minister to because the differences seem too great to overcome, but Eddie advocates instead developing win-win strategies for both groups."

—Herman R. Yoos, Bishop, South Carolina Synod,
Evangelical Lutheran Church in America

"Eddie Hammett has done it again! He's taken the basics of a wonderful book, updated the thoughts to today, and brings a treasured and timely resource to the church. Since the 30 somethings of today are quite different than the 40 somethings when the book first came out, Eddie has rewritten strategic portions to give us fresh ideas and insights. I'm grateful for his coaching and leadership. I'm grateful for his love for the church and the Christ!"

—Bo Prosser, Coordinator of Organizational Relationships,
Cooperative Baptist Fellowship

"Edward Hammett has had a profound and lasting impact upon my ministry. The most influential work of Hammett, in my opinion, has been *The Gathered and Scattered Church*. After reading his book I knew I had to meet this man who crystallized for me what I was struggling with in ministry. His work has been both an inspiration and a source of fresh ideas and insights. Edward's newest book, *Reaching People under 30 while Keeping People over 60* will be a welcome addition to pastors and lay leaders who are looking for strategies to sustain church growth. The blending of Traditionalists, Boomers , X'ers and Millennials is a challenge for any pastor. Take the time to read and digest this work and then invite your leaders to study it with you. Your thinking and ministry will be transformed as you discover new ways of doing ministry."

—Geoffrey V. Guns, Second Calvary Baptist Church,
Norfolk, Virginia

"Effective church leaders need many tools to make the most of their opportunities. Sometimes a whole shelf of resources is needed, given the challenges leaders face. On such a shelf, this book goes right in the center. On one end of the shelf a set of titles speak to the changing age composition of our communities and congregations. On the other end, a set of titles explain church life cycles and the organizational challenges aging presents. This book is an expanded version of a very helpful original. In it, Eddie describes a gift from his grandmother: a real-life experience that inspires older members to see how their seniority gives them the power to open their church to others as no one else can. That story alone is worth the price of the book. Younger members do not have the patience or staying power to engineer needed changes in most churches. Older members seldom appreciate how very different the needs and interests of their younger members are. Hammett describes these differences with the clarity of an experienced consultant. His coaching and books have helped many churches."

—Carl George, Author, Consultant, Church Planter

"Eddie has the pulse of the twenty-first–century church. *Reaching People under 30 while Keeping People over 60* accurately identifies every pastor's challenge. He presents new approaches that adequately mix theory and practice built upon a theological framework suitable for clergy and laity alike."

—John Hill, Winterville Free Will Baptist Church, Winterville,
North Carolina

- Liberal / ecumenical
- Very little Scripture mentioned
- Bad take on Jesus (?) and the Church (?)
- A book about Jesus' church uses "C.E." dating
- Ch 1 & 2 filled with other peoples statistics, stories, and ideas.

  Lots of vague words but no specifics at all about
    "reaching people <30 while keeping people >60"

  So far just a long-winded book saying nothing new and
    yet to offer any actual ideas.

Reaching
People under 30
while Keeping
People over 60

Creating Community Across Generations

EDWARD H. HAMMETT

WITH Paul L. Anderson AND Cornell Thomas

Key Leadership Resources from
www.TCPBooks.info

George W. Bullard Jr.

Every Congregation Needs a Little Conflict

FaithSoaring Churches

Pursuing the Full Kingdom Potential of Your Congregation

Richard L. Hamm

Recreating the Church

Edward H. Hammett

Recovering Hope for your Church:

Moving beyond Maintenance and Missional to Incarnational Engagement

Making Shifts without Making Waves:

A Coach Approach to Soulful Leadership

Reaching People under 30 while Keeping People over 60:

Creating Community across Generations

Spiritual Leadership in a Secular Age:

Building Bridges Instead of Barriers

Gregory L. Hunt

Leading Congregations through Crisis

Cynthia Woolever and Deborah Bruce

Leadership That Fits Your Church:

What Kind of Pastor for What Kind of Congregation

The Sustaining Pastoral Excellence Peer Learning Team

So Much Better:

How Thousands of Pastors Help Each Other Thrive

Larry McSwain

The Calling of Congregational Leadership:

Being, Knowing, Doing Ministry

For more leadership resources, see
www.TheColumbiaPartnership.org
www.TCPBooks.info

Other Books by Edward H. Hammett

(available at www.amazon.com and www.transformingsolutions.org)

Making the Church Work:
Converting the Church For the 21st Century, 2nd ed.

The Gathered and Scattered Church:
Equipping Believers for the 21st Century, 2nd ed.

Reframing Spiritual Formation:
Discipleship in an Unchurched Culture

Spiritual Leadership in a Secular Age:
Building Bridges Instead of Barriers

The Gospel According to Starbucks
Leonard Sweet, contributor

Making Shifts without Making Waves:
A Coach Approach to Soulful Leadership

Recovering Hope for Your Church:
Moving Beyond Maintenance & Missional To Incarnational Engagement

You can order audio and video presentations, small-group leader guides and PowerPoint presentations for some of these books online.

✳ You can also find FREE handouts and podcasts to support your journey.

Visit www.TransformingSolutions.org

Copyright ©2015 by Edward H. Hammett

All rights reserved. For permission to reuse content, please contact Copyright Clearance Center, 222 Rosewood Drive, Danvers, MA 01923, (978) 750-8400, www.copyright.com.

Bible quotations, unless otherwise noted, are from the *New Revised Standard Version Bible*, copyright 1989, Division of Christian Education of the National Council of the Churches of Christ in the United States of America. Used by permission. All rights reserved.

Cover art: Getty Images

Cover and interior design: Elizabeth Wright

TCPBooks.com

Print: 9780827233041   EPUB: 9780827233058   EPDF: 9780827233065

Library of Congress Cataloging-in-Publication Data

Hammett, Edward H.

 Reaching people under 30 while keeping people over 60 : creating community across generations / by Edward H. Hammett, with Paul L. Anderson and Cornell Thomas. — First [edition].

    pages cm

Includes bibliographical references and index.

 ISBN 978-0-8272-3304-1 (pbk. : alk. paper)

1. Communities—Religious aspects—Christianity. 2. Intergenerational relations—Religious aspects—Christianity. I. Title. II. Title: Reaching people under thirty while keeping people over sixty.

BV4517.5.H36 2015

262.001'7—dc23

                    2015033130

Contents

Editor's Foreword

Inspiration and Wisdom for
21st-Century Christian Leaders

You have chosen wisely in deciding to read and learn from a book published by TCP Books from The Columbia Partnership.

We publish for

- Congregational leaders who desire to serve with greater faithfulness, effectiveness, and innovation.
- Christian ministers who seek to pursue and sustain excellence in ministry service.
- Members of congregations who desire to reach their full kingdom potential.
- Christian leaders who desire to use a coach approach in their ministry.
- Denominational and parachurch leaders who want to come alongside affiliated congregations in a servant leadership role.
- Consultants and coaches who desire to increase their learning concerning the congregations and Christian leaders they serve.

TCP Books is a sharing knowledge strategy of The Columbia Partnership, a community of Christian leaders seeking to transform the capacity of the North American Church to pursue and sustain vital Christ-centered ministry.

Primarily serving congregations, denominations, educational institutions, leadership development programs, and parachurch organizations, TCP also seeks to connect with individuals, businesses, and other organizations seeking a Christ-centered spiritual focus.

We welcome your comments on these books, and we welcome your suggestions for new subject areas and authors we ought to consider.

George Bullard, Senior Editor, TCP Books
The Columbia Partnership
332 Valley Springs Road, Columbia, SC 292236934
Voice: 803.622.0923, Website: www.TheColumbiaPartnership.org

Foreword

I've known Eddie Hammett for more than two decades. During that time I've watched him hone his coaching skills and develop into one of the best church coaches I know. What I really like about Eddie is that he keeps current with our ever-changing world. His adaptability is most recently evident in this revised version of the older book *Reaching People under 40 while Keeping People Over 60*.

I was privileged to write the Foreword for that book because I thought the principles in it were spot on. Well, the world has radically changed again since publication of the first book. We have been introduced to the most secular generation and culture I've ever seen. In wholesale fashion these under thirties are avoiding the established church in favor of the likes of Starbucks. While spiritual, they don't have a religious bone in their body. We thought the Gen-X crowd was anti-establishment. But to our surprise they are tame compared to the under thirty crowd. People under thirty require totally new approaches to outreach, worship, and discipleship, and all of them will upset the average person over sixty. I know because I attend one of those churches reaching this under thirty crowd in record numbers. So Eddie's book is profoundly relevant to the current crises.

Now add to the new mix the multicultural, multiracial changes over the past decade and you have a recipe for disaster for most established churches. Eddie not only addresses both issues in this revised version of his book but also has coauthored the book with two African American friends who offer perspectives from differing generations.

I was born in 1939 into an Ozzie and Harriet world. Most people were baptized, married, and buried by a church. In most areas of the country the church played such a significant role in the culture that America was considered to be a "churched" culture. Even though you might not have attended church, you felt as if you should. In many ways twentieth-century America was a "one size fits all" culture. And to top that off, most of my world was white. I had never seen a Muslim or an Asian person in my life. My high school was integrated my senior year, but with only one black student name Elmo. Elmo was elected president of the student body. Compare that to what we've seen in Ferguson, Baltimore, and the like.

All that has changed today. No longer is America considered a white, Ozzie and Harriet "churched" culture. No longer does life revolve around the church. No longer do people expect to be baptized, married, and buried by a church. For the first time in our history, civil marriages outnumber church weddings in some parts of the country. New parents are far less likely to bring their babies to church to be baptized just to please their parents. No one feels guilty if they aren't in church on Sunday, not even most Christians. As a result, the public's knowledge of Christianity has significantly waned. Many people are cynical toward organized religion or they are cultural Christians.

The cultural revolution has been so effective that in order to survive, much less thrive, established churches must learn how to reach and disciple people from this unchurched diverse culture without losing the over sixty generation. Few established churches are winning this challenge. Some simply aren't willing to entertain any level of change. Others are so frightened by the cultural changes that all they can do is retreat behind their walls. Still others are so comfortable with what they have that they consider congregational death more desirable than disruption of their comfort.

In all fairness to established churches, the changes they need to make to reach the new world are so daunting that the best of us wilt a bit under the prospect. But here is where the authors' work offers hope to established churches. They describe a win-win strategy for reaching this new culture while maintaining the established church.

What I like about this book is every section is augmented by some of the best coaching, grounded in concrete, practical church examples that every church leader in an established church will quickly recognize as part of their dilemma. The authors recognize that many churches have no clue how to start, and so they probe the everyday issues facing churches that are fixated on the past, yet desire to reach into the future.

Those who read this book and follow its coaching will find a win-win approach to reaching this new culture.

Bill Easum
The Effective Church Group
www.effectivechurch.com

Preface

Reaching People under 40 while Keeping People over 60 (2007 edition) has touched churches of many denominations across the country and in a few foreign countries. Leaders, both lay and clergy, have found value in the practical principles and tools about *Being Church for All Generations*. I'm grateful for all the readers, churches, and leaders who have embraced this challenge and watched God bear much fruit. Amid a host of seminars and workshops across the country, I've heard leaders struggling not only with "being church for all generations" but also "being church in an increasingly diverse world." I recall a middle-aged, seasoned pastor in the Midwest who came up to me after the seminar and asked for some of my time. I was delighted to listen to her story. She served as pastor for a midsize church that once was homogenous and now "the community is changing rapidly, and the church does not know how to deal with the growing diversity of ethnic groups, value systems, economic realities, different family systems, and a host of different beliefs and views of spirituality." After I heard her struggles with "learning to lead amid diversity without destroying their church," she asked with tenderness in her voice and a tear in her eye, "Can you help us know how to create community across generations and diversity?"

That conversation, and many other similar conversations, over the last seven years provide the distinctives in this updated edition. Even as I work on this revision, the world is filled with protests from people of all cultures and ethnicities due to what some see as injustices around racial, political, and law enforcement issues. Ferguson, Missouri, and Berkeley, California, are only two examples where African-American young men have been shot and killed, often by an older white police officer. As this goes to press our country has experienced the tragedy on the Emmanuel 9 in Charleston, SC. A brutal and senseless murder during a local church Bible Study. Where is the reconciliation, redemptive voice, and ministry of the church? Emmanuel AME church is showing to the world a glimpse of living from and into grace and redemption as they live out of deep faith and trust in God and create community across the diversities of culture and generations. I am excited to have two friends, former students and professional colleagues, Paul Anderson and Cornell Thomas, as contributors to this edition. They bring an urgently-needed African-American perspective from differing generations.

What Differences Will Readers See?

While this volume attempts to stay loyal to the principles and practices introduced in the 2007 edition, we are also committed to bringing the challenge of leading and being church amid diversity into the manuscript. You will find about fifty pages of new material, and in many places throughout the book, you will see guidance for being church amid increasing elements of diversity. Since we are addressing people under 30 and the increasing diversities in our culture we are retitling this revision. *Reaching People Under 30 while Keeping People Over 60: Creating Community Across the Generations* sustains proven principles from the previous book but builds upon these from new challenges and lessons learned.

We will address several topics that surface repeated in our experiences and travels: (1) What are the distinctives of doing church in a multicultural, multiethnic, multigenerational community? What are the challenges? What are the benefits? (2) What are the challenges of creating a parallel structure for the younger generation in a multicultural and multigenerational faith community? (3) How does a multisite, multiworship service church retain focus, community, and unity without forced uniformity?

You will also find supplemental information on my personal website that allows you to stay current with teaching supplements from the authors and other readers. My hope is that this information will bring freshness, teaching materials, and connections with other leaders and churches facing the challenges reviewed in the book from our own personal and professional ministries inside and outside the walls of the church. We want to speak to this topic in the framework *in*, *through*, and *as* the church. (I speak more to the biblical framework of these issues in *Spiritual Leadership in a Secular Age*.)

Acknowledgments

Reaching People under 30 while Keeping People over 60 is a personal book for me in that I've lived through the struggles and successes shared in this manuscript. The insights shared here come from my professional and personal journey experienced over the last thirty-five-plus years of involvement in the local churches in various volunteer and paid leadership positions. These lessons began in my home church and in my own family of origin and extended family.

The title of this book came from an elderly lady in eastern North Carolina who desires to remain anonymous. I knew when she asked me during an interview, "How can my church reach people under forty while keeping people over sixty?" that she had described the challenge of many churches in North America. I wrote an article by that title for *NetResults Magazine*, and the e-mails and phone calls poured in. The book was then born through seminars, online forums, and countless coaching conversations with churches across denominational lines throughout North America.

I have invited two of my former students—both colleagues and friends—to contribute to this manuscript to bring a younger and multicultural perspective. Both are engaged in multiethnic and multicultural and multigenerational ministries. They are seasoned and yet fellow learners on the journey of knowing how best to lead in and minister to a diverse, fast-paced world. Cornell Thomas, a Millennial, is involved in inner-city ministries in Charlotte, North Carolina.. Cornell is married and has three beautiful, energetic daughters. Paul Anderson, a Boomer, is founding pastor of The Fountain, a multicultural, fast-growing congregation in Raleigh, North Carolina. He and his wife are parents of two creative millennial men.

Because this book is a part of a series of my books seeking to speak to "a church in need of conversion," I will reference my other books here. I simply am trying to acknowledge that many of the ideas presented here are complex and have received additional treatment in my other writings. We hope this book offers everyone greater understanding for the differences in our generations and cultures. We all need one another for healing and movement toward health and wholeness. We can teach one another so much if we can only remain open and seek to understand and be understood.

A final note of appreciation for Judi Hayes, Trent Butler, Judith Pierson, and Gail Stobaugh, who helped with editing, the support of The Columbia Partnership, Chalice Press, and the continuing support I receive from Cooperative Baptist Fellowship of North Carolina where I serve as church and clergy coach. I am founder and president of Transforming Solutions, LLC. We are committed to offering coaching and consulting services to for-profit and nonprofit organizations, denominations, and churches across the country. We work with our clients to discover and implement solutions that bring transformation of heart and organizational structures to ensure a deeper impact on the culture in which we are called to work.

Edward Hammett
Hendersonville, North Carolina
August 2015
www.transformingsolutions.org

Introduction

A woman came up to me after a conference at a church in eastern North Carolina. She had listened attentively and was clearly concerned about her church. She said, "I just need to know one thing: How do we reach the people under forty without losing those over sixty?"

Many established churches are facing a number of challenges in today's increasingly secular and diverse culture. No longer are North American churches living and serving in a churched culture. Recent research has suggested that the number of unchurched persons in America increased 92 percent between 2005 and 2014. Not only do we have a category of "nones" (those who claim no affiliation to a church), but we also now have the "dones" too! (those who have been active in church leadership in the past but now are "done with the church" for a variety of reasons. We now find ourselves in a pluralistic, often pagan culture that is more often than not insensitive to traditional church culture values. Traditional church times, programs, buildings, music, staffing, dress, and manners are frequently diminished rather than elevated. Such a shift in many communities creates a challenge to church growth and church health. It seems that satisfying the needs of one group creates barriers to reaching another group. So, many are asking, "How do you keep people over sixty years of age—who often hold traditional church culture values—while at the same time reaching people under thirty—who often hold postmodern values on a vast array of subjects?" If a church is interested in growing, this situation and generation (the Millennials, who generally became adults in the first decade of this century) become a major challenge—one that confronts most established churches today.

This book contains some of the understanding I've gained from more than thirty years of church ministry and denominational service. We'll look at the church as it seeks to function in a new world—what has changed, what has not, and why reaching people today is so much more difficult than it once was. We'll look at the differences in the generations we serve, and we'll look at postmodernism—not just generational differences but a global change involving a shifting demographic, value system, and understandings and expressions of faith and spirituality. Then we'll look at what a church can do in this new age to help the church survive—even thrive. Finally, we'll celebrate what God is doing in the church today.

Some grieve the demise of the church. I'm not one of those persons. My 2014 *Recovering Hope for Your Church* gives all the signs of hope I see. In fact, I have more hope for the church than I have ever had. I'm certain the journey of recovery and reconnecting with this modern-day culture will be tough for most, but it is essential to carry on the message of hope, healing, and reconciliation into the next generation. Since the journey of revitalizing and retooling churches for a 21st-century world is not a quick fix and is complex I wrote this book that lays out eight basic principles and concepts. *Spiritual Leadership in a Secular Age* provides information about the rapidly changing culture in which we minister; *Making Shifts Without Making Ways* provides leadership a toolkit to implement the principles and concepts; and *Recovering Hope for Your Church* frames a congregational process of education and coaching that focuses and mobilizes a congregation around God's call, their discernment, gifting and passions to be and do church in unique ministry contexts.

Edward H. Hammett

Lessons Learned from Churches Using
Reaching People under 40 while Keeping People over 60

1. The principles work when you work the principles.
2. Introducing the book to staff and leaders and dialoguing with them about it before the congregation hears about it adds support and needed legitimizers.
3. Using the book as a teaching/dialogue tool during small-group studies brings insight, encouragement, hope, and opportunities for intergenerational dialogue.
4. Engaging in an ongoing coaching relationship ensures sustained momentum and helps those involved gain clarity, establish focus, and set priorities.
5. Providing a congregational seminar generates excitement, deepens ownership of the principles, and illustrates the impact.
6. The work is hard but can ensure the future of a congregation for the next generation.
7. The degree of effectiveness depends on the level of intentionality, follow-through, and focus of the remnant leadership.
8. Engaging in individual and group prayer provides an essential element of spiritual discernment and unity to keep moving forward

PART I: Understanding the Church's Multidimensional Challenges

1

Pastors Burn Out, and Churches Die

If you grew up in the church, as I did, you can probably remember a different day in the church. Doing church was pretty easy. Programs ruled. Everyone participated in just about everything, and most congregations and communities were homogenous. Everybody used the same curriculum, studied the same Scripture. Whatever the church leaders asked the congregation to do, they did. Well, almost. It probably wasn't as wonderful and easy as we sometimes recall it, but it was a different day.

The Dying Church

We lived in a churched culture. We counted our progress by the four *B*s: bodies, budgets, baptisms, and buildings. We were usually more concerned about where we would put all the new babies than with whether we had the budget to keep the lights on and the staff paid.

Most of our competition was friendly rivalry with the church down the street to see who had the best youth ministry. Almost everyone went to church somewhere, at least on Sunday morning. If not, they at least knew they should. When you visited newcomers or hardcore nonattenders about coming to church, they knew the church language, knew what you were talking about, and appreciated your visit. An annual revival was certain to draw a crowd and reach some people—perhaps some the church had been praying for and trying to reach for years.

This wasn't just a simpler time of your childhood memories. It was really like that. Churches really were thriving in a friendly environment. A denomination could program for A Million More in '54 (a Southern Baptist emphasis).

That day is gone. What once worked, no longer does. Hardly anyone has a revival anymore because it's almost impossible to get busy members there, much less the unchurched. Many churches no longer have a night of planned visitation for the same reasons. Church members often won't come, and church guests sometimes fail to appreciate surprise visits. The age of knowing what to do, how to do it, getting great support, and seeing results is a thing of the past.

Perhaps even worse is that many people today have a negative image of Christians, of denominations, and of the church in general. In the past, even people not involved in church had great respect for it. Today many secular adults see the church as neutral or negative. Before someone can be reached for Christ, that negative image must be overcome. Often this takes a long time and is accomplished only by gradually building relationships.

Cultural Challenges

Culture is now specific to a group. That's what culture is—shared values, characteristics, beliefs, goals, and practices. Church attenders tend to find people much like themselves in the church. They feel comfortable there. A few decades ago, most people who attended church had that experience. Today, at the same time the world seems smaller—meaning we have access to products, information, events, and even travel with relative ease almost anywhere in the world—our world is also much more diverse. The world has come to our doorstep with a myriad of beliefs, customs, habits, ideas, and ways of understanding. People know where they feel comfortable and where they don't, where they fit in and where they feel like a stranger.

Each community, church, people group, family, or Sunday school class has a culture created by its participants over a period of time. People who helped fashion it usually embrace it and value it, while those who were not part of creating it often feel alienated or even repelled by that culture. This is often one reason a newcomer to a group doesn't fit in and often doesn't join the group. (I discuss the impact of culture on the church in more detail in my books *Spiritual Leadership in a Secular Age* and *Making the Church Work*.[1])

In the last several decades, cities, states, organizations, and institutions have found themselves challenged by a growing multiculturalism and a pluralistic society. Language, rituals, traditions, and values are not as clear and readily accepted as when we were in a church culture with people from the same or similar backgrounds and belief systems. Now the world has shifted—families have changed, and schools have children who may speak many different languages (but not ours), and who may come from a number of different countries. Businesses have become culturally sensitive, while churches for the most part haven't changed at all. In fact, many churches believe that remaining the same as they were when their culture was formed in the 1950s or earlier is their godly responsibility. For many, they are not looking for a church but rather for a life mission.

Cultures Coming Together

John Bingham makes a fascinating observation. He wrote that places of worship and sporting events lead the way as places modern Britons are most likely to mix with people of other races, classes, and generations:

Groundbreaking new analyses of the friendship networks of almost 4,300 people aged from 13 to 80 has identified churches and sporting events as the last bastions of neighborliness and integration in Britain. Overall, it found that churches and other places of worship are more successful than any other social setting at bringing people of different backgrounds together, well ahead of gatherings as parties, meetings, weddings, or venues such as pubs or clubs.[2]

Church is a vital institution and experience in our increasingly diverse world. I suspect what is true in Britain is equally true in the United States.

Don't misunderstand. I'm not suggesting that churches change their biblical message. I am suggesting the church is intricately valuable in our culture when it connects faith in the midst of the diversity. I am also suggesting that we might need to consider altering our methodology so that those in our new world might be able to hear the Good News in ways they can understand and embrace it. That's really what this book is all about. Ultimately, it's about reaching people, evangelism, making disciples, carrying out Jesus' command to reach people. Here's the pinch: when you begin trying to make the needed adjustments, church members—usually sixty and over from the church culture, and certainly of that value system regardless of age—become angry, resistant, intolerant of change. They withhold their money and leadership. They vote collectively to keep things the way they are, for, "If the way things are is good enough for me, it should be good enough for others." Now what does a church or leader do?

In most communities, if the congregation decides to keep the over-sixty crowd satisfied (to keep their money?), the church will not grow numerically. In time, the congregation will die (unless the community demographic can support a church focused on senior adult ministry). In all probability, keeping the sixty-plus crowd happy almost always assures that the church will reach few new people under the age of thirty. (By the way, those who are fifty or so are transitional persons—some join those with under-thirty characteristics, and others join the over-sixty group and their characteristics.)

The reality here is that most denominations have not been reaching many people under thirty for decades. Most people thirty and under are from a world with different values, traditions, rituals, and personal preferences—a different culture. Tension escalates, leaders resign or become disgruntled, money begins to dry up, and the church community becomes more and more introverted—focused on caring for people within the church rather than being concerned about reaching out to those outside the church to people they don't understand and really aren't sure they want in the church anyway. So begins a cycle of maintenance and survival for most churches. What's a leader to do?

Leadership Challenges and Solutions

While principles remain intact for an effective New Testament church, the design of programming and the approach to leadership face many seismic shifts. Quite often these shifts prove threatening; most always they bear fruit for those who persevere in leadership development. Both volunteers and paid staff find themselves overwhelmed by challenges in this situation. They love the church and most sincerely want the church to grow.

At the same time, they experience conflict: church is a place where they are comfortable, where they come for fellowship with lifelong friends, where they worship in a setting and style that easily helps them connect with God. In my travels across the country I increasingly hear a refrain from clergy and lay leaders alike: "I'm tired of working harder and not making any progress." "I am tired of fighting with those who want to stay the same while my call is to fulfill the Great Commission." "I just cannot do any more. My plate is full and running over. I've got to have a break!"

To reach out to younger people may mean that this place of familiarity will change so radically that they no longer know how to function, and so they are torn. Do they change to reach a new generation, or do they keep doing what once worked but no longer does. Do they welcome under thirties into their fellowship, or do they watch the church continue to decline and perhaps even die? Others feel they are not honoring their past and present leaders or family members if they allow things to be changed. Still others control the pace of change as much as possible in the church because they cannot control the rapid rate of change in their workplace or community. The challenges church leaders face are immense.

The solution is often complicated and messy. Heart-held beliefs and identity-giving rituals and practices may have to change. Tension may erupt, challenging relationships. Church leaders may be torn between loyalty to friends and taking a risk to find a new way of doing church. Generations of family members within a church may strongly disagree. Personal preferences may have to be discarded to try to reach younger people. Even with the best planning and research, change is a risk. Your change may attract younger people, and it may not. Trading the secure for the unknown may mean losing the older generation, while it may or may not reach the younger crowd.

Transitioning puts heavy demands on church leaders, both paid and volunteer. The church must continue as it always has, which is demanding in itself, while researching, dreaming, praying, seeking God's guidance, and giving birth to a new direction—all at the same time. Workloads and stress may increase exponentially.

While stress levels and workloads are rising, leaders must continually communicate love for all. Leaders are to demonstrate a desire to hear each member and an effort to communicate openly with the entire church. They must find a way to be inclusive with existing members while knowing that many will dislike any changes that are made. Such an inclusive spirit is both Christlike and practical. Jesus' example is to love everyone, even enemies. Church leaders need to remember that opposition in the church isn't usually the enemy. People within the church who disagree may have the same goal in mind but different ideas about how to get there. Alienating senior adult leaders may mean that they withdraw their substantial influence and finances.

Cultural Sensitivity Creates Community

Church leaders who are sensitive to what is happening both inside and outside the walls of the church have a growing awareness that the world outside the walls of the established church is changing and that new methods and strategies are needed to remain relevant. Such sensitive leaders have probably also noticed, over time, that the pews are not as full as they once were, fewer children come to the front for children's sermons, not as many high school students are recognized in graduation events each year, the pastor is performing and members are attending more funerals than weddings, across the congregation on any given Sunday a lot more gray heads appear than blacks, browns, and blondes.

The Builder Generation's aging out. Church and denominational loyalists, we love local church ministry. Proudly we narrate how we built our church as institution and as facilities. We explain the way it was done in the fifties and the sixties, almost unaware we Builders are dying out. These are the leaders who were around for the "million more in '54" (a Baptist campaign) when the church was thriving, growing, building new church buildings. Institutions and publishing agencies were soaring. During that time churches basically looked alike, studied about the same thing, had basically the same type worship service. Like it or not, that's just not true anymore. The Builder Generation, people over sixty, are beginning to age out of leadership pretty rapidly. With them goes the tithing base and the leadership base. With their retirement, funds are diminishing in the local church. Today a growing number of churches are merging because they do not have enough members to keep the doors open. Other churches are "building poor." That is, they have a small congregation in a large, aging facility. Maintenance and building upkeep surpass their budget. Many churches and denominations are downsizing staff and merging congregations due to economic struggles. Money always talks. I don't care what business you're in, what church you're in, too often we don't pay attention until the money drops. Membership can drop, but as long as we've got a lot of rich people or a big endowment, we're OK. When the money starts to drop, we pay attention. And the money is dropping. The tight economy might just be of God. It is forcing churches and denominations to streamline and "cut away the fat" of our organizations.

I was at a meeting of 121 church leaders from twenty-one denominations. One of the leaders asked, "How many of you in this room have already experienced an economic drop or a downsizing of your staff in the denominations in which you serve?" Everybody except one person raised a hand. During the dialogue and debriefing session, the person who did not raise his hand , said,

"It hasn't happened yet, but it's coming." The dialogue that ensued that day confirmed what most of us already knew: we're losing our Builder Generation. They're taking their money and leadership with them, and we haven't replaced them with people under thirty. Mutual understanding of culture helps in creating community.

Ignoring Cultural Changes at Your Own Risk

The longer churches delay adapting their structures and programming, not their message, to the changing world around them, the more difficult church life becomes. When a church moves from plateaued to declining, it will first try to maintain the same level of ministries; but this becomes increasingly difficult. Leaders are harder to find. The faithful few are stretched. Limited time, energy, and resources, which could have been directed toward finding a future, are now focused on survival. At this point the church has moved from mission to maintenance. Carey Nieuwhof, a pastor in Canada who speaks and writes about culture and change, explains "12 Cultural Trends Church Leaders Can't Ignore (But Might)": *Liberal*

Online as a New Default
Wifi and Smartphones
Dialogue
Loyalty
Lack of guilt
Declining trust in authority
Declining trust in institutions
Personalized, eclectic spirituality
A desire for greater purpose
Personal mission
Trust in user reviews
The death of cash and cheques[3]

Churches through the years have faced change in a variety of ways. At one time in recent church history, the biggest challenge was a changing or transitioning neighborhood. Churches decided to move, to embrace the newcomers, or perhaps to have two campuses. Change wasn't easy, but it wasn't too hard to understand. The challenge today is more complicated. Understanding how postmoderns, Millennials, and Gen X want to worship is complicated. It may mean a lot more than doing away with the hymnals in favor of a big screen. Just figuring out how to change is a challenge. Even change with the best intentions may not guarantee the desired results. Change is likely going to be ongoing as churches learn to connect with people in a secular, unchurched culture. Still, for a strong percentage of churches, change is essential for survival.[4]

Such challenges of change are real and ever-present in the hearts and minds of church leaders. The leaders fear moving forward, for they may destabilize a group or church that is already suffering. They are not sure how to take calculated risks, which risks to take, or whether they have the skill set needed to introduce and manage this cultural change.

Choosing to Survive

Often they opt just to survive and keep people as happy as they can. In making this decision, they continue to do much good. Individuals and families inside the church receive much-needed ministry. The church may continue to be involved in worldwide evangelism. Some inside the church may be growing in their personal journey. But, ultimately, while I can understand this logic and feeling, *the flaw in being satisfied with the status quo is that it does little to follow the biblical mandate* given to all Christ followers—and thereby to all churches—to "go…and make disciples" (Mt. 28:19).

Now if you just want a holy huddle and a hotel for saints instead of a hospital for sinners, then tie all your staff up, turn all your lights on, and turn on all your air conditioning and heating at the same time. Burn all your money up to make those ten people who come comfortable. Eventually you'll kill your church. My granddaddy would say that what I am saying is heresy. I believe it's just good Bible preaching out of the book of Acts.

Can the Staff Survive?

Part of what we're often dealing with is an overwhelmed staff. I've recently completed a study of leadership models throughout the Bible. The Scripture's clear: church leaders have a biblical mandate to equip the saints for the work of the ministry, as Ephesians puts it. *Equipping* means teaching people to go out to where the people are to do whatever it takes to connect people with the Good News of Jesus Christ. Jesus spent more time at parties than he did in the synagogue. His culture was similar to ours. The people in 30 C.E. weren't knocking down the doors to come to the synagogue. If we don't do something, we're going to continue to overwhelm our staff. They will sense that the church expects them to deal with this diverse and growing problem. The staff will see an emerging population. All the while, our staff will look at themselves as ill-equipped and hamstrung by the same structures and in the same value system that worked in the fifties.

For many church leaders the stress has already become overwhelming. Some of the brightest and best of our ministers are e-mailing me to say that they are leaving their churches for other occupations. It's not just that they don't see their families because they work seventy hours a week. It's because as hard as they work, they feel what they do has no positive results in growing the kingdom. They have told me they are burning out. They are overwhelmed. They have said the churches' expectations on their time and on results are unrealistic. And they have said, "I'm tired of beating my head up against the wall with these church people I'm trying to serve. They really don't want to go on mission into the world. They want me to be a caregiver for them. God called me to go into the world and to reach the world for Jesus, and my church people really aren't interested in doing that. They want to keep things the way they are, and I feel that God is calling me to go out into the secular world."

Many ministers are doing that successfully. I believe God is birthing a whole new church out there that I call the scattered church, and he's taking some of our best and brightest clergy and building that church.[5]

handwritten margin notes: "why would God want no model no model"; "/ Oyrs later, the clear answer to 'No, He wasn't'"

The Plight of the Pastor

Pastor-bashing

"Pastor-bashing is my church's focus" were the words from a sincere but deeply wounded coaching client. He was so hurt, angry, and tired that he needed a retreat, a compassionate listening ear, and encouragement in his coaching session. God did bless our coaching time, but his words and story continue to work in me.

His words have haunted me for days. I have had many faces and experiences rush to my mind that would likely fit into this "pastor-bashing" category. In a decade when most numbers associated with church—finances, membership, baptisms, new members, visitors, etc., are declining, pastor-bashing seems to be on the rise. While some pastors and staff and churches are having a fulfilling and fruitful relationship, many others are in the fierce tensions of pastor-bashing.

Pastoring a church or serving on staff in a church of any size, in any setting, with any demographic is challenging at best these days. Most pastors and staff find themselves living in the pinch. They feel the pinch of finances, demographic challenges, philosophical and theological challenges, control issues in the church, community, and often the denomination or judicatory of which they are a part. Permit me to share personal observations based on my experience consulting with churches for more than twenty years, serving congregations in denominational work for fifteen-plus years, coaching pastors and staff for six years, and serving in various church roles as a volunteer. I've found the burning issues to include:

1. What is pastor-bashing?
2. How does pastor-bashing manifest itself?
3. What does it mean?
4. What methods might bring some resolution to pastor-bashing?

From my client's perspective and from my observations through the years, pastor-bashing can be characterized by at least these experiences:

- Accusations, and sometimes threats, that "the church is not growing because of you!"
- Spreading of rumors that question the pastor's integrity, work habits, loyalty to church traditions or disregard of ancient church values, etc.
- Withholding of tithes, offerings, leadership, and participation because of personal disagreements between church members and pastor/staff.
- Accusations, uncalled-for personal references or ridicule of pastor/staff's

family members and their participation or lack of participation in church activities.
- Isolation of the pastor/staff from friendships, loyalty, and the support of leadership.
- Tearing down of pastor/staff's self-esteem, confidence, and sense of call or pastoral skills.
- Forcing pastors' families to live in a fishbowl before church and community families.

How does pastor-bashing manifest itself?

Sometimes physical threats even enter the picture. Believe it or not, I know directly of a church where three deacons visited the pastor and threatened him in the presence of his teenage son. They were "going to take him behind the barn and teach him a lesson." What do you think that teenage son learned about deacons and church that day?

I had been working with this pastor and church to assess what would make them more effective in a rapidly growing community. The pastor was growing the church and bringing in people, but these deacons did not like the people he was bringing in. The pastor was bringing in new members who were unlike the natives of the community. That fueled the congregation's anger. The church leaders feared that the influx of new members would jeopardize their control, so they sabotaged the growth and bashed the pastor! Who would have ever thought it! Such brash actions illustrate living in the pinch of times. The pastor/staff is caught between at least two value systems, two worlds, two cultures, and two philosophies of church.

What does pastor-bashing mean?

How could church leaders and congregations bash their pastor? What does this mean? Christians are supposed to be kind, courteous, forgiving, loving, self-controlled, patient, long-suffering, and the list of virtues from Galatians 5 continues. So how do we get into this tragic situation where no one really wins?

Seems to me that pastor-bashing displays some patterns that frequently occur and may reveal meaning and motive to this traumatic situation:

- Personal preferences create tensions. The pastor's vision and preferences conflict with those in leadership or in the pew.
- Spiritual warfare and immaturity emerge in people, families, and often the congregation at large.
- Past and future collide in ways that create tension. Often the congregation (sometimes the pastor) wants things to stay the way they are rather than face the demands and opportunities of the present and future.
- Control and leadership are challenged. So often the bashing is over control issues. Who will lead the church? Whose vision will drive the congregation's decisions or programming?

- In earlier phases bashing—and awareness of the bashing—is limited to a small number of leaders.
- Incompetence and impatience collide. This can be seen on one or all sides involved. So often fear emerges before patience is cultivated, and stones begin to be thrown in efforts to protect "our way."
- Families take sides, and boundaries are set. Again, this can be on one or all sides of the issue. When such polarization occurs, the intensity increases, and the bashing becomes visible to a larger group.
- Emotions escalate, and facts become blurred. So often emotions drive the dialogue and bashing and not the real facts. The emotions are often driven by perceptions, not necessarily the facts. People think such and such is true, or they "heard it from many people," but they never name the people.

What methods might bring some resolution to pastor-bashing?

Most pastors are living out a calling to "go into all the world" and a belief that Christ wants the world to know him and his love. The pastor believes that the church is on mission and is to grow in Spirit and in number. However, increasingly pastors and staff are finding that they are called by congregations who do not share this same value system. The members may mouth the words and loyalty to the Great Commission during the interview and negotiations. The reality becomes clear in time that their words mean: "only if the mission doesn't inconvenience me, doesn't change our church's traditions, or challenge the leadership base's personal preferences." That is living in the pinch!

I recently heard Eugene Peterson, a pastor to pastors, has explained the situation:

> Pastoring is not a very glamorous job. It's a very taking-out-the-laundry and changing-the-diapers kind of job. And I think I would try to disabuse them of any romantic ideas of what it is. As a pastor, you've got to be willing to take people as they are. And live with them where they are. And not impose your will on them. Because God has different ways of being with people, and you don't always know what they are. The one thing I think is at the root of a lot of pastors' restlessness and dissatisfaction is impatience. They think if they get the right system, the right programs, the right place, the right location, the right demographics, it'll be a snap. And for some people it is: if you're a good actor, if you have a big smile, if you are an extrovert. In some ways, a religious crowd is the easiest crowd to gather in the world. Our country's full of examples of that. But for most, pastoring is a very ordinary way to live. And it is difficult in many ways because your time is not your own, for the most part, and the whole culture is against you. This consumer culture, people grow up determining what they want to do by what they can consume. And the Christian gospel is just quite the opposite of that. And people don't know that. And pastors don't know

that when they start out. We've got a whole culture that is programmed to please people, telling them what they want. And if you do that, you might end up with a big church, but you won't be a pastor.[6]

David Olsen echoes these thoughts:

Recent studies indicate clergy have more stress-related health problems than the general population and work longer hours, an average of 51 hours a week according to one study. In response, some religious denominations are either adding or expanding health and counseling programs, while urging clergy to take more time off. Denominational leaders say stress and the damage it can cause personal relationships often end up harming not only clergy but the congregations they sacrifice so much to serve.[7]

What Can a Pastor-bashing Church Change?

So what's a church and pastor to do? How can we move from pastor-bashing to pastor blessing? How can a congregation and pastor become partners in ministry and learn to work through personal and philosophical pinches and fears? Let me make some suggestions:

[handwritten margin note: nothing in either category has any Scripture refs to support all are man-centered]

As a pastor

- Acknowledge that implementing and managing change in a congregation calls forth a unique set of skills that most pastors need help in refining.
- Enlist a certified coach to walk with you through the trials of change and the learning curves you are faced with to move forward your congregation and leadership style.
- Read, reflect, and pray before you embark on introducing change in a congregation.
- Join a peer learning community of pastors in similar situations for support, encouragement, and guidance.
- Clarify what you need during times of negotiating with the church before you come.
- Be honest about your strengths and weaknesses as a pastor, leader, preacher, administrator, counselor, and other roles that might be expected of you
- Commit to ongoing self-care and continuing education.
- Be faithful in taking your time off and vacation. You and your family deserve it.
- Negotiate and make plans that ensure an uninterrupted time away.
- Build a partnership with area pastors who can help in times of crisis.

As a congregation

- Acknowledge, as church and pastor, that these are rapidly changing times and that introducing and managing change is inevitable if churches are to remain relevant, faithful, and fruitful in the twenty-first century.

- Be honest with candidates about the state of your church, community, staffing, finances, and expectations. Hiding them only sets all up for disappointment and struggle.
- Require and resource continuing education and coaching for all pastoral staff and key church leaders. Budget for it, schedule it, and build it into the culture of your leadership circle. Such will help the leader and congregation to face and walk through the learning curves that come with change and challenge.
- Plan regular pastor/staff appreciation days/months. Resources online and in print are available to help with this special time when the church blesses, encourages, and supports pastor/staff and their families. Surprise them, and be authentic. Enlist persons to tell stories of how God has used the staff personnel in personal ministry efforts.
- Encourage pastor and staff to take their days off and all their vacation time. *Then make plans so you do not have to interrupt their time away.* So often pastors can't relax because they live in the reality that they might be expected to return for funerals, etc. A local pastor can help with this. Give your pastor uninterrupted rest time.
- Be faithful in scheduling, planning, and resourcing sabbatical times for your pastor/staff.
- Provide the needed support staff that will allow the professional staff to maximize their time and focus their ministry.
- Stand up for your pastor/staff when they are accused, ridiculed, or judged by others. They need friends, support, and people who are willing to stand up to the few who are against them.
- Be a trustworthy friend for your pastor/staff. Many pastors and staff persons and their families are lonely and stressed people. They are often afraid of ridicule and judgment if they make friends of a few in the congregation, so they live lonely lives. Be their friends, allow them to have other friends, and take the initiative and reach out to them regularly.

Certainly the church should not have to fall into the trap of pastor-bashing, and the pastor and the pastor's family should not have to be victims of pastor-bashing; but more than that, the world, the nonbelievers, should not have to hear of pastor-bashing. Such ridicule and bashing are not the image we want to present of Christ's church. They tarnish the church's witness to the world. Will you join me in focusing on blessing rather than bashing our pastors?

Economic Challenges

Many churches today struggle not only with keeping existing members (those over sixty) and reaching new members (those under thirty); they also struggle with their expenses and their financial base. These provide economic challenges for both the church and the pastor.

Some of the Issues:

For the pastor

- Pastoral salaries and annuities create dependency on ministry as a lifelong source of income, resulting in some pastors working out of a need for money rather than out of empowerment or fulfillment.
- Clergy face a major gap between retirement age and income and housing. Retired ministers need extra income and meaningful service. Denominations need to find ways to use/employ retirees as chaplains or in other positions.
- Pastors face stricter requirements to maintain denominational ties. Various boards and agencies attach economic strings to ensure pastors (and churches) pass a litmus test for orthodoxy. Thus they generate a self-serving agenda rather than God's agenda.
- New standards of measuring success are greatly needed for pastor search/ appointment staff committees, churches, denominations, judicatories, districts, conventions to move beyond bigger buildings, attendance, budgets, staff as defining effectiveness.

For the church

- Preserving family heritage and hope becomes more central than faithfulness to biblical teachings.
- For most members, maintaining buildings is the essence of church, not biblical mandates or mission.
- Creative funding of ministry moves beyond traditional church-based giving plans (which many have made a sacrament) to multiple-funding streams and collaborative ministries and fruitful partnerships.
- Many churches are businesses with massive overhead to sustain services valid in another age but that often are a financial and leadership drain today (for example, travel when the cost of gas is high; large staff in an age of downsizing, etc.).
- How can partnerships/alliances be established to offer services without current denominational and associational agencies, boards, etc.?

Statistics on Church Involvement

Is the picture as dire as I've painted it so far? Let's look at some research statistics:

- The nation's largest Protestant denomination saw stats for 2014 suggesting "decline evidence in recent years will not only continue but likely accelerate. Follow the current trend line and soon the Southern Baptist Convention will be declining at 2 percent a year, then 3, then…"[8]
- Southern Baptist membership declined for the eighth straight year in 2014, according to an annual report released June 14, 2014. An article

reporting on the 2013 decline said, "The report by the Southern Baptist Convention's publishing arm, Lifeway Christian Resources, puts total membership in the Nashville-based SBC at 15.7 million. That's down from 15.9 million in 2012, a decrease of a little less than 1 percent. Weekly church attendance decreased more than 2 percent last year, falling to 5.8 million as a weekly average for the year. The report also notes a 1.5 percent decrease in the number of baptisms, falling to 310,368. Baptisms are an important measure for the denomination because of its strong commitment to evangelism."[9]

- "'Unchurched adults are very much like churched adults . . . except they don't attend church,' says David Kinnaman, who served as a general editor alongside George Barna in the recent book *Churchless*. . . . ' While a few of the demographic differences between churched and unchurched are statistically significant, there is no such thing as a can't-miss strategy for appealing to them. In fact, the data uncover so many similarities between churched and unchurched people that we have to conclude that a number of the stereotypes about both groups are not valid.

  "'The fact remains, though, that more Americans than ever are not attending church,' Kinnaman continues. 'Most of them did at some point and, for one reason or another, decided not to continue. This fact should motivate church leaders and attenders to examine how to make appropriate changes—not for the sake of enhancing attendance numbers but to address the lack of life transformation that would attract more people to remain an active part."[10] A recent study's results document this.[11]

- "Five Trends among the Unchurched" from the Barna Group says that the percentage of unchurched adults in America has increased from 30 percent to 43 percent of the population since 1990. Barna points to five trends that are contributing to this increase:

  The research reveals the big picture: Today's unchurched are much less likely to come from a church background than ever before. Furthermore, unchurched people today have different expectations of church involvement from those of previous decades. These changes are the result of shifting personal attitudes as well as significant changes in the broader cultural landscape.

  1. Secularization Is on the Rise

  — Nearly two-fifths of the nation's adult population (38%) now qualifies as post-Christian (measured by 15 different variables related to people's identity, beliefs and behaviors . . .). That includes 10% of Americans who qualify as highly post-Christian. Another one-quarter is moderately post-Christian (28%). Examined over time, our research shows that the proportion of highly secularized individuals is growing slowly but steadily.

  — In other words, in spite of our 'Christian' self-descriptions, more than one-third of America's adults are essentially secular in belief and practice. If nothing else, this helps explain why America has experienced a surge in unchurched people—and presages a continuing rise in this population.

— Among the churchless, the proportions skew even more heavily: Overall, more than three-quarters of unchurched adults fall in the heavy-to-moderate range on the secularization scale. That compares to about one out of eight among the churched.

— As you might expect, the data show some striking generational differences when it comes to secularization. The pattern is indisputable: The younger the generation, the more post-Christian it is. Nearly half of Millennials (48%) qualify as post-Christian compared to two-fifths of Gen Xers (40%), one-third of Boomers (35%) and one-quarter of Elders (28%).

2. People Are Less Open to the Idea of Church

— Barna research shows that the unchurched are becoming less responsive to churches' efforts to connect with them. For example, conventional wisdom says the best way to get people to visit a church is to have friends invite them—and the conventional wisdom is right. The churchless we interviewed were most open to 'a friend of yours inviting you to attend a local church,' with one-fifth expressing strong interest and nearly half willing to consider a church based on this factor. An invitation from a friend is the top-rated way churches can establish connections with the unchurched.

— However, while the conventional wisdom remains true today, the road ahead shows challenging signs. Barna Group's trend data raise questions about the long-term durability of this approach. *Twenty years ago, two-thirds of churchless Americans (65%) were open to being invited to church by a friend. In 2013, that percentage has slipped to less than half (47%).*

~ It's not only the efficacy of personal invitations that is changing. Barna's tracking data stretching back to the 1990s reveal a slow-growing calcification of unchurched people toward churches. For every outreach method surveyed, the unchurched are less open to it today than they were two decades ago. While churchless people continue to show moderate openness to high-touch, relational connections— pastoral home visits (27%, down from 34%), a phone call from a church (24%, down from 34%)—they are resistant to other forms of outreach. This is especially true for advertising, including TV, radio or newspaper (18%, down from 20%), direct mailings (16%, down from 24%) and billboard ads (14%, down from 21%).

3. Churchgoing Is No Longer Mainstream

— Churchgoing is slowly but incontrovertibly losing its role as a normative part of American life. In the 1990s, roughly one out of every seven unchurched adults had never experienced regular church attendance. Today, that percentage has increased to nearly one-quarter. Buried within these numbers are at least two important conclusions: 1) Church is becoming increasingly unfamiliar to millions of Americans, and yet 2) the churchless are still largely comprised of de-churched adults. . . .

4. There Are Different Expectations of Church Involvement

— Another intriguing shift among the churchless has to do with their expectations of church involvement. In the early 1990s, our research showed that nearly seven out of 10 adults, if they were to visit a church, would be most interested in attending the Sunday service. In 2014, weekend worship services remain the most common entry experience, but only slightly; now, only 57% of churchless adults say they would be interested in Sunday worship as their starting point. In 2013 unchurched are more likely to say they are simply not sure, reflecting their disinterest in churches generally, or are more likely to say they would prefer attending some activity other than the Sunday service.

— A similar shift is afoot in terms of the number of churches they would attend. The churchless were asked in both 1993 and in 2011 if they would prefer to be involved in one church or multiple churches in their area. Two decades ago, even the unchurched expressed some sense of church loyalty (albeit hypothetical): 85% said they would expect to attend just one congregation. The recent study reflects a slight loosening of this potential loyalty, but the more notable shifts are among those who don't have a preference and who aren't sure. *Together, these percentages doubled from 8% to 16%, reflecting growing cultural indifference to church involvement.*

5. There Is Skepticism about Churches' Contributions to Society

— Although many of the churchless hold positive views of churches, a substantial number also have no idea what Christians have accomplished in the nation, either for the better or for the worse. When the unchurched were asked to describe what they believe are the positive and negative contributions of Christianity in America, almost half (49%) could not identify a single favorable impact of the Christian community, while nearly two-fifths (37%) were unable to identify a negative impact. Of those who could identify one way Christians contribute to the common good, the unchurched appreciate their influence when it comes to serving the poor and disadvantaged (22%), bolstering morals and values (10%) and helping people believe in God (8%). Among those who had a complaint about Christians in society, the unchurched were least favorably disposed toward violence in the name of Christ (18%), the church's stand against gay marriage (15%), sexual abuse scandals (13%) and involvement in politics (10%).[12] Reflecting on the skepticism about churches it is critically important to see that this is not just a current issue. These statistics are for the last two decades. The trend is now a clear and continuing pattern.

- "According to the latest research, more than 1 out of every 3 adults (33%) in America is unchurched. This means they haven't attended a religious service of any type during the past 6 months. This represents approximately 73 million adults, plus roughly 27 million teens and children for a total of 100 million Americans."[13]
- "For most of the past 300 years, 35%–40% of the population has participated in church with some degree of regularity."[14]
- "Despite what people SAY about weekly attendance, the true weekly rate is closer to 25%. If we use lesser frequencies, more than 60% of American adults have attended a service at a religious congregation in the last year."[15]
- "While it's debatable whether the attendance is going down or remaining level, the data is unambiguous that overall church attendance is not increasing. More specifically, religious service attendance declined in the several decades leading up to 1990 and seems to have been essentially stable thereafter."[16]
- "However, the percent who say they 'never' attend church has risen steadily over the last 30 years as people shift from infrequent attendance to nonattendance."[17]
- "Finally, the Protestant portion of the U.S. population is in decline, due to the rise in 'nones' (no religious preference), decline of mainline denominations, and rise in the percent of recent immigrants claiming a religion other than Christian. The Protestant makeup was 62% in the early 1970s to just over 50% [in 2014]. If that trend continues, we will soon be a Protestant-minority country."[18]

This latter conclusion may be hard for many churchgoing Christians to believe. But it's true: Even though the cultural trend is toward less church-friendliness overall, the vast majority of unchurched adults still have at least some level of personal experience in a church.

- Interest in spirituality in the United States is growing, but this has not translated into greater church involvement.[19]
- At the present rates of change, Islam will become the dominant religion in the world before 2050.[20]
- At the present rate of change, most Americans will be non-Christians by the year 2035.[21]
- Interest in new religious movements (e.g. New Age, neopaganism) is growing rapidly. In particular, Wiccans are doubling in numbers about every thirty months.[22]
- The influence of the central, program-based congregation is diminishing as more cell churches are being created.[23]
- Many Christians have left congregations and formed house churches: small groups meeting in one another's homes.[24]
- Only three out of ten adults in the U.S. in their twenties (31 percent) attend church in a typical week, compared to four out of ten of those in their

thirties (42 percent) and nearly half of all adults age forty and older (49 percent).[25]

- Eight million adults who were active churchgoers as teenagers will no longer be active in a church by the time they reach thirty.[26]
- Only three out of ten adults in their twenties donated to a church in the past year, whereas 61 percent of older adults reported having donated to a church.[27]
- Only 30 percent of those in their twenties have read the Bible in the past week, compared to 37 percent of those in their thirties; 44 percent of those in their forties; 47 percent of adults in their fifties; and 55 percent of those age sixty and above.[28]
- Just one-third of adults in their twenties (34 percent) claim to be absolutely committed to Christianity. That compares to more than half (54 percent) of all older adults who claim such absolute devotion, including more than six out of ten adults who are age fifty and older.[29]
- More than eight out of ten adults in their twenties (80 percent) said that their religious faith is important in their life, and nearly six out of ten (57 percent) claimed to have made a personal commitment to Jesus Christ that is still important in their lives.[30]
- Three-quarters of young adults in their twenties (75 percent) said they had prayed to God in the past week.[31]
- Since 1991, the adult population in the United States has grown by 15 percent. During that same period the number of adults who do not attend church has nearly doubled, rising from thirty-nine million to seventy-five million—a 92 percent increase.[32]
- In the American context, 2009 was a turning point in regards to the perception of Christianity's health in the U.S. That year, the results of the American Religious Identification Survey (ARIS) was released. It showed the percentage of self-identified Christians had fallen 10 percentage points, from 86 to 76, since 1990. It also showed that the "nones"—those who claim no religious affiliation—rose from 8 to 15 percent in the same period.[33]
- Men constitute 55 percent of the unchurched.[34]
- The unchurched are also younger than the norm. The median age of U.S. adults is forty-three, but it is just thirty-eight among the unchurched. Born-again adults are substantially older than either group (median: forty-six).[35]

Reflecting on Statistics

At first glance, the impact of these statistics is depressing, staggering. The stats certainly shine the light on the world's diversity and the need for community building. But take a closer look. Younger adults aren't coming to church; but they do claim to be Christians, have faith that is important to them, and to pray. That's encouraging. The challenge is to get those who claim Christianity involved in a church they find relevant and meaningful and, through them, to reach other young adults. A seventy-eight-year-old, former member of a Presbyterian church, and later in life an Episcopalian, is now an active part of Jubilee Community Church in Asheville, North Carolina. When interviewed about her church and church attendance, she explained,

> "I think people either grow up in a church and stay there, or they search for what they need. And I think most people have found Jubilee because they were searching."
>
> When asked why the younger generations are leaving traditional mainline church pews, she says: "You all are diverse. You are accepting of all kinds of people, all kinds of lifestyles. You know when something happens on the other side of the world immediately and you react to it, and that's different from what we knew. We knew our little town and that was about it."[36]

Dr. Molly Marshall reflects on and frames the future church with sharp and challenging insights after reading the Spring issue of *Abby Banner*, in which

> Abbot John Klassen describes what the emerging church will look like: "It will be browner and poorer, more sensuous and feminine, less clerical and more collegial and inclusive, less concerned about the works of charity and more aware of the need for change in structures, more multilingual and polycentric." I find his words extremely hopeful, especially if the marginalizing impulses that arise from hierarchical structures are quelled. He is describing a major shift in all quarters of his ecclesial tradition, and his words are perceptive for the larger church.[37]

Dr. Marshall continues her reflection by declaring, "I believe that the coming church will be a better blend of youthful and senior, more liturgical, more theological, less bounded and more permeable, and less self-interested."[38]

The Potential

Years ago in many communities of this country, especially throughout the South—the Bible Belt—everyone went to church. Church growth came from children growing up in the church, occasional newcomers, and the transfer membership of a few disgruntled church members. On Sunday everyone got up and went to one church or another. That's no longer true today. Today we live in a secular culture in which the church's competition doesn't come from another denomination down the street but from work, golf, NASCAR, football, community soccer, Little League sports, caring for aging parents, gardening, or just a treasured day with family without the weekly rapid pace of life.

Ed Stetzer's work suggests we may have three different categories of Christians today:

Cultural Christians—people who believe themselves to be Christians simply because their culture tells them they are. Christians by heritage. Makes up about one-third of the 75 percent who call themselves Christian.

Congregational Christians—similar to the first group, except these individuals at least have some connection to congregational life. They make up another one-third of the 75 percent in the research sample.

Convictional Christians—people who are actually living according to their faith. Another one-third of the 75 percent.[39]

The potential is great. Every community is filled with people who do not know Jesus Christ, and those who are from the other categories mentioned above. The church has work to do, people to reach. To do that, the church will need to build relationships and community, getting to know the needs of younger generations, and make changes in the church to appeal to people under thirty.

Is changing worship the answer? Perhaps. Some have changed to blended or contemporary worship. For some this has worked, and for others it has not. Many who have tried blended worship in an attempt to please everyone have found that there was a greater likelihood of making everyone angry.

Jubilee, a diverse community of faith, incorporates a variety of arts, styles, traditions, and ethnic and cultural rituals and traditions.

Throughout the service, there are multiple opportunities to hold your neighbor's hand, greet them, embrace them. A poem spiced with personal, social and political flavors is offered by one of the members whose birthday it is; a local singer-songwriter performs; sage is burned as the 300–400 attendees turn in unison to face the four directions in the traditional Native American manner as [their leader] leads in prayer. Those present range from Millennials to elders in their 70s and 80s, plus parents of many ages in between accompanied by their children."[40]

If a congregation discerns change is needed, the key to change is to change values and beliefs before changing behavior. We'll deal in depth with these concepts later in this book.

COACHING QUESTIONS

- What issues in this chapter do you most identify with now?
- Who are other persons who might identify with the same or similar issues?
- What actions might you take to begin to work through some of the identified issues?
- What is your next step now?

2

Church: A Hotel for Saints or a Hospital for Sinners?

Does your church have a mission statement? What is its purpose? It probably includes something about reaching people for Christ and growing disciples. Although each church is unique and must minister in its culture and context, ultimately it gets its commission from Matthew 28:19–20: "Go therefore and make disciples of all nations, baptizing them in the name of the Father and of the Son and of the Holy Spirit, and teaching them to obey everything that I have commanded you. And remember, I am with you always, to the end of the age." Jesus' last words to his followers were to go and make disciples.

Although we are expected to care for one another, the New Testament says much more about making disciples than about nurturing and providing fellowship for those already inside the church. Yet many churches have turned their focus inward instead of outward. How does this happen?

Growing churches are dynamic and exciting. They reach people and care for one another as well as those outside the church. Plateaued or declining churches get used to the status quo. They lose their first love of reaching people and make priorities of the building, the budget, the cakes baked for fellowships, and the baked chicken for folks who are sick. Eventually the pastor's primary job becomes keeping everyone inside the church happy, while Scripture calls pastors not to keep members happy but to equip and challenge them to be missionaries of the Good News.

Breaking out of that cycle means taking risks. Very often the most authentic ministries are rooted in the greatest risks. Could it be our ministries are limited because of our fear of taking risks? For some churches and staff members the price is just too high or the threat of pastor-bashing is too great. Most church leaders don't get together and decide that they'll choose the safe road of keeping the older folks happy rather than upset everyone by trying to make changes to reach a younger group, but that's what happens. If an idea doesn't produce great results, or the power brokers—mostly people past sixty—complain enough, leaders settle into the secure tasks that mean complaints die down and tithes keep coming. So church leaders give the existing church culture what they need, want, and desire.

Entrepreneurial Leaders

Some believe the church for today and tomorrow calls for more entrepreneurial leaders. Carey Nieuwhof suggests five things this type leader can bring to the church:

1. The willingness to risk

The early church took incredible risks. People risked their health, safety, financial security and their very lives for the sake of the Gospel.

In a time when too many churches are trying to figure out how to survive, we need leaders who will change the question to how the church is going to thrive.

You can't do that without risk. Being willing to risk what you have today is the best way to get to a different tomorrow.

2. Experimentation

Have you ever asked yourself what it would have been like to be in the New Testament church?

It was an audacious experiment that God was completely behind. Everything changed in a generation; the place of worship, who worshipped, where people worshipped, how they worshipped, how they connected to each other, how they gave and how they forgave.

There isn't a single element of everyday life that looked the same after a decade of life in the church.

If the church is going to grow, it's going to have to change.

3. A restless discontent with the status quo

Entrepreneurs and apostles are never satisfied. While it can be frustrating to work with someone who is never satisfied, it's an essential gift both in birthing what's new and in expanding a current mission.

Entrepreneurs are not only discontent with what others have created; they're soon discontent with what they've helped create.

Paul died in prison longing to do more. Why do we make fun of church leaders today who have the same sense of urgency?

4. Boldness

If you search the New Testament, you'll see boldness as a hallmark of early church leaders.

You can hardly describe the church culture of many churches today as bold. Anemic, maybe. Bold, no.

And when people become bold, people criticize them for being arrogant or in it for themselves. Well, sometimes yes. But often no. They're just exercising a God-given gift. Paul, after all, was no stranger to that criticism.

After all, boldness moved the cause of Christ forward in a remarkable way, changing millions of lives.

5. A bias for action

We have plenty of thinkers and prayers in the church and not nearly enough doers.

Entrepreneurs bring a bias for action that is often astonishing. Spiritual entrepreneurs accomplish things nobody else accomplishes because they do things nobody else is willing to do.

If you think about the (much criticized) innovations in today's church (video venues, multisite churches, online campuses etc.) you realize that you open yourself to a world of criticism when you start bold new things. So what?". . .

I'm not saying the gift of apostleship is the only thing, but it is a missing thing.

Conventional seminaries are mostly addicted to producing shepherds. If all we get is shepherds stepping into leadership, then what you get is people who will (mostly) care for small groups of people.

Organizationally, it makes some sense to hire leaders and have shepherd volunteers. That's what we've done at Connexus. You can care for hundreds, or thousands, of people through volunteer shepherds (we call them small group leaders) and let the leaders lead.

Do we need the gift of shepherding? Absolutely.

But we're desperately missing the gift of spiritual entrepreneurship in the church today.

The church has plenty of opinions but not nearly enough capable leaders.

So here's my challenge . . . why don't you tap an entrepreneur you know on the shoulder today and ask him or her, 'have you ever considered ministry'?

Think about it.

Who do you know who might be in business today who could be in ministry tomorrow? My guess is that there are people who are running businesses and leading in organizations who have the gifts for ministry but have never thought about ministry.

And maybe they've never thought about ministry because they've never seen anyone with their gift set use it for ministry."[1]

I'm confident leadership style and philosophy make the difference in most churches and in the lives of most people (churched or unchurched). Too often our leadership seems to fall into the traps of tradition, established expectations, or comfort zones rather than moving into the unknown as a person of faith, hope and vision.

The desire for harmony frequently outweighs the desire to be obedient, faithful followers of Christ. *Reaching People under 30 While Keeping People over 60* depends on two critical factors: (1) practicing proven principles of effective intergenerational ministry; (2) practicing consistent leadership styles and practices that creates a pull more than a push strategy that deepens the faith and function of the body of Christ. *Pull* is about what draws and compels people forward. *Push* is about feeling dictated to and by others. Bill Habicht's dream and model creates a pull by doing church as a social enterprise. His presentation at Next Church conference in 2015 represents a working model that holds great promise for the mission of God in the world in a culture in which we now live.[2]

The Power of One

The pain and struggle I/we went through during tough days of transitioning a small church has now been used of God in powerful ways in my journey and in the journey of others who identify with the feelings, situations, and challenges. Everywhere I go people ask me to share my grandmother story. Here it is.

My maternal grandmother was a member at my home church in South Carolina, a little mill village church. My mother went back to work when I was four years old, and I stayed with my grandmother. She cared for and nurtured me. There was deep love between us.

When I was about seventeen years of age, I accepted the call to ministry. I didn't know exactly what that meant at the time, but I knew God was doing something in my life. I had been involved in church life, raised in a Christian family. I didn't feel called to be a preacher. I had no idea what a minister of education or other staff person was because we didn't have staff ministers in my small church, but I went forward and said to my congregation, "I really believe I'm supposed to go to college and I'm supposed to study ministry," and that was all I said.

The motto of my church became, "Let Eddie do it." Anything that needed to be done, let Eddie do it. I tried to do whatever they asked me to do. (I was a people pleaser during those days.) Right before college when I was as green as a gourd and didn't know anything except what I had seen lived out in front of me, they asked me to join the staff to "help our Sunday school grow." They didn't call me a minister of education. They just gave me an assignment: "help our Sunday school grow."

I said OK and got to work. The small salary they were giving me would help me in my first year at Furman, and I saw the practical experience fitting in with my plans to major in religion. Then the pastor told me that one step in helping the church grow was to provide more space for babies. To reach young families in our area, we needed a bigger preschool area. The way he saw it, I needed to move my grandmother's group out of their customized Sunday school class so the babies could have that room.

That was my assignment—to move my grandmother's Sunday school class that had been meeting in the same place for about twenty years. She was in her sixties at the time, and hers was the last class before heaven in our church. It was pretty sparse in membership, but they had a nice big room, pictures on the wall of all of those who had gone before. They had little chairs with cushions that they had all made and had their name on them. They had put carpet down and put wallpaper on the walls. It was a nice little mausoleum for them. I was stupid enough to walk into that room one Sunday morning with those ladies, most of whom had diapered me in the church nursery, and say: "We've got a lot of new babies coming into our church. The nursery is packed, and your room is bigger than their room. We would like you to swap rooms."

It made good sense to me but not to them. Those five women were ready to kill me. Before we got out of church that Sunday morning, the whole community knew that my grandmother's grandson had upset the older women's Sunday school class. That was long before cell phones. I don't know how they got the word out, but it was terrible. During that week I went in and out of stores in the community, and wherever I went I would see people pointing to me. I knew they were talking about what an awful person I was to upset that bunch of old ladies and to try to take away the room they had worked so hard to call their own.

Our family used to go to my grandmother's house after church for Sunday dinner. She told me that Sunday not to come—no more fried chicken. It crushed me. I don't know which was worse, no fried chicken or knowing that my grandmother was mad at me. And I couldn't even understand what the problem was. I thought they'd want more babies in the church. I thought they liked babies. I couldn't believe those women were so mean.

I came to understand through great pain and suffering over an eight-month period that those women were family for one another. That classroom was a sacred space for them. I didn't understand any of that at the time, and I had to do some confessing and repenting to my grandmother through the years as I gained a better understanding of what I, in my innocence, had done.

My grandmother and I loved each other so much that we covenanted to talk once a week, pray together once a week, and study Scripture together once a week until we could find some sense of reconciliation in this broken relationship. It was very painful. I can't tell you how painful it was for both of us.

After about eight months of these weekly dialogues, she called me one afternoon and said, "I want you to come over here." It was not an appointed hour that we had agreed upon previously, but I said OK and went immediately to her house. When I got there, she sat me down in the same little place we used to sit when I was four and five years old, on the front stoop of the porch. She put her arm around me and said, "You've told me about some mistakes you've made as a young and inexperienced minister of education. But I've been praying a lot and studying a lot and have been talking to some of my class members. God has convicted me of my position in this matter. I have come to understand that my personal comfort is not as important as this church's mission." She shifted and said, "I'm going to walk into class on Sunday morning"—her Sunday school class that was still meeting in that self-made "mausoleum"—"and I'm going to tell those ladies, not ask, that we need to move down the hall; and I want you to be with me."

I looked her in the eye and said, "There's no way I'm going back in that class. I love you, Grandma, but I'm not going back in there again."

She said, "Well, at least stand outside the door."

So I stood out of the other women's sight outside the door. I listened to my grandmother, and I got my first real lesson of what a power broker looks like in a Baptist church. My grandmother was one. I didn't know it until then.

She walked in and said to those other four women: "Ladies, I've come to understand that our personal comfort is not as important as this church's mission and its future. I want us to move today to the class down the hall, and I want us to take a little money out of our kitty (which was bigger than the church budget), and I want us to fix up our new room. But I also want us to fix up this room that we are leaving for the new babies that are coming in. I want it to be nice, and I want us to start an adopt-a-grandchild ministry in this church for all these new families coming in that don't have grandmas and grandpas locally. I want us to learn to love these babies. We need them as much as they need us, and I want us to be a part of the future of this church instead of the stumbling block to keep it where it is."

Then she picked up her chair and walked down the hall, and every one of those women followed her. They didn't say a word. They didn't ask a question. They followed their leader.

I know the pain and risks that come when church leaders take a stand to help the church move forward, but I also know the reward that comes when risks are taken and people are reached for Jesus Christ.

My grandmother eventually went into a nursing home as an Alzheimer's patient. And I eventually preached her funeral. As a result of her decision, her courage, her leadership, and her spiritual maturity and conviction, not only does my little mill village church have a thriving children's ministry today, but they have a brand-new children's building because of her. Not that she gave the money, but she gave the leadership to reach that generation.

One day before she died, I visited her in the nursing home. I was trying to find one of those open windows to her memory through the Alzheimer's, and I was retelling this story. Together we caught a little glimpse of reality. She got up out of her little chair and walked to me with her wobbly cane. Her frail body reached me, and she hugged me. Then she whispered in my ear, "We got those old women to go on mission, didn't we?"

My grandmother gave me a rich legacy for church leadership. I told this story at her funeral. After the service five women came down to speak to me. They were from different churches. I didn't know any of them. They stood at the end of her casket as we were trying to put it in the hearse. They each said, "Son, I don't know you, but I knew her. Your story today is going to help our churches because I've been a roadblock in my church, and I didn't know it until today."

I love the church, but we church people are killing many of our churches to preserve our comfort. My challenge for you: Are you trying to preserve the church for yourself and your generation, or are you trying to do church in a way that reaches out to a new generation?

COACHING QUESTIONS

- With what parts of this story do you identify?
- What are the internal shifts you are facing if your church is to grow forward?
- Who can help you make the needed shifts?
- What next steps are you willing to take now?

A Model from Luke's Writings in Luke and Acts

Sam Hobson, a retired Presbyterian minister believes that "historically, the church has been too acquiescent to society's dominant culture and often ends up promoting the status quo when it should be questioning it.

> "If a culture is not seeking social justice, if it is not seeking inclusivity, then the church should question it—both within and outside the church itself. The perfect church would be one in which every nation of the Earth could be seen represented—worshipping in one place.[3]

Rev. Milly Morrow of The Cathedral of All Souls in Biltmore Village, North Carolina, explains, "The people gathered in remembrance of Christ and Christ's work in the world. And it's for us to continue that—which is work of justice and mercy."[4]

For the church to be on mission, reaching people under thirty, it must be following the Great Commission and be as outwardly focused as it is inwardly focused, concerned as much about "them" as "us." Jesus' final words were the culmination of his earthly ministry—his example, his teaching, his mentoring. I see a progression of four steps in Jesus' example that the early church followed, as recorded in the New Testament books by Luke, namely Luke and Acts.

1. Come and See

Jesus connected with people and invited them to follow him. He built relationships. He got to know people and invited them to get to know him before he talked with them about taking up their cross and following him.

For example, look at Zacchaeus. Jesus saw him in a tree, called him down, and said that he was going home with Zacchaeus. Let's look at this brief story from the Gospel of Luke:

> He entered Jericho and was passing through it. A man was there named Zacchaeus; he was a chief tax collector and was rich. He was trying to see who Jesus was, but on account of the crowd he could not, because

he was short in stature. So he ran ahead and climbed a sycamore tree to see him, because he was going to pass that way. When Jesus came to the place, he looked up and said to him, "Zacchaeus, hurry and come down; for I must stay at your house today." So he hurried down and was happy to welcome him. All who saw it began to grumble and said, "He has gone to be the guest of one who is a sinner." Zacchaeus stood there and said to the Lord, "Look, half of my possessions, Lord, I will give to the poor; and if I have defrauded anyone of anything, I will pay back four times as much." Then Jesus said to him, "Today salvation has come to this house, because he too is a son of Abraham. For the Son of Man came to seek out and to save the lost." (Lk. 19:1–10)

Zacchaeus was curious about Jesus. He didn't come to worship him that day; he just wanted to look at him. Jesus wanted to build a relationship with a sinner, so he abandoned all the religious leaders and went home to spend the day with Zacchaeus. Luke doesn't tell us that Jesus preached to him, scolded him for his sins, or reprimanded him for not going to synagogue every week. A relationship with Jesus changed Zacchaeus. He voluntarily told Jesus what he was going to do to make his life right. Such change in behavior shows conviction and repentance. Jesus saw that seeking and saving the lost was not what the temple leaders expected, but it was Jesus' mission.

In Acts we can see where Paul followed Jesus' example:

In Lystra there was a man sitting who could not use his feet and had never walked, for he had been crippled from birth. He listened to Paul as he was speaking. And Paul, looking at him intently and seeing that he had faith to be healed, said in a loud voice, "Stand upright on your feet." And the man sprang up and began to walk. When the crowds saw what Paul had done, they shouted in the Lycaonian language, "The gods have come down to us in human form!" Barnabas they called Zeus, and Paul they called Hermes, because he was the chief speaker. The priest of Zeus, whose temple was just outside the city, brought oxen and garlands to the gates; he and the crowds wanted to offer sacrifice. When the apostles Barnabas and Paul heard of it, they tore their clothes and rushed out into the crowd, shouting, "Friends, why are you doing this? We are mortals just like you, and we bring you good news, that you should turn from these worthless things to the living God, who made the heaven and the earth and the sea and all that is in them. In past generations he allowed all the nations to follow their own ways; yet he has not left himself without a witness in doing good—giving you rains from heaven and fruitful seasons and filling you with food and your hearts with joy." (Acts 14:8–18)

Paul related to the man who could not walk. He focused on him. He saw his need. He perceived his faith. Then when he responded to the crowd who had mistaken him and Barnabas as gods, he gave Jesus the rightful credit for deeds the people had attributed to their gods—creation, rain and harvest, and a personal relationship that leads to happiness. It is one of the few times Paul did not immediately proclaim Jesus' death and resurrection. Rather *he met the people at their point of need and understanding and connected with them there.* He offered them an invitation to come and see his God, the God who was truly responsible for all the good in their lives.

Many churches and leaders miss the vital significance of the "come and see" phase of ministry for this postmodern and pre-Christian culture. Many are afraid or even resistant to shifting to this phase of discipling for fear of "entertaining others." Jesus knew that you have to attract people before you can reach them. Meeting people where they are, rather than where we want them to be, is the first step we take in ministering in a pre-Christian world. *Yes, it's risky, sometimes messy, but always essential for those who are pre-Christian and from an unchurched culture.*

People under thirty are on a spiritual journey, but often they don't know Jesus. They may just be curious about him. Reaching them will mean building relationships with them and inviting them to a relationship with Jesus.

2. Come Follow Me

Jesus invited people to follow him—just as they were. He didn't begin the journey with a lot of preconditions or stipulations such as, "If you're going to follow me, you'll need to dress this way, read this translation of the Bible, fill out these forms, come three Sundays in a row, and bring an offering." No, he just said, "Follow me." With some people he did see what blocked them from following him and invited them to give away riches or forsake family because those things prevented them from following him.

> After this he went out and saw a tax collector named Levi, sitting at the tax booth; and he said to him, "Follow me." And he got up, left everything, and followed him.
>
> Then Levi gave a great banquet for him in his house; and there was a large crowd of tax collectors and others sitting at the table with them. The Pharisees and their scribes were complaining to his disciples, saying, "Why do you eat and drink with tax collectors and sinners?" Jesus answered, "Those who are well have no need of a physician, but those who are sick; I have come to call not the righteous but sinners to repentance." (Lk. 5:27–32)

Jesus didn't go to the synagogue or temple to spend time with the scribes and Pharisees and to choose his disciples from the church crowd. He called people from their everyday routines. He called sinners. He called tax collectors, who were among the least popular people of the day, to follow him and become his disciples.

Acts records a great discussion among the disciples, the early church leaders, about taking the Good News of Jesus Christ to the Gentiles, to the pagan people of the world. Some people thought Jesus came just to the Jews. Others thought that if Gentiles were to come to Jesus they must first become Jews. However, Peter had a dream that was confirmed when he met with Cornelius, an Italian centurion. All who came to Jesus were to be welcomed without any conditions, such as circumcision or first becoming a Jew. When Peter saw the Holy Spirit enter the lives of new Gentile believers, he was convinced.

> While Peter was still speaking, the Holy Spirit fell upon all who heard the word. The circumcised believers who had come with Peter were astounded that the gift of the Holy Spirit had been poured out even on the Gentiles, for they heard them speaking in tongues and extolling God. Then Peter said, "Can anyone withhold the water for baptizing these people who have received the Holy Spirit just as we have?" So he ordered them to be baptized in the name of Jesus Christ. Then they invited him to stay for several days. (Acts 10:44–48)

Jesus also used teachable moments to instruct those who engaged him in conversation. Even though he knew their need, he timed his teaching to meet their ability to grow in understanding. One example is his response to the rich ruler.

> A certain ruler asked him, "Good Teacher, what must I do to inherit eternal life?"
>
> Jesus said to him, "Why do you call me good? No one is good but God alone. You know the commandments: 'You shall not commit adultery; You shall not murder; You shall not steal; You shall not bear false witness; Honor your father and mother.'" He replied, "I have kept all these since my youth." When Jesus heard this, he said to him, "There is still one thing lacking. Sell all that you own and distribute the money to the poor, and you will have treasure in heaven; then come, follow me." But when he heard this, he became sad; for he was very rich. Jesus looked at him and said, "How hard it is for those who have wealth to enter the kingdom of God! Indeed, it is easier for a camel to go through the eye of a needle than for someone who is rich to enter the kingdom of God."
>
> Those who head it said, "Then who can be saved?" He replied, "What is impossible for mortals is possible for God." (Lk. 18:18–27)

Jesus used teaching opportunities to connect life principles with spiritual truths. The rich ruler may have kept the letter of the law, but he had not made the connection to love God and love others. Instead, he loved his money. The man didn't ask about money or compassion or loving your neighbor, but Jesus saw his real need and used his question to speak to his life situation.

In the book of Acts, Philip, guided by the Holy Spirit, used the Ethiopian eunuch's interest in reading Isaiah to tell him how to be saved.

Now there was an Ethiopian eunuch, a court official of the Candace, queen of the Ethiopians, in charge of her entire treasury. He had come to Jerusalem to worship and was returning home; seated in his chariot, he was reading the prophet Isaiah.

Then the Spirit said to Philip, "Go over to this chariot and join it." So Philip ran up to it and heard him reading the prophet Isaiah. He asked, "Do you understand what you are reading?" He replied, "How can I, unless someone guides me?" And he invited Philip to get in and sit beside him. Now the passage of the scripture that he was reading was this:

"Like a sheep he was led to the slaughter,
and like a lamb silent before his shearer,
   so he does not open his mouth.
In his humiliation justice was denied him.
   Who can describe his generation?
   For his life is taken away from the earth."

The eunuch asked Philip, "About whom, may I ask you, does the prophet say this, about himself or about someone else?" Then Philip began to speak, and starting with this scripture, he proclaimed to him the good news about Jesus. As they were going along the road, they came to some water; and the eunuch said, "Look, here is water! What is to prevent me from being baptized?" He commanded the chariot to stop, and both of them, Philip and the eunuch, went down into the water, and Philip baptized him. (Acts 8:27–38)

A part of Jesus' invitation to follow him—to listen to him, to learn from him how to be saved as well as how to live—meant entertaining the crowd, capturing and holding their attention using the best skills of the day. He taught, he used examples, and he told stories. The crowd's interest is obvious, for they stayed with him well beyond dinnertime. During this phase of discipling, Jesus responded to questions those around him asked. *He didn't impose himself on others; he looked for, prayed for the teaching:*

The crowds . . . followed him; and he welcomed them, and spoke to them about the kingdom of God, and healed those who needed to be cured.

The day was drawing to a close, and the twelve came to him and said, "Send the crowd away, so that they may go into the surrounding villages and countryside, to lodge and get provision; for we are here in a deserted place." But he said to them, "You give them something to eat." They said, "We have no more than five loaves and two fish—unless we are to go and buy food for all these people." For there were about five thousand men. (Lk. 9:11–14a)

Peter also attracted a crowd when he preached in Jerusalem after Jesus' ascension. They responded to his powerful, and likely entertaining, message:

"So those who welcomed his message were baptized, and that day about three thousand persons were added. They devoted themselves to the apostles' teaching and fellowship, to the breaking of bread and the prayers" (Acts 2:41–42).

3. Come Be with Me

Jesus spent the most time with those he called to be with him, to be his disciples, his closest followers—these included the twelve as well as others. He mentored them. He let them try their ministry skills with him nearby to coach and console.

First he commissioned the twelve:

Then Jesus called the twelve together and gave them power and authority over all demons and to cure diseases, and he sent them out to proclaim the kingdom of God and to heal . . . They departed and went through the villages, bringing the good news and curing diseases everywhere (Lk. 9:1–2, 6).

Later he sent out seventy of his followers:

After this the Lord appointed seventy others and sent them on ahead of him in pairs to every town and place where he himself intended to go . . . The seventy returned with joy, saying, "Lord, in your name even the demons submit to us!" (Lk. 10:1, 17).

Barnabas first took a chance with a man who had a dramatic conversion, one who went from persecuting the church to planting churches—the missionary Paul.

When he had come to Jerusalem, he attempted to join the disciples; and they were all afraid of him, for they did not believe that he was a disciple. But Barnabas took him, brought him to the apostles, and described for them how on the road he had seen the Lord, who had spoken to him, and how in Damascus he had spoken boldly in the name of Jesus. (Acts 9:26–27)

For a time after that, Barnabas mentored Saul. Barnabas was willing to risk his reputation on a young man who had been a leader in killing those who followed Christ. Barnabas was even willing to train Paul and let him go on to surpass his own ministry. No wonder he was known as the encourager.

Paul mentored Christ followers like Priscilla and Aquila, and they in turn mentored others:

Now there came to Ephesus a Jew named Apollos, a native of Alexandria. He was an eloquent man, well-versed in the scriptures. He had been instructed in the Way of the Lord; and he spoke with burning enthusiasm and taught accurately the things concerning Jesus, though he knew only the baptism of John. He began to speak boldly in the synagogue; but when Priscilla and Aquila heard him, they took him aside and explained the Way of God to him more accurately. And when he wished to cross over to Achaia, the believers encouraged him and wrote to the disciples to welcome him. On his arrival he greatly helped those who through grace had become believers, for he powerfully refuted the Jews in public, showing by the scriptures that the Messiah is Jesus. (Acts 18:24–28)

Paul also mentored young leaders like John Mark and Timothy by taking them on missionary journeys with him. Then, unable to be with all the churches all the time, he continued to disciple new believers as well as church leaders through the letters he wrote: "Keep on doing the things that you have learned and received and heard and seen in me, and the God of peace will be with you" (Phil. 4:9).

Certainly Jesus was not always pleased with what the disciples did, and sometimes he had to correct them.

People were bringing even infants to him that he might touch them; and when the disciples saw it, they sternly ordered them not to do it. But Jesus called for them and said, "Let the little children come to me, and do not stop them; for it is to such as these that the kingdom of God belongs. Truly I tell you, whoever does not receive the kingdom of God as a little child will never enter it." (Lk. 18:15–17)

Yet even in correcting his disciples, Jesus was teaching them, showing that he loved them enough to want them to grow.

Paul also instructed those he mentored:

Continue in what you have learned and firmly believed, knowing from whom you learned it, and how from childhood you have known the sacred writings that are able to instruct you for salvation through faith in Christ Jesus. All scripture is inspired by God and is useful for teaching, for reproof, for correction, and for training in righteousness, so that everyone who belongs to God may be proficient, equipped for every good work. (2 Tim. 3:14–17)

Developing leaders requires love for them and love for the church. It takes time and patience. It requires a desire to multiply leaders to continue to go and make disciples.

4. Abide in Me

Jesus' ultimate goal was for his disciples to become like him, to become one with him, to have learned so completely from him that they would know what to do. To reach this goal, Jesus promised his ongoing presence with them:

Abide in me as I abide in you. Just as the branch cannot bear fruit by itself unless it abides in the vine, neither can you unless you abide in me. I am the vine, you are the branches. Those who abide in me and I in them bear much fruit, because apart from me you can do nothing . . . . If you abide in me, and my words abide in you, ask for whatever you wish, and it will be done for you. My Father is glorified by this, that you bear much fruit and become my disciples. As the Father has loved me, so I have loved you; abide in my love. If you keep my commandments, you will abide in my love, just as I have kept my Father's commandments and abide in his love. I have said these things to you so that my joy may be in you, and that your joy may be complete. (Jn. 15:4–5, 7–11)

Such abiding love does not happen overnight. Jesus spent three full years with these men before he reached this point with them.

Paul also taught others to abide in Christ:

For we do not proclaim ourselves; we proclaim Jesus Christ as Lord and ourselves as your slaves for Jesus' sake. For it is the God who said, "Let light shine out of darkness," who has shone in our hearts to give the light of the knowledge of the glory of God in the face of Jesus Christ.

But we have this treasure in clay jars, so that it may be made clear that this extraordinary power belongs to God and does not come from us. . . .

Grace, as it extends to more and more people, may increase thanksgiving, to the glory of God. (2 Cor. 4:5–7, 15b)

This is a model not only for the disciples or for the early church but also for us today as we seek to stay on mission, reaching and engaging the unchurched—especially those under thirty—with the Good News of Jesus Christ.

We must invite them to *come and see*. We must honor their curiosity and tolerate what we might perceive as irreverence. We must build relationships so that we can communicate. We must know their greatest needs and show them that Jesus cares about them and can fulfill their deepest longings, heal their deepest hurts. We must be willing to spend time with them and patiently guide them to the cross. Creating a safe place for persons to explore life questions, issues, and struggles is key at this point of the journey. A question that might guide us here is,

- How would Jesus deal with curious persons who are different from him?

We must invite them to *come and follow* Christ. We must do this without asking them to conform to our way of doing church or worshiping God. We must hear and learn about their world even as we seek to involve and include them in the life of the church. We must watch for opportunities to teach and to entertain, to find the teachable moments to help them connect lifestyle issues with eternal truth. We must be prepared to show them the relevance of God's Word and the Savior it proclaims. Key questions that might direct us here are:

- What not only attracts persons but leads them to deeper places and higher levels of leading, loving, and learning?
- What are people ready to learn now?
- How do we respond to their life questions in ways they can understand and that fuel their souls?

We must invite them to *come be with me*, mentoring them, teaching them, helping them discover their gifts, allowing them to try on leadership positions, and assisting them in growing as leaders, thereby equipping them to reach others of their generation in the postmodern world. We must be willing to turn over leadership to them, guiding them but also realizing that they can take the church to places those over sixty cannot, and those new directions will win others to Christ. Key questions that might guide us here are:

- How can I be the presence of Christ in the midst of the world, family, job, and community I live in?
- How can the Christ in me meet and address the need in the world?

We must love them and nurture them and pray for them until they *abide in Christ* as mature believers. As we grow in relationship with these younger leaders, we will all be branches of the same vine, abiding together in him. Guiding questions here might be:

- What does it mean to rest in God's care and vision for you now?
What are the ways he directs you now?

Dr. Jolene Erlacher provides three keys for engaging Millennials on your intergenerational ministry team:

Take time for team relationships.

Trust is the foundation of any healthy team, but it takes time and effort. Amidst the urgency of ministry demands, team building requires intentionality and prioritization, especially for those whose personalities or perspectives do not naturally resonate. Millennials desire ministry teams that feel like a family, not a business. When was the last time your team sat around and discussed why they feel called to this ministry? Do you know what is going on in each other's families? Is there regular discussion of what dreams God is putting in the hearts and minds around your church office? While team relationships are critical, even more important to Millennials is how team members relate to leaders. Accustomed to engaged parents, Millennials expect leaders who want to coach and mentor them. Is there a culture of honesty, trust, mentoring, and encouragement between leaders and those working with them? Without healthy, authentic relationships, young adults will quickly become disengaged.

Encourage questions and honest dialogue.

"'Why?' is the question of childhood and youth. "Why?" has become the question of young adults. In many leadership contexts, questions arise from those holding dissenting opinions. They come as a form of challenge to decisions or goals. As a result, we sometimes develop a resistance to questioning, seeing it as a sign of conflict to resolve and thus additional work in our already busy lives. When young adults ask 'why?' however, they genuinely want to understand the reasons behind traditions, decisions, and initiatives. Like a three-year-old who wants to know why the sky is blue, Millennials are not asking to annoy us. They truly desire to understand.

Consider the young man who asked, "Just when was it decided and who decided that a church service consisted of singing a few songs and then having to sit and listen—bored or not—to someone speak to me for 30 minutes to an hour?" His leader explained to me that in her experience, "The act of "'going to church"' was the important thing—not necessarily what we got out of it. The loyalty was built into me—going to church was important. I just did not question if it was the right thing or not." She said, "I see Millennials more concerned about the content. That's a good thing." Strive for Socratic interactions in your conversations and meetings. Create an environment where young adults feel safe to ask questions. Embracing the "why" questions vocalized by Millennials creates an opportunity to truly reflect on reasons for ministry practices being what they are, analyze them in light of Scripture, and pass on valuable truths to the next generation! Honest and thorough answers will accomplish much in helping young ministry leaders make sense of important values and ideas.

Give and request timely and consistent feedback.

Gone are the days of annual performance reviews. Millennials are accustomed to instant and specific feedback. This generation has been conditioned to receive a gold star or trophy just for showing up and participating, so an absence of affirmation communicates something is wrong. When her pastor asked Nina if she needed more feedback, she responded, "Yes! If I don't hear what you are thinking, I automatically assume something negative. If I don't get any encouraging words, I automatically think I've done something wrong." Thus, feedback not only encourages, but also contributes to the ability of young leaders to serve confidently. Millennials also appreciate the opportunity to give feedback. They are used to engaging with information by "liking," "commenting," "sharing" or "retweeting," so asking for their input on ministry initiatives and decisions will do much to engage them on your team.

Adjusting our leadership styles or team dynamics to engage and empower young leaders is an investment into their ministries for years to come. Blessings as you correct, encourage, and inspire the leaders of tomorrow![5]

COACHING QUESTIONS

- What did you learn about the four phases of Jesus ministry that you did not know before?
- How can you follow Jesus' example in your circle of friends and family?
- What are your next steps?
- What are the implications of ministry in the midst of diversity?

Missions or Maintenance

Check the following statements that are true for your church to see if your church has a missions or a maintenance mentality.

_____ 1. Our buildings are very important to us. We maintain them well and use them often.

_____ 2. Our staff reports on the number of pastoral visits they make.

_____ 3. We are always offering new opportunities for participation in ministries.

_____ 4. We get people involved in disciple-making and growing groups.

_____ 5. We work to fill every program position in our organization.

_____ 6. Our church tries to help Christ followers find places to use their gifts both inside and outside the church.

_____ 7. We try not to upset our senior church leaders.

_____ 8. The leaders in our church work hard to make the church a stable, unchanging anchor in our world.

_____ 9. Our church has a great fellowship, loving one another and taking care of each member's needs.

_____ 10. Our church looks for ways to meet the needs of people in our community and even around the world.

1, 2, 5, 7, 8, 9 are maintenance statements.

3, 4, 6, 10 are mission statements

PART II: Discovering Points of Tension

3

When Generations Collide

People are living longer. A church might minister to five or six generations of a single family at the same time. Not long ago I sat on a church platform and observed the congregation. Part of the service was a baby dedication. Near the front in one row, sat five generations of one family. Watching their participation in this traditional service, I observed that the older the members of this family were, the more they engaged in the service. They sang with gusto, using their open hymnals. They opened their Bibles when Scripture was read. They listened intently, nodding in affirmation. As I glanced down the pew, I saw that being engaged in the worship service diminished with each generation, rapidly reaching boredom and apparent total disinterest.

For the first time in history, most churches face the challenge of ministering to five or more generations at one time. Most churches in America participate in worship, Bible study, and just about everything else in much the way they have for more than fifty years, when the Builder Generation took the lead and began to build buildings and programs. We are rapidly losing our Builder Generation. They've been faithful in building our churches and our institutions and in financing local church ministries and missions around the world, but the Builders are retiring and dying. Churches are not replacing them with younger generations of leaders. Baby Boomers are left trying to figure out what to do to grow a new generation of members and of leaders. They quickly find that what pleases one generation often doesn't satisfy the next generation, much less the third, fourth, or fifth.

Part of the challenge of reaching people under thirty while keeping those over sixty is a generational issue because generations have different preferences for how they worship, minister, learn, lead, relate, and interact with one another. They have different personal preferences and lifestyles, styles of music, and attire. They also experience community in different ways.

Many churches, and even denominations, have not yet figured out that we are in a different culture and that if we don't change things, we're not going to reach younger generations. What many term a lack of commitment is usually more rooted in a lack of understanding of shifting cultures and community.

Americans are living longer, resulting in most of our church leadership base remaining in office so that an older generation continues to determine the directions in which our churches grow. In many cases the Builder Generation is still leading the denomination, but they are dying out rapidly. Some aging Baby Boomers are also in leadership roles and are beginning to feel the pinches of a leadership void because funding is dropping and existing leaders are aging out. Tithers are retiring and dying. Churches and denominational agencies have less money than they once did. It's happening in all Protestant and mainline denominations across the country.

The overlooked generation currently ranges in age from thirty-four to forty-nine, which may be one reason they're so often missing from stories about demographic, social, and political change. They're smack in the middle innings of life, which tend to be short on drama and scant of theme. Churches that learn to effectively engage aging Boomers have a bright future.

Other explanations have nothing to do with stage of the life cycle. George Bullard observes,

> Back in the 1970s a lot of congregational prognosticators warned that the Church, in general, was in the process of losing a whole demographic generation known as Baby Boomers. Existing congregations, new congregations, and denominational approaches to ministry were losing the ability to appeal to this numerically largest generation ever born in North America. Generally the birth years of this generation were 1946 through 1964.
>
> As this generation approached their 20s during the 1960s they became a generation known for their rock music, pursuit of mind altering drugs, guilt free sexual love, and demand for peace. While not nearly all—or even a majority—of this generation connected with all these issues, the segment of the Baby Boomers who did was loud. They rejected institutions and authority and saw the Church, in general, and congregations, specifically, fitting into their perception of irrelevant.
>
> I was part of this generation, but missed out on most of the experiences. The only parts that infected me were a pro-peace bias, a belief popularized by Jacques Ellul that institutions do violence to individuals, and some learnings from Saul Alinsky about community organizing that have helped me work with congregations to organize them as social systems.
>
> As the public crescendo of warnings by the congregational prognosticators reached its zenith and full volume in numerous places around North America, a new style of congregation known as contemporary was gaining traction. The most well known of these were

Saddleback Valley Community Church and Willow Creek Community Church. Since you know exactly who I am talking about when I name these two congregations, it is obvious their approach worked.

The power of the response to these contemporary congregations was so great that with some modifications many of these congregations adapted to the next generation known as the Baby Busters. Generally the birth years of this generation were 1964 through 1982.[1]

Ten thousand Baby Boomers turn sixty-five each day. Approximately 70 percent of senior adults need some kind of assistance as they age. Richard Eisenberg reviews emerging communities for aging Boomers: (1) co-housing; (2) niche retirement communities; (3) NORC—naturally occurring retirement communities—like communities where groups of people have aged where they live; (4) shared housing; (5) and "The Village Model"—where neighbors help one another.[2]

Pew research indicates, "Gen Xers are bookended by two much larger generations—the Baby Boomers ahead and the Millennials behind—that are strikingly different from one another. And in most of the ways we take stock of generations—their racial and ethnic makeup; their political, social and religious values; their economic and educational circumstances; their technology usage—Gen Xers are a low-slung, straight-line bridge between two noisy behemoths. Millennials outnumber the boomers and busters in our 2015 culture"[3]

I was in a church one Wednesday night during a business session. The topic was new choir robes. The church was more liturgical than many in its denomination. Members liked choir robes and formal worship. I observed the reactions among the different generations in that meeting. Many of the younger adults were disengaged. Those actually focused on the discussion may not have said anything; yet any observer could clearly discern that the silent majority disagreed with the whole direction. The topic was which new choir robes, but what the younger group was clearly thinking was whether to have choir robes or even a choir. The older church leaders seemed oblivious to the discontent of nearly everyone under forty in that room that night.

Later I met with the church staff. They knew the church wasn't growing and wanted it to grow. They were looking for insight and new direction. I asked them what the nonnegotiables were, what they were not willing to change in their church. That question made them a little uncomfortable. After a few moments of nervous silence, I mentioned the choir robes. They had a new young staff minister whose age-group assignment was students and young adults. Most of the other staff members were in the over-sixty group or close to it. The pastor got nervous, jittery. The longtime minister of music crossed his legs, uncrossed them, then crossed them the other way. Another staff member folded his arms across his chest and looked at the pastor. Finally the new young guy broke the tension and said, "I think we probably need to change worship if we are going to reach any young people."

The pastor said, "Change worship? Why do we need to do that?"

The new staff person, respectful but direct, answered the pastor, "Well, now that I'm building relationships with students and young couples in the area, they're telling me they are bored in worship."

"Bored? With what? What's wrong with our worship? What's their problem with it?" The pastor was trying to remain calm but was clearly getting increasingly agitated.

Then the new staff person started squirming. The worship leaders hadn't even considered changing worship, yet they wanted to reach younger adults. The same could be said for other areas of the church. Worship is the most visible and the entry point for most people into the church, so it is often the focus of change. Too often the worship experience is only community for a small group of attendees.

This staff group interaction is taking place in many churches, if they are talking at all about change and reaching people under thirty. The generational tension that was evident in that meeting is just a fraction of what can be seen in churches when they consider changing. Those over sixty often can't see a need to change, and those under thirty think it is so obvious it hardly needs discussing.

Leonard Sweet offers some significant insight in these general observations:

While traditional worship has tended to be:	Contemporary worshipers seek worship that is:
Rational or linear	Experiential
Performance-based (choir/preacher)	Participatory (congregational)
Centered on words	Image-rich
Focused on individual	Connected

Finding and Connecting with God and Others on the Journey

North American churches find themselves in an increasingly pagan and secular world; church images, careers, language, concepts, values, traditions, rituals are losing influence among the churched and the unchurched at a frightening pace. This is not to say that people are not spiritual, for they may be more spiritual than in recent decades; however, the power and influence of the institutional church is fading. As the church-culture of the Builder Generation dies out, so do their values in most situations. Their children and grandchildren have lost or changed their connections with traditional family church values.

Christopher Ingraham writes:

While the number of religiously unaffiliated Americans has risen dramatically in recent years, measures like belief in God and church attendance have appeared remarkably stable. Researchers have hypothesized that people were turning away from religious institutions and taking more of a 'cafeteria approach' to belief.". . . But these poll findings suggest that many more people are simply not going to the cafeteria at all.[4]

The article explains that such behavior is consistent with the trend for Americans to choose "none"—or to refrain from affiliating with a church.

How do we move on and meet the needs of all those on the journey without sacrificing the integrity of the Good News? It seems to me that much of this rests on the way we define church, conversion, faithfulness, fruitfulness, and what it means to be the people of God in an increasingly secular world.

Many churches today want to reach the younger generations—Millennials and Gen X and Y. However, most seem to want the youth to change to the existing leadership's core beliefs, values, and traditions without much, if any, conversation, much less negotiation. Bruce Gourley writes,

> Roughly one in three Millennials claim no religious affiliation.... A large and growing segment of Millennials pointedly identify conservative/fundamentalist theology as that which steered them away from organized religion. . . . Nevertheless, spirituality is not at all unusual among Millennials, although not always easily definable.[5]

Much of the challenge today is the array of generational and cultural distinctives in the faith journey. What seems to work for one age or cultural group does not always seem to work for another age group. The older generations desire to preserve what has worked for them, and their children and grandchildren are their hope for making this happen. The reality seems to be that we can't get to where we want to go unless we are willing to leave where we are. Indeed, there's only one faith, but we are all learning there are many different and valid expressions of that faith. Such expressions often depend on the heritage or mindset of the person. In many families, children and grandchildren have dropped out of church or moved to a more generationally friendly church/worship style. Such collisions bring deep conflict and disappointment for many and often fuel family tensions that can sabotage faith journeys. How sad!

Community Building Learning Experiences to Deepen Understanding of All Generations

We can build bridges rather than barriers between the generations and thus create community. Consider these ideas.

Create and facilitate interview cycles among persons of all generations. Provide forums in a casual but structured atmosphere for parents/grandparents to interview children and grandchildren. Sample interest starters might include:

- In what setting do you experience God the most?
- What makes these experiences meaningful to you?
- Describe the most meaningful experiences you have in life. Is God included?

- What distinctive elements from your culture/ethnicity/family impact your faith walk at the deepest level?
- What is missing in your church life or spiritual life?
- What do you think would make your faith more alive?
- How can our church change to enliven faith and worship for you?
- Which persons inside or outside the church most nurture your faith life?
- What do you remember most from your teenage years about church, times of worship and Bible study?

Plan for each generation to visit various styles of worship, Bible study, and mission involvement together. Be sure to include various music styles. Arrange a multigenerational setting to critique these experiences. Find a thirty- or forty-something to serve as a neutral facilitator to help pull the best learnings from each experience and group. Open the meeting with Builder music—piano or organ prelude, a hymn from a standard hymnbook, special music from a robed choir. At uncharted intervals, let a rock group, Christian band, or other contemporary source begin playing.

During discussion time, as a topic creates mutual interest, have the facilitator invite each group to find more information on the topic. What sources would each group expect to use? The younger generation(s) can lead in a search on Google. (The younger generation might have to explain "Google search" to the older generation.) The older generation could then introduce the traditional way of finding information. The older generation might search the Yellow Pages, find a volume of an encyclopedia set, or conduct a survey of their church friends to gain knowledge on the topic. (The older group might have to explain "Yellow Pages" to the youth.)

Questions the facilitator might ask to create community among generations include:

- What experience touched your life in an ongoing way beyond the service?
- How did you respond to the music?
- What made each visit meaningful for you?
- What elements led you to experience worship? What elements hindered worship?
- Where did you experience the presence of God in the worship, Bible study, mission project?
- What was missing for you in this experience?
- How would you have changed the experience to make it more significant for you?

Review music of the generations. More often than not, certain generations have their distinctive music preferences. They like certain types and dislike others. This provides fuel for the worship wars. Plan family times to attend a modern Christian music concert and a symphony or choir concert. Gather the family to discuss responses to the music programs. Let a member of the younger generation ask these or other questions to help uncover some new understandings:

- What type music do you listen to during your leisure times? How does it compare to the music concerts?
- What makes this music meaningful to you?
- Does this music evoke memories? What kind?
- What feelings surface?
- Who was with you when you first experienced this music?
- How do you connect with this music?
- What appreciation have you developed for the other generation's music?

Explore visual arts. Members of the younger generation often wear their faith story and personal uniqueness on their bodies via tattoos, dress style, jewelry selections, hairstyles, etc. These are not acts of rebellion as the older generation too often thinks. They represent ways the younger group uses to communicate who they are to the world. Other generations treasure different visual arts:

- stained-glass windows often tell the faith story of the church culture;
- church dress (coat and tie and best dress) communicates reverence and respect for God and the church;
- personal pieces of art help a person express personal dedication.

Visual arts are venues of worship, identity, etc., in many different ways. See what you might discover in dialog with a different generation over topics like these:

- When and how did you decide on your visual art preferences?
- What visual representations help you in worship? Why?
- What is meaningful to you about your preferred visual art?
- What would be missing if your visual symbols were not allowed or respected?
- What visual symbols do you think would enhance your understanding or experience with God and his movement in your life if they were more often utilized ?
- What are the places our stories connect or find similar connections?
- What might happen if families, churches, and friends were to engage in this kind of dialogue in an intentional and sensitive manner?

As I write this we are in Advent. My local community of faith built Advent around intergenerational dialogues seeking to help generations learn from the faith journey of others. We've discovered this approach is not only a family builder, but it also engages singles and those without biological family present into the intergenerational dialogue about hope, peace, and other Advent themes. Everyone wants to do this again!

Capturing Your Learnings

Now, what are the mutual learnings you want to lock in from these dialogues? Capture them for history as building blocks for future dialogues and next steps in your spiritual journey and spiritual friendships. As a group consider and capture in print:

- What did we learn from this experience?
- What are the things we have in common?
- What are our distinctives?
- What new understandings do we have about each generation's distinctives?
- What did you learn that you did not know before about persons of another generation?
- What did you learn about their spiritual journey that brings you encouragement and hope?
- How can you continue to build on these learnings?
- What are your personal next steps as a result of this experience?
- What false impressions did you have about another generation?

Learning to build bridges and value bridge-building more than arguing is essential if we are to be community and watch God continue to move in all ages and generations. Everyone's journey is important and unique. Everyone's encounter with God has highly distinctive and personal ingredients. Persons who are not church people, more often than not, have experiences with God. Learn to ask about them rather than judge them. Persons who like different music often find great hope, healing, restoration, and the presence of God in music that speaks to them. Learning to embrace them, even if not their music, helps the human community mature and the faith community grow deeper and wider and more authentic. The people of Scripture certainly encountered God in a variety of ways—in gardens of good and evil; standing on the banks of major challenges; some when they picked up a snake; some when they struck a rock; others when they saw a fire in the sky and decided to follow it; some who encountered God in the whirlwind and others in the quiet whisper; some who encountered God in the acts of nature and others in the power of quietness while doing their job on the hillside of a desert. Yes, God comes to us in a variety of ways.

I cannot help but wonder what aspects of God we might have missed through the years because we have limited the way God comes to us by our own familiarity of preferences. What would happen if we opened ourselves to encountering God in all of life, through all mediums of art, dress, music, worship styles, etc., that he provides through the gifting he gives to his people. Learning to treasure our uniqueness just might help us find and experience God in deeper ways and places than we have ever known. Think about it.

Creating Community among Generations

Churches that change to reach people under thirty generally experience generational tension unless they have no younger adults who are engaged enough to care. Sadly, in many churches nearly everyone under thirty has given up being actively involved in the institutional church. Change is difficult and risky. Knowing what to change is difficult and different for each church, so we have no easy answers. We can begin by gaining a greater understanding of the differences in the generations.

The oldest Americans were born into a horse-and-buggy world; children today don't even look up when the TV shows a space shuttle lift off. Many of the oldest generation started life without indoor plumbing and read at night by light from an oil lamp. Today's children begin learning on computers long before they can read or go to school. Some members of the oldest generation were born before World War I; they believed the world was getting better and better with every technological advancement. Children born today live in a world of terrorism and Internet predators who prey on children. The oldest generation was born in a modern world; the youngest is born into a postmodern world.[6]

Between the oldest and youngest generations stand several more who have their own set of formative experiences making them distinct in many ways. The older people are, the more experiences they have in common. For example, older Baby Boomers, nearing sixty, have lived three-quarters of the same years as their eighty-year-old Builder parents. Formative events that took place during their childhood and youth make them see the world a bit differently, but they have lived through many of the same world events. They have differences, but they also have many experiences in common. People under thirty have fewer experiences in common with the oldest generation. The younger they are, the less they have in common and the greater the difference in the way they see the same events. These differences are made even greater because the generations interact less than they did in the past. Many of the younger generations are well educated but cannot find consistent work due to economic challenges. Consequently, many Millennials and Gen Xers are staying at home with parents longer, or they are living in cohabitating situations and often delaying marriage or ignoring marriage as an option for their present and future.

Grandparents, their children, and their grandchildren once lived together on the farm or nearby in town and saw one another regularly. Today several states may separate the generations, and they get together only a few times a year on holidays and weekend visits. Those visits are so quick that they seldom have time to connect, much less learn to value one another's life stories.

Generations are not distinct entities that stand alone, entire within themselves. They overlap. Older generations have lived through all the years the younger generations have, but they have been shaped by events and world changes that the younger generation has not. For example, the oldest generation was shaped by the Great Depression and the rationing of vital supplies during the world wars. The majority of children and even young adults in America today have more than enough of everything; they have little concept of delayed gratification, much less doing without.

Even though the majority of senior adults today no longer have to worry about getting the things they need, many of them buy in quantities and hoard items like paper goods as if they anticipate a shortage any day. They know they can get what they need, but years of economic hardships when they couldn't get many basics shaped them. Younger generations have no similar experiences. Even though the generations overlap, we are shaped by the world into which we are born. Today's younger generations have life issue landmarks related to security because of the events of September 11, 2001. Wide use of the Internet has issued in an invasion of personal privacy issues.

Looking at each generation in greater detail helps us achieve our goal of understanding that generation and what each brings to community. A danger in such knowledge is labeling or making assumptions about individuals, stereotyping individual persons of a generation as all having the exact same characteristics. Each person, of all ages and generations, is uniquely created by God with gifts and personality matched by no one else. Knowing generalities about generations should jump-start understanding to aid in building relationships among generations, not replace the time needed to get to know individuals.

The "Builders"

Builders were influenced by the Great Depression, rationing, World Wars I and II, Pearl Harbor, the automobile, radio, and big band music. Born before 1946, this "generation" (more accurately described as the combination of the GI Generation [1900–1924] and the Silent Generation [1925–1946]) of Americans built the country as we know it today—economically, morally, and religiously. Many of them continue to hold powerful positions with both wealth and influence. The women built airplanes and other products in factories during World War II while the men were fighting a war.

Both physically and organizationally, this generation has shaped the church and most of the church-related institutions. Builders are known for their faithful stewardship, loyalty, and leadership—not only to the local church but also to the denomination, the workplace, the social community.

The GI Generation overcame the Depression and the Second World War. They would say that what they survived only made them stronger. They took charge and built homes, businesses, schools, civic organizations, and churches.

Most of the Silent Generation were too young to serve in World War II, too old to serve in Vietnam. The war they did serve in (Korea) is often overlooked. They are known for their stability and dependability. They have faithfully served and supported the institutions the GI Generation worked so hard to establish.

The family life of the Builder Generation meant loyalty. Divorce rates, though higher for the Silent Generation than the GI Generation, are lower than in subsequent generations. They lived on one income. The father often stayed with one company all of his life. Hierarchy was accepted and expected in all organizations; bureaucracy gave order and stability. Many saw the beginning of change at the end of their careers, when loyalty between a company and employees became less valued than the bottom line, and seniority was often seen as a liability instead of an asset.

Gender roles were clearly distinguished, with the family also having the stability of hierarchical leadership. They had children and supported their schools and bettered their communities through civic organizations. This is the family that stayed together and prayed together.

They believed in and supported missions and evangelism. A higher percentage of Builders call themselves Christians than any subsequent generation. In some churches they continue to lead—and even control—the way the church is organized, the style of worship, and how the money is spent.

Some of them are frustrated in churches today. They don't see younger adults supporting the church with the same determination and unquestioned loyalty they had. Many are overwhelmed by change. With all the changes they have experienced in their lifetime, more of that change has come in the past ten years than in all the prior years. They see that same change going on in the church, and many times they don't understand the reason for the change. They don't necessarily want everything to be the way it once was, but they do long for stability. The changes they see happening in the church seem to be a risk; leaders don't know whether changes will have the desired result. This generation would prefer to stay with the tried-and-true methods they've seen work in the past.

Today members of this generation are retired or soon will be. They don't have the funds to finance the church ministries as they once did.

The Boomer Generation

Baby Boomers—a lot of them—were born after World War II, between 1946 and 1964. Influences that shaped this generation included television, the Cold War, assassinations, the civil rights movement, Vietnam, Kent State, rock and roll, the sexual revolution, the birth control pill, legalized abortion, illegal drugs, Kennedy's "new frontier," the Peace Corps, the space race, Watergate, and the resignation of President Nixon. Is it any wonder this generation mistrusts authority and government?

On a local scale, they began to see parents, who had been loyal to a company for a lifetime, lose their jobs. Drafted to serve in a war many didn't believe in, they came home to find disrespect for their efforts. Disillusioned by the institutions their parents honored and served, Boomers quickly became known as the "Me" Generation, no longer willing to sacrifice for the good of the community.

Their relationship with the church became more personal than institutional. They would rather go to China on a mission trip than to give to send people they don't know associated with an agency they don't care about affiliated with a denomination they often don't agree with and may not trust. They want relationships. The church has to provide fellowship and community. Boomers support individuals but not institutions. They are more tolerant of differences among people than are their parents. While their parents lived to work, this generation works hard and plays hard.

In the family, both spouses work. This generation is the first in which more than 50 percent of marriages end in divorce. Despite equal college education, gender differences abound in the workplace and in the home.

Boomers have thrived on technology and are quick to buy the latest gadget. Their motto is, "Buy now, pay later," sending consumer debt soaring. Self-focused, they have responded to marketing slogans that proclaim, "Get it now. You deserve it." A wealthy generation, they are known more for their spending than for their saving.

At this point in their lives, Boomers are concerned about traditional values, a second career and looming retirement, spiritual search, health and fitness, leisure activities, and trying to slow the pace of their hectic lifestyle. Midlife transitions reveal the death of the American dream. Expecting to soar at midcareer, they face layoffs, downsizing, starting over again, or just giving up. Many accept early retirement and a lifestyle significantly less than what they'd always assumed. Retirement funds disappear to pay debts, mortgages, and college loans and to the care of aging parents. Meanwhile adult kids sometimes just won't leave home.

Having radically changed the world, Boomers aged and become more conservative while remaining unpredictable. According to the Barna Report: The first generation raised with omnipresent television and computers, now reads for pleasure more than any other generational group. The "sex, drugs and rock-and-roll" generation are now only one-third as likely to have extramarital sex as are Busters. They form the generation least likely to get drunk and are no more likely to illegally download music from the Internet than are the Net-impaired Seniors. Only three percent of Boomers engage in yoga in a typical week (compared to 10 percent of Busters).[7]

Made to go to church as children, many quickly abandoned the church at their first opportunity, only to return to it when their children were born. Today they control many churches. Sixty percent of Protestant senior pastors are Boomers, while fifty-eight of current lay leaders are Boomers. Half the money given to churches last year came from Boomers . (That's more than double the amount any other generation gave.)[8]

As their children leave home, a lot of Boomers are dropping out of the church even if they have held leadership positions. In late middle age and looking toward retirement, they find that church doesn't meet their needs the way it once did. Their friends were the parents of their kids' friends. Without their children to keep them connected, those relationships are falling apart. Boomers look outside the church for essential relationships. Instead of mentoring the next generation of church leaders, Boomers continue looking for personal fulfillment. They leave it to the church to search for the next generation of church leaders.

Expressing his concern about this, George Barna writes to "fellow Baby Boomers." He notes the years they have "sweated, argued, fought, manipulated, analyzed, partnered, prayed, and strategized to get our own way,"[9] believing the nation's values should reflect their own. They demanded decision-making authority and key positions. Having blamed the system for problems, they commandeered the system and became the system. Now two generations following the Baby Boomers see control as a serious issue. Boomers are not good at sharing. The richest generation in history, we are the most selfish. One value defines us: power. We have no intention of relinquishing it. Soon we must.

Boomers at age 65:

2011	First Boomer
2015	15 million
2020	31 million
2025	48 million

"The Builders were a can-do, get-it-done generation," Barna says. "But the Boomers are the ultimate take-no-prisoners generation when it comes to shaping society—and, in some cases, the world."[10] You'd think the richest generation in world history would be excited about helping our children to follow in our footsteps. But Boomers revel in power and will not share it, reasoning that quality must be maintained rather than admitting an unhealthy desire for control. Most Boomers—even those in churches—"have no intention of lovingly handing the baton to Baby Busters,"[11] who once again are leaving the church as they did as teenagers. Sometimes the only one to note their disappearance is the church treasurer.

George Bullard adds another dimension to this challenge, introducing his 60-40-20 schema referring to people 60 years old, 40 years as Christians, and 20-year members of the same congregation. Thirty percent of active membership fitting this pattern identifies an overly churched culture congregation. Deeply grounded in how to do church from a perspective of the past, 60–40–20 people are having trouble understanding how to do church in a rapidly changing future-oriented culture. Rather than change, they reinforce church as it has been.

This is often not intentional. They believe the way things have happened in the past should continue forward into the future. They do not realize they are out of touch with reality.[12]

Another perspective comes from Carol Howard Merritt, author of *Tribal Church* and a blog for *Christian Century*, who points to the impact of Baby Boom retirements on our denominations:

- increased number of people on a fixed income.
- with effect on giving;
- an increased volunteer force;

What will we do if there are more willing hands, eager to serve? Many churches are responding by starting low-cost, high volunteer-hour projects, like starting community gardens, farmer's markets, or food pantries. Is your church prepared for a greater influx of volunteers? What dream has your church put off because you did not have enough people to pull it off? This could be an exciting time for you.

A church's governing bodies will need to stay mindful of the employed. Many situations prevent employed people from participating fully in the life of the church. Holding meetings during work hours or not providing child care (a spouse may not be available to watch the children) are two things churches do commonly. Merritt goes on to say,

> Churches need to be aware of even more systemic things. Like in the [Presbyterian Church (USA), pension incentives are given] for employees to put off retirement. This is great for those who are not willing or able to retire, but it's difficult for seminary students who are entering a difficult job market filled with people working past their planned retirement age.
>
> We have talked about putting some energy into going through all of the hoops to change this, but we smash into a wall—church governing systems. Who runs our governing bodies? Retirees or people very close to retiring! Young minsters have no power or influence. Too often they hold on to system control and do not seem to have new, employment-age pastors in mind. For a healthy church, we need to make sure that our young (or even not-so-young) pastors have calls.
>
> Retired pastors will need to be careful about their work. This is such a tough one. I have seen second-career pastors who have a teacher's retirement income and income from their pastor's pension They view the double income as a blessing and as a divine call to work for free. Not needing an extra income seems like a good thing, but it can become very damaging for the church, overall. Churches that could afford to pay full-time ministers (or churches that could become more generous and grow their budget) become dependent on very able and gifted ministers who work for a little bit of nothing.
>
> This can end up hurting the church, because the congregation doesn't have the challenge to be more generous or welcoming to a new generation. It can damage the employment-age pastors, who have seminary debt and need jobs. And it can undermine the overall income level of pastors. After all, why would a church pay a full salary for someone who has a mortgage, kids, and student loans, when you can get a retired pastor with a lot of energy who will eagerly work for far less than minimum wage? As Jesus said and First Timothy echoes, "The laborer deserves to be paid."[13]

A super opportunity awaits the church. We can

1. reconnect and reengage the aging Boomer population;
2. think creatively,
3. move beyond what is to what can be, and
4. take off the blinders that inhibit deepening the faith and function of Boomers in the next twenty years.

Amy Hanson is one of many consultants who are taking on this challenge from a church perspective. Through her blog, she is stretching the institution but is also energizing the Boomers' faith life.[14]

An article in *The Baptist Standard* discusses retiring Baby Boomers:

The generation preceding the boomers—the builders—tended to commit to an organization or group, such as church or a civic club. "Boomers and subsequent generations tend to want to volunteer for a certain project or a cause that is near and dear to their heart,'" noted [Amy] Hanson, author of *Baby Boomers and Beyond: Tapping the Ministry Talents and Passions of Adults Over 50.*

Many boomers move away from volunteering once their children leave home or as a result of downsizing their lifestyle, said Frank Fain, director of educational services for The Baptist Home in Missouri. Some give up volunteering for school events and church functions geared for children and youth because they gave their time when their own children participated in those activities. . . .

The key to enticing baby boomers to volunteer is to tap into their passions. . . . congregations must recognize and respect that boomers prefer short-term commitments, rather than signing up for a multiyear stint.

"While the builder generation was willing to sign on and teach the Sunday School class for 20 years, the boomers want to know that they can be gone to see their grandkids play soccer or take a spontaneous trip with their spouse," Hanson pointed out. . . .

"'Boomers have an entrepreneurial spirit and an attitude that they can change the world,' Hanson added. . . .

Churches looking to the boomer generation to bolster or revitalize senior adult ministry may be disappointed. . . . While most congregations think boomers will move right into the ministry, they likely will not, because they view it as something for their parents and grandparents.

Boomers do not want a connection to anything labeled "senior." . . .

Just as volunteerism needs to be focused, so does giving. . . . But appeals to the generation need to strike the same chords—passion and specific projects or social concerns.

Boomers—just like all believers—must be reminded of the biblical mandate to give, Hanson noted.[15]

The Distinctives of Generations Chart is a quick generalized summary of generations today. A review of the values, preferences of each helps us begin to understand and embrace in ways that creates community.

Churches have a great opportunity to maximize Boomers in ministry efforts as we explore new possibilities for the second half of life. Will churches cling to the past models of ministry and go bust, or will churches engage in innovative dreams and birth the new. God is birthing the new. Will the churches take the

Generational Distinctives of 6 Living Generations—Reflection Exercise for Your Church & Community
For All Generations: 1 Corinthians 9; Mathew 28:19–20;
(Based on presentation in local church)

Characteristics	Builders	Silent	Boomers/Bridgers	Generation X Survivors	Millennials/Gen Y	Generation Z/Homeland Generation?
Birth	1901-1924	1925-1945	1946-1965	1966-85	1986-2003	2003- present *(Now 10 yr old)*
Religious expression	Presbyterian	Episcopalian	New Age	Religiously Independent	Not yet clear	Yet to see
Percentage of US population	2%	7%	30%	21%	28%	13% *(under age of 10 now)*
Typical of your church statistics *(raise hands of those present)*	2%	54%	28%	10%	3%	9%
Relate to your community demographics	2%	19%	22%	26%	20%	11%
Defining events	WW I & II, Great Depression	Korean War, WWII, Space Race, Moral Majority, Communism	Vietnam, human rights, never dealt with Great Depression	Challenger Disaster, AIDS, never dealt with Great wars, affluence, educated, 9/11	Iraq, Columbine, War on Terror, affluence, digital age, recession, educated, 9/11, Iraq War, Global warming realities, 2008 elections	Not yet known

©2015 Edward H. Hammett, *Reaching People under 30 while Keeping People over 60.* www.TransformingSolutions.org.

plunge? Boomers are also seeing the church as an arena for another career and calling. A recent newspaper article speaks to this issue,

> Although many industries are intent on attracting a young workforce, churches have realized the benefits of also recruiting people with real-life seasoning. 'The life experience they bring with them is a great advantage to the churches,' said Carrie Carroll, dean of students at Luther Seminary in St. Paul, Minnesota.
>
> "Nearly a third of the students enrolled in local seminaries are considered baby boomers, defined as those born between 1946 and 1964. Not only is that above the national average—which is pegged at 25 percent—but the state has been ahead of the curve of what's been a relatively recent phenomenon in many places.
>
> "I think it started here 10, if not 15, years ago," said Glen Herrington-Hall, director of admissions at United Theological Seminary in New Brighton, Minnesota. "The seminaries have reached out to older students with innovative formats. United has a program in which classroom training is concentrated in two back-to-back days a week; there even are motel-like dorms on campus for students who drive in from out of town. At Luther, there's a program offering intensive training on campus twice a year—January and June—while everything else can be done online."[16]

The Buster Generation

Busters were born between 1965 and 1983. The Boomer Generation exploded in numbers of births. Then in 1965, the birth rate in the United States dropped from 3.8 million in to 3.1 million, a real bust in numbers, hence the nomenclature Busters or Generation X or Gen X.[17] This generic generation remains largely unknown and not understood. The X seems to indicate that the world is still waiting to see what will be the distinguishing characteristics of this generation.

Busters have been shaped by the AIDS epidemic, legalized abortion (the 1973 decision of *Roe v. Wade*), technology, a varying economy, video games and television, the Challenger disaster, the fall of the Berlin wall and the end of the communist threat, the first Persian Gulf war, and music. This generation accepts situational ethics, truth that is in the eyes of the beholder, and living in shades of gray instead of black-and-white. They are well aware that absolute truth and morality no longer exist in the United States. One Buster said it this way, "No rules, no boundaries, no wacko religious morality."[18]

Not only were Busters the end of the boom of births in the United States, but this generation has also delayed marriage. Disillusioned by their parents' divorces and not wanting to bring children into the world to live as latch-key children the way they were brought up, Busters have sometimes had an attitude of "what's the use?" This attitude is reflected in the workplace as well as the home and the church, if they attend any form of the latter. They are turned off by their parents' work ethic and the lack of resulting rewards. Many move from job to job, changing careers if they don't feel good about what they are doing or to move ahead. They didn't see companies honoring their parents, so they see no reason to stay with an employer when they decide it's time to move on.

Some researchers have concluded that this generation has a short attention span caused by their television viewing habits. They quickly tire of one electronic gadget and want the next, the newest, and the best. Their generation is not known for one type of music. They like different kinds and move from one to another. They are tolerant of diversity, partly because they can't decide what is true. Relationships are important, but they often discard them at the first sign of conflict.

Many Busters see the values of their parents' generation as empty, meaningless, and unrewarding. They see leaders who lack even basic ethical values. They seek truth but don't know where to find it. Since their perception, and perhaps experience, is that one truth is as good as another, many bounce from one church, denomination, or even religion to another or begin to incorporate a little of each into their lives.

If they go to church, they prefer one that has definite beliefs, "clear and convictional doctrine."[19] But most Busters don't go to church; perhaps only one in seven is an active churchgoer.[20]

The Millennial Generation

Born since 1984, this generation, also called "the next generation" or "the mosaic generation," has grown up in an age of technology and prosperity, the children of two-parent-income or single-parent families. Because both parents worked, they have grown up in institutional settings. Their generation has seen adults in significant positions fail to measure up. They have been shaped by live reporting on television, even from war zones; the World Wide Web; the loss of integrity—and therefore respect—for authority figures, government officials, sports heroes, and even clergy, with sex scandals rocking the Catholic Church as well as some local churches; a multiethnic, multicultural world; and violence and terrorism. The issues that have formed Millennials have led to their being known as the most serious, stressed, and worried generation as they begin their adult lives.

They worry about everything—grades, getting into the right college, finding the right spouse, choosing the right career, finding the best job, staying fit and taking care of their health, the economy, the environment, and terrorism. To deal with their stress they often turn to drugs—both legal and illegal—and alcohol. Their generation has seen more teenage crime than other generations. But they are braced for change, ready to take on the world, which is multicultural and global. They're highly mobile and highly tolerant of others' ideas. And they are shaped by the multiplicity of ideas they encounter.

This group is spiritual but not religious. They are truth seekers, but they generally want to determine for themselves what is true, accepting all religions as valid. Even if they call themselves Christian, they determine for themselves what beliefs they hold, and those beliefs may or may not be based on the Bible.

This generation is seeing the family redefined. Families are no longer parents and children or even blended families as a result of divorce and remarriage. Now there are single-dad families, children being raised by grandparents, multiethnic children, children from *in vitro* fertilization, and even homes with two mommies or two daddies. In 2015 same-sex marriage is now legal in the USA and transgender lifestyle issues are rapidly gaining recognition and acceptance too.

This generation moves in groups rather than in singles or pairs. Prom night often doesn't mean a special date, but rather a large group going together, perhaps not unlike the teenage years of their grandparents.

They are materialistic. They want the best of everything. As complicated new items come on the market, they don't have time to determine by a product's attributes which one they want, so they just buy "the best," which is usually defined as the most expensive with the most options. Many no longer are content with one home and one car; they aspire to have two or more cars and a vacation home. They grew up with everything they wanted, and they anticipate continuing that lifestyle as adults. They often expect to enter adult life on the same financial and social stage at which their parents arrived after forty years.

And they're wired. As media consumers, they may choose the car they buy depending on the best sound system. You may search far and wide to find one without a wire or a smartphone attached to an ear. And the media they consume—movies and music—in turn shapes them, their ideas, and values.

Millennials need unconditional love, a safe place for building relationships, leaders who won't abandon them. In the church they will do well in teams with shared responsibilities. They will demand the best at church as they do in their personal lives. They will expect technology and media to have an important part in both worship and education.

Since Canadian church culture shifts preceded shifts in the United States a Canadian perspective on Millennials might offer insight and challenge.

> An exclusive survey of 1,004 Canadian millennials conducted for *The Huffington Post Canada* found 51 per cent of respondents said they never attend a religious institution. Just 12 per cent said they attend weekly, with attendance highest among millennials in central Canada (23 per cent) and lowest in Quebec (3 per cent). Weekly attendance was most common among Christian denominations, followed by Jews and Muslims. . . .
>
> In 2005, Statistics Canada found that a third of Canadians aged 15 to 24 had never attended a religious institution, compared with 25 per cent in 1985.

"What we're seeing . . . is that there is a significant percentage of Canadian teens and young adults who are abandoning religious orientations after being involved in them as children," explained James Penner, an author and sociologist based in Lethbridge, Alta.

In his 2012 report *Hemorrhaging Faith*, which analyzes why and when young Christian Canadians leave and return to church, Penner found that, for every three young people who attended church as a child in the 1980s and 90s, only one regularly attends now.

Moreover, he found that only 23 per cent of young Canadian Christians are "religious engagers," meaning they still associate with the Christian tradition.

"One reason for the drop in church attendance," Penner said, "is that Canadian society has become more individualistic, while young people are more focused than ever on attaining the credentials, internships and education required for good jobs."

When Ian Vandaelle was 12, he started to referee hockey on Sunday mornings. He said he got the job specifically so he would not have to attend church with his family.

Vandaelle's family attended a United Church in Lacombe, Alta., a small town in what he calls 'Canada's bible belt.'

Now 22 and living in Toronto, Vandaelle has completely stepped away from his religious roots: He jokes that he will go to church only to make his mother happy.

"There's a man in the sky, or a woman in the sky, or some kind of creature sans gender in the sky, that gave us free will but has already determined everything we're going to do," he said sarcastically.

"There's this disconnect. It doesn't make sense to me. I'm a guy who likes to reply on what makes sense in my own mind."

Penner said young Canadians often step away from religion to do what he calls "getting a life."

All the pressures of setting up your apartment, roommate relationships, finding a new community, new church. [Church] lifts off the radar," he said.

He cites Tim Clydesdale's book *The First Year Out* which examines the identities of young adults just as they leave high school. The book explains that young religious people often keep their faith hidden.[21]

While the challenges are deep and wide in reaching the younger generation, it is possible—*if* churches are willing to respond.

The problem is, I believe, the church has largely failed to take stock in this generation because they are different. A lack of knowledge breeds fear. In relation to the Millennials, many churches do not take the time to know the next generation, so they are stuck with attaching stigmas (many untrue) to them. Some churches in different locales are thriving with Millennials. I've seen a number of churches struggle with this issue and make significant progress as they work with all generations. A church in a Virginia college town invited texting during worship as a way to engage the college generation and followed it up with "on the spot responses" and a blog. Such engaged the group to the point of not only attending church but starting another service. An inner city church in Charlotte, North Carolina, has renovated space, retooled staff and is working on adjusting attitudes and structures to engage an explosion of Millennials moving into residential apartments blocks from their plateaued church. Their future is bright as they reframe church for all generations (www.pritchardmemorial.com).

So, what differentiates a church culture that attracts Millennials and one that repels them? There are many factors, but I want to highlight ten really important ones. If you are a church that has been asking why it is so hard to get the next generation to become part of your culture, the ten explanations written by Frank Powell in a blog post, and paraphrased below, might shed some light on your struggle:

1. Our churches have a strong resistance to change.

This Millennial generation does not understand the refusal to change a program, activity, or even an entire culture if it is not working. Traditions are not something most Millennials treasure. Many see traditions as the enemy because churches allow their traditions to hinder them from moving forward. No matter how you feel, this lack of appreciation for our traditions is a reality.

A very strong value of this generation is changing the world. Many times traditions hold them back from their mission of change. The next generation understands change as necessary to remain focused on the vision of being externally focused.

2. A compelling vision is lacking or nonexistent.

If your goal is to drive away the next generation, especially those with any initiative and talent, then refuse to cast vision in your church.

In virtually no other arena of life do we refuse to vision and plan, but for some reason the church is different.

Millennials see example after example of an infinitely powerful God doing amazing things through normal people. You might think they are naive, but most Millennials do not believe they have to wait until they receive a certain degree or reach a certain age to start non-profits, plant churches, or lead businesses. They will not invest in a church that doesn't dream big.

3. Mediocrity is the expectation.

The next generation is not content with mediocrity. They are very optimistic about their ability to excite change in the world. They have a strong desire to do something extraordinary and are not scared to fail. They believe churches should operate with a similar mind-set. They understand we serve a God who works beyond our ability. The Millennials want to make the world a better place, and mediocrity has no place in those plans.

4. Our churches take a paternalistic approach to leading Millennials.

If you want to push the next generation away from your church, refuse to release them to lead. Titles are largely irrelevant to the next generation. They want to be trusted to fulfill tasks, not given titles or committee assignments.

If you micro-manage them, treat them like a parent and refuse to believe they are capable of being leaders because of their youth, lack of experience, lack of wisdom that comes only with age, etc., they will soon be gone.

Millennials will not allow age to keep them from leading…and leading well. If you refuse to release them to lead, the next generation will quickly find another church or context where they can use their talents and gifts to their full capacity.

5. Our churches display a pervasive, insider-focused mentality.

This mentality is evident in the issues we discuss. Traditional or contemporary worship? High church or low church? Plurality of elders or board of directors or staff-led church? Millennials don't care.

What is important to Millennials is how a church responds to the lost in the world, both locally and globally, and how a church responds to the poor, homeless, needy, and widowed.

If you want to ensure your church has very few Millennials, answer the questions nobody is asking, spend most of your resources on your building, and have a lot of programs that do little to impact anybody outside the church walls.

Most of the next generation has a very pessimistic attitude towards institutions…the church included. Church leaders can get mad or frustrated about this reality, or they can change some things.

6. Transparency and authenticity are not high values for our churches.

Most Millennials value transparency and authenticity. Portray "holier than thou" mentality and make everyone feel they are terrible people, and your church will be largely devoid of the next generation. Millennials know church leaders are not in their position because they are absent of sin, temptations, or failures. They do not expect people to be perfect. Millennials are looking for people to be real and honest about struggles and temptations.

7. Mentoring is not important in our churches..

While Millennials do not like paternalistic leadership, they place a high value on gleaning wisdom from generations past.

Millennials are not standoffish towards those who have gone before. They place a high value on learning from people who have a strong desire to be a sage instead of a dad. If your church is generationally segregated and refuses to pour back into the next generation, you can be sure your church will not attract Millennials.

8. Our churches view culture as the enemy.

Millennials are tired of the church viewing the culture as the enemy. Separationist churches who value creating "safe" places for their members and moving away from all the evil in the city are highly unlikely to attract the next generation. The next generation is trying to find ways to engage the culture for the glory of God.

Millennials are increasingly optimistic about the surrounding culture because they see Jesus loving all types of people, loving cities, and engaging culture. The church needs to stop believing the goal of Christian living is to escape the evils of culture and finish life unharmed and untainted. To reach people today, the church must be immersed in the community for the glory of God.

9. Community is not valued in our churches.

Forming community stands among the greatest values of Millennials. Community is a non-negotiable part of their lives. They are not looking for another group of people to watch football with on Sunday or play softball…the next generation desires a Christ-centered community. They value a community that goes beyond the surface and yields transformation. Community keeps Millennials grounded, keeps them focused, and challenges them to reach heights never imagined alone. They see Jesus living in community with twelve men for most of His earthly ministry. They see Jesus spending much of His time pouring into people and initiating transformation. Community is not a passive, optional part of a Millennial's life . . . it is essential.

In a culture that is becoming increasingly independent and disconnected, Millennials are modeling something important for the church. There is power in numbers. As an African proverb states, 'If you want to go fast, go ALONE. If you want to go far, go TOGETHER.'

10. The church is a source of division and not unity

Nothing frustrates Millennials more than a church that does not value unity highly. For years church leaders have preached on Jesus' final recorded prayer on earth in John 17. Too often churches miss a central theme in that prayer—unity. On four separate occasions, Jesus explicitly prays for unity. It was important to him. He brought together tax collectors and Zealots (read about both of these groups if you want to know how difficult it would have been to bring these two together). He talked to prostitutes. He brought people together. This is why places like coffee shops are grounds for scores of Millennials. They provide an atmosphere for all to come and feel welcomed and accepted.

Churches that value racial, generational, and socio-economic unity are going to attract Millennials. Why? Because most next gens believe the gospel is most fully reflected when all of these groups are brought together, and most of the next gens are just crazy enough to believe the power of the Spirit is sufficient to make it happen.[22]

While I do not completely agree with all of Powell's observations, I do think he surfaces critical issues that churches need to explore and make decisions about as a path to reaching the younger generation. It always distresses me that every church I work with or visit always says, "We want to reach younger families," and yet they all but refuse to make any significant adjustments of structure, attitude, or policy that would attract and retain younger generations. What is worse, they usually deny or ignore this disconnect!

This quick review of today's generations serves as a reminder of the formative events that shape people of different ages, providing a little insight into why we are the way we are. You may even want to sit down with different generations and read these descriptions together. What do individuals agree with or resent? What resonates and what irritates? Do differing responses split down age lines? What other factors are important in creating opposing responses? Use the responses to start getting to know one another in the church and to work together to make your church one for all generations—those over sixty as well as those under thirty.

One reason Xers have trouble defining their own generational persona could be that they've rarely been doted on by the media. By contrast, Baby Boomers have been a source of media fascination from the get-go (witness their name). And Millennials, the "everybody gets a trophy" generation, have been the subject of endless stories about their racial diversity, their political and social liberalism, their voracious technology use, and their grim economic circumstances.

Molly Worthen, assistant professor of history at the University of North Carolina at Chapel Hill, makes a valuable observation that guides and frames these shifts and challenges on all fronts. "Christianity has been around for 2,000 years. Over the centuries, the faith's center of gravity has shifted many times: from Palestine and Northern Africa to Rome and Byzantium; from Western Europe to America.[23]

COACHING QUESTIONS

- What insights did you gain from this chapter that you want to remember?
- How will these insights impact you and the way you do church in the future?
- What options are available to you for acting on these insights?
- What are you going to do to engage the retiring Boomers?
- Which generation is God calling your church to engage now? in three years? in five years?
- Who else might you dialogue and work with to move forward in ministering to all generations?
- Can you name three people from generations other than your own with whom you might spend time and from whom you learn?
- When will you make contacts with these people?

4

When Mission Challenges
Personal Preferences

In 2015 many are not looking to join a church. They are looking to be engaged in a mission. Being faithful in a postmodern world means, among other things, influencing, engaging or penetrating the culture like salt, light, and leaven. One of our problems and the reason we are not reaching the people under thirty is because we stay in our "holy huddles" in our little traditional meetings to which we all are accustomed and comfortable. Coming to these meetings makes us feel good, but we rarely leave the meetings to penetrate or engage the culture. Most often we insulate and isolate ourselves from the culture. We're focused on the folks inside the church instead of those wandering in darkness outside the church. All those people in a lost and hurting world are dying without experiencing fulfillment and hope because we think we've got to keep the lights on in the church even when nobody comes. Leaving the lights on might work for Motel 6, but it isn't working in the average church today.

Nor is Physicians Mutual's motto working for the church: "We're here when you need us." That kind of "y'all come" mentality may work for some businesses, but it's not working in the church today. The staff people are there, ready and willing to work, serving those inside the church; but those they serve are getting fewer and fewer. Most churches don't even advertise with a "we're here" slogan; they just think everyone knows what a warm and wonderful atmosphere people outside the church would find inside the church. After all, the church is essential in the lives of seniors over sixty, and they think that's also true for folks under thirty. The function of the church is different to different generations.

In many ways the church has become like a business. That model began in the 1950s and has persisted. Is the church a business? If it's not run like a business, should it be? If it is run like a business, is that good or bad?

Is the Church a Business?

"The church is not a business!" declared a frustrated pastor as he responded to a deacon's explanation as to why the church was not growing. The deacon's position was the church needed more intentionality about managing the business of the church more effectively. Better management of funds, personnel, schedules, mission, and leadership would result in a growing and thriving congregation.

Is the church a business? Would better management make better churches? Let's explore balancing business and ministry instead of debating about business or ministry.

Balancing Business and Ministry

The church certainly has a business side, but the pastor's point is that the church also has a ministry side and that sometimes the two are incompatible. When a church functions more like a business than a community the younger generation loses interest fast. More often than not, business leaders and managers in the church have a business and management mind-set and value system. They frequently see the solution to many church problems only through a management lens. They only look at the bottom line—the numbers: how many members, how much money, how many visits, how many staff, how much on buildings and grounds, etc. While these numbers certainly are indicators to consider, they are not the only indicators of an effective church. Sometimes you can have all the right numbers and still have an ineffective church when it comes to fulfilling the biblical mandate. Disciple-making, caring for the poor, being an advocate for justice, and creating centers of redemption and spiritual renewal are not often in the formula for success for most managers.

How can churches and leaders (clergy and lay) collaborate rather than compete? How can effectiveness as a business *and* as a ministry center and faithful people of God benefit from the best of management and ministry, from the business mind-set and the ministry mind-set?

The Mission of the Business

The church is the business of the heavenly Father. The people of God are to be about God's mission of fulfilling the Great Commission and the Great Commandment. The question, "Is the church a business?" can be answered in this regard with a resounding yes! However, many churches and leaders lose sight of God's "business mission" and make the church into our human image to meet our human desires and needs rather than in God's image to bring pleasure to God. When management concerns turn meeting agendas toward us rather than God, we are in trouble.

For instance, some church business meetings make the financial report and the Bible study attendance report the focus of the meeting. Others make how many visits the pastor has made a critical piece of the meeting. Still others spend much energy and time on building concerns, upkeep of grounds, and sticking to proper constitution and bylaw concerns. While these things are of interest to some, they are **not** the business of the church that should take priority of our time, energy, or money if we are meeting the Father's desires for his church.

A meeting agenda that focuses on God's mission would begin with mission reports about volunteers in ministry in the community, state, and nation. . In fact, in our church we no longer talk about members; we endorse, equip, and mobilize missionaries into the world. In our "business meetings" you hear stories from people who had benefited from the benevolent ministry of the church, reports from those who had shared the Good News with neighbors, family, and work colleagues. Reports would flow about how the church had been an advocate for the poor and those treated unjustly. Putting this type of report first on the agenda moves us in the right direction of pleasing God. The budget, attendance, and other numerical goals can be shared or worked on in committees, ministry teams, or a leadership community and shared as information in the business meeting, but not lifted up as the priority of the business of the church. What kind of business is your church focused on these days?

Leadership in the Business

Who is in charge of the church anyway? Who's the boss of the business? Such questions surface often in my consulting with deacons, elders, sessions, and congregations. A simple yet profound answer is that God is in charge of his church! God is the head of the church. God writes the mission!

A more complex answer has unique features related to the denominational affiliation of the church, the church's polity or governance as stated in charter and constitution, or the core values of the congregation. Some are congregationally guided; others are pastor/staff driven; others are denominationally guided or directed. Some have deacons; others have elders; others have a ministry leadership team that provides administrative guidance on a day-to-day basis.

Whoever is in leadership needs to be clear about the mission of the church. Each leader needs to be clear about the DNA of the church—the core values, core beliefs, and practices of the congregation. Unless the leaders are clear about these essential characteristics of the church, over time the church will drift and weaken in its mission.

Today many congregations, particularly those reaching a younger generation, want to streamline decision-making, engage in hands-on ministries, and not get trapped in jumping through a lot of hoops to get something done.

Finances of the Business

"Money follows mission" was the mantra of many churches in the past decade. In other words, if you want people to give, they must be clear about and engaged in the mission of the church. Today it seems we are moving to "money follows ministry and community." Unless people feel they are a part of the congregation's mission and feel their money is helping the hurting and spiritually thirsty, they don't give time, energy, or money. People of our mobile age are seeking community and want to give as they experience community.

This has much to say about how and when we assimilate and orient newcomers, new members, and prospective attenders and members. Notice I'm not just focusing on membership. Church membership is not a high value for many today; joining a small group or community is of high value. (I discuss this in more detail in *Spiritual Leadership in a Secular Age.*)

Now churches are creating multiple paths for funding ministry. Creating multiple avenues for attenders, guests, community members, businesses, and members to give toward ministry and mission projects they believe in is a growing phenomenon. Invite people to give—not to buildings, programs, or staffing needs, but to humanitarian, mission, family, community needs. (For help with this, contact www.TransformingSolutions.org.)

Membership and Staffing of the Business

Who are the members of the business/church? How do we get the job done in today's world? I've spent much time putting my thoughts about this into print over the last few years, so I'll simply briefly summarize. (For other thoughts, see www.transformingsolutions.org for other book titles and leadership newsletters.)

A business exists for its clients. Without clients there would be no business. The church is different; the church exists for those outside its walls and membership. Jesus died for the world, not just the church (Jn. 3:16). This is a distinct place where ministry and business values shift and often create much conflict and confusion. Members sometimes feel they give their money and hire their staff and create their programs to take care of them. That is not the biblical design Jesus had in mind for his church.

In fact, the real ministers of the church are the persons in the pew, not the people behind the pulpit. Peter Wagner's great book *The Church in the Workplace: How God's People Can Transform Society* begins by saying the church is "a bride and an army"[1] He is right! This is a real difference from the management of a business too. (I discuss this in detail in my book *The Gathered and Scattered Church* and in chapter 6 of this book.)

Policies and Practices of the Business

The policies, practices, and programs of the business are to be in keeping with the biblical mandates of the mission of the church and not just what's hot and will reach many of our people or even what we need for our families. The policies, practices, and programs that bring favor to God are those that are designed and crafted to reach people outside the walls; to mature believers, not just to keep us happy; and to empower and mobilize the army of God in the world. I'm keenly aware that this is not generally and quickly embraced by many churches, but I do feel it is in line with the biblical mandate for the church. My books *Making the Church Work* and *Reframing Spiritual Formation* go into this in much more detail for those who might be interested. The management challenge is balancing the books, energy, and focus on "ministry for us" and "ministry to reach those outside the walls of the church." This is a real tightrope for many;

but, unfortunately, it is ignored by most who see the ministry of the church as being for those inside the walls, those who give the money, and those who are in the membership.

ROI in the Business

The return on the investment (ROI) is clear management language from the business world. The ministry world often has no immediate tangible return on our investment of time, energy, or money. Reaching out and ministering to the poor does not put much in our offering plates, and yet are mandates of God for his church. Building a ministry for single-parent families or persons with AIDS or the disabled or disenfranchised in the community often brings little financial return to the church, and oftentimes does not bring persons into the pews during the traditional church meeting times. So the church's ROI is often measured differently. Learning to measure what matters is a real challenge for many churches. (I have written much about this, and do a workshop around this from my book *Spiritual Leadership in a Secular Age*.)

Mission of the Business

Is the church a "business"? The answer to the question is not simple, but it does seem to rest in your church's response to another question: What is the mission of the business/church? Is it God-honoring, or is the church really focused only on keeping its members happy and ignoring the call of the hurting, lost, ill, and broken of the community around you? What business is your church in? How do you measure effectiveness and success? What are your next steps as a leader that will move your leaders and church forward in pleasing the heavenly Father and participating in his mission in the world?

What might happen if a church turned from an inward to an outward focus? What would happen if, instead of keeping the lights on and the air flowing for the faithful few, they sent the staff and volunteers out to where the people are? What would happen if your church decided to be salt and light in your community?

A church in western North Carolina has figured out that the best use of their time and resources to evangelize their rural community is to figure out where the young families and their children congregate. Rural western North Carolina is made up of pretty small towns, and there aren't a lot of places to go, not a lot of places for people to congregate, no Starbucks or Barnes and Noble. However, by using a survey in the community, the church discovered that while the church was open and ready on Sunday and Wednesday nights, most of the town was at the local skating rink. All the young families were skating in the skating rink, so they decided to close down their Sunday night worship, turn off the lights at the church, and go to the skating rink to do and be the church there. They partnered with the skating rink owner in a win-win deal. Church leaders said, "If you'll let us come in forty-five minutes before you open the door to skating, we'll bring in a lot more people."

The skating rink owner said, "That sounds good. Let's try it. I'll give a discount to all those who come early for your worship service; and since they'll already be here, they'll be allowed to skate first."

The church developed a family Bible study for parents and children at the skating rink, and I hear they're going to have a baptism at the skating rink because that's where people were led to Christ.

For those over sixty, that's a real shift of values and a real change in the way to do church. For those under thirty, it's practical and it works. They may not want to do it that way forever, but right now it's a good way to reach new families, some of whom would never have thought about going inside a church building. Now, because they had a good experience at the skating rink, they will probably come to the church building and feel comfortable there when they see familiar faces and connect with those who have already formed a relationship with them. People over sixty in some congregations, like this one in western North Carolina, are beginning to realize that there's more than one way of worshiping, more than one way of doing church.

Then there are those "cowboy churches" and those who are developing a ministry and church for bikers. Boy, that is a stretch for those over sixty and even some under thirty, but it meets people where they are and provides them an experience that moves them forward in faith and function. Lifeway Christian Resources summarizes these unique churches in their *Facts and Trends* magazine in January/February, 2007, www.lifeway.com. Grace United Methodist Church in LaSalle, Illinois, found a way to preserve their traditions while reaching the younger generation of men and their families.[2]

And that's OK. It's OK with God, and if we reach the decisions lovingly and deliberately in our churches, it can be OK with people from all generations. If seniors remember why they built the church, they can see that those under thirty have the same goals—winning people to faith in Christ and teaching them to be disciples, bringing them into the church and helping them grow—that the seniors did fifty years ago; those under thirty just have different action steps to meet the goals.

Some churches haven't changed in a long time. The pastor, having exhausted his/her energy and his/her time during the week doing church maintenance, pulls out a sermon for Sunday morning from the already-been-preached file; and, if he/she has time, updates the illustrations. The minister of music pulls his/her notebook of church bulletins off the shelf, looks at the same Sunday two or three or more years ago and uses the same hymns. Why can they do this? Because worship is the same Sunday after Sunday, year after year, and that's just fine with seniors over sixty. In fact, many of them come week after week and park in the same place and sit in the same pew. They like the routine, the sameness. The predictability provides security in a world that many of those over sixty feel they no longer understand, while providing deadly boredom and irrelevance to those under thirty.

One question those inside the church—not just those over sixty—need to ask is, Do we believe the primary purpose, the mission, of the church is to care for those inside the church or to reach those outside the church? That's a real big difference.

My granddaddy believed deeply that the Bible taught that the church existed for him. I can't find that anywhere in Scripture. It took me a long time to understand that because I just assumed my granddaddy knew what he was talking about. I finally asked him, "Where did you come up with that?"

"Oh, that's what my daddy told me," he said.

It didn't come out of his study of Scripture. It came out of his lineage, and he was just passing it on down to me. That's where a lot of our faith traditions have formed—not from Scripture but from practice. We just trust that granddaddy was right.

My granddaddy was in this camp of equating practice and tradition with the Word of God struggle. My granddaddy was a deacon of his little mill village church, and he would talk to us on the Sunday afternoons when we ate together. He would snap his suspenders after eating, that big old potbelly of his bumped up against the table, and he would say, "Well, I wonder what I'm going to get to vote no on tonight at the deacon's meeting." That was how he saw his role as a deacon because he didn't want anything to change. He liked church the way it was. It worked for him. That's what he liked.

During those same conversations I also heard him say: "We don't need to change nothing. If those people really love Jesus, they'd come at 11:00, the same time I do, and they'd be back on Sunday night just like I am." He didn't go every Sunday night, but he had that value system. That's what, to him, made him a Christian. That's what made him a good church person—showing up on Sunday morning whether he liked it or not.

I knew he didn't like his preacher most of the time, but he showed up at church every Sunday. Then he ate him for lunch every Sunday I was there.

Some church leaders tried to close down the Sunday night service because only a little handful came on Sunday night. But others in the church opposed the idea because their definition of being faithful as the church and that faith community was to keep the lights on. They didn't really care if anybody was in there or not; at least they didn't do much to try to get more people to join them on Sunday night. They just had to keep the lights on, and the people who wanted the lights on were the very people who didn't come.

That's not what being faithful is about in a postmodern world. We've got to learn to do more than keep the lights on. Church is more about transforming lives than about lighting up a building and staffing programs.

My granddaddy left a legacy for me that he was more interested in a church that served him than a church that reached those outside the church. As a grandson, I have to live with that. If he had caught his pastor at a skating rink on Sunday night and if he'd had the power, granddaddy would have fired him for not being at the church and having the lights on, ready to receive anyone who might show up. My granddaddy rarely went on Sunday night; but he wanted those lights on, and he wanted that preacher preaching. For my granddaddy that's what it meant to be faithful; that's the way he defined faithfulness.

Granddaddy believed that if what the church was doing, what it had always done, was good enough for him, then it was good enough for everyone else. If they didn't like it, they didn't have to come to his church. They didn't come to his church, either. In fact, I went to his church a year or so ago. Granddaddy has been dead for several years, but the church invited me back to do the last service at that church. It went out of business. I said to that group that day, "I'm sorry my granddaddy helped kill this church." I really believe he did his part to set that church on a course that led to its demise because he popped his suspenders and voted no on everything. He didn't want his church to change with the times. He wanted it for him, not them, and the church went out of business.

Churches across this country are going out of business, closing their doors, because they've lost their relevancy. They chose not to change with the times. They chose to keep people over sixty happy and forget about reaching people under thirty. They, like my granddaddy, measured faithfulness by doing things the same way year after year, regardless of the response or the results.

How do you define faithfulness? It gets back to what you see as the primary mission of the church. Is it rooted in the Great Commission, or the church's tradition? Is it maintaining the status quo, or taking a risk to get out of the comfort zone and try to reach a new generation, a new age, for Jesus Christ?

God is eternal. The church is ongoing. The truth of God's Word never changes. The Good News is for all people of all ages. But how we communicate that truth and reach those people with the Good News of Jesus Christ is different for each generation.

When missionaries go to cultures and countries that are different from their own, they have to learn how to relate. They have to find out what makes these people tick. They spend months, sometimes years, learning the native language. And they shape their Bible teaching and worship to fit that culture.

The builders of the church, those over sixty, are being called to become missionaries to a younger generation. They need to learn to speak this other "culture's" language, develop relationship bridges, and discover ways to communicate the truth about our awesome God to the next generation. Yes, I'm aware this is a mutual issue and that the postmoderns need to meet the Builder Generation on level ground by learning something of their values and language too. However, Scripture does declare that the "old shall teach the young." We also see through biblical narratives that the older generation does have responsibility for leaving a legacy, sharing their faith with the next generations. We also see illustrations, throughout Christian history, that the language of faith and church has shifted many times as believers find more effective ways to share in new cultures and new generations. Still, knowing this reality, it's tough to change our personal preferences, even to reach a new generation.

Getting Honest about Our Personal Preferences

"What do I do with my preferences? Do I simply ignore them to reach someone else? I helped found this church," exclaimed a faithful church leader during one of my seminars. I had hit a nerve. Was I suggesting that the style and preference of worship, music, etc., to which she was accustomed was wrong? Certainly not. What communicates the Good News effectively to various generations needs to be valued and strengthened. My point is that to be a New Testament church, serious about fulfilling the Great Commission and the Great Commandment, we are challenged to find the way of communicating and worshiping for other generations, just as we do for our own. The message of the gospel is of no value if it's not voiced in ways others can hear it and embrace it.

How can we do some self-assessment about our personal preferences? Consider these questions:

- Does the way I choose to worship move me to a deeper walk with God?
- What influence does my life and walk with God have on others?
- How can I grow my faith and my ministry in the world to the next level?
- How do my personal preferences serve as barriers to others seeking God?
- How might I be a bridge-builder for persons who do not share my personal preferences but are on a serious spiritual journey, just at a different place from where I am?

What are the personal preferences I want to protect? Consider these areas:

- Role and function of pastor and staff
- Dress codes for church events
- Music style and preferences
- Appearance of the church
- Solitude and reverence in the church
- Translation of the Bible used in church
- Role of men and women in the church
- Role of divorced and single persons in the church
- Programs offered and sponsored by the church
- Schedules for church meetings
- Where and who offers us our training
- Who is allowed to lead in our church
- Role of single adults and people of all ethnic groups
- Affiliation with denomination and judicatory
- Presence and leadership of a choir
- Use of hymnal in worship

How did you do? What personal preferences are dear to you? How can you embrace what meets your needs and still create other venues and styles that reach and communicate the Good News to those who have preferences that differ from yours?

Bridge-building and creating new and varied opportunities is critical during these days of diversity of population and levels of spiritual maturity. Challenges leaders face include:

- Learning to create nonthreatening entry points for persons at different levels of the spiritual journey. A nonthreatening entry point is an activity or relationship that attracts seekers and persons not yet connected to the faith or the church. It's nonthreatening to them, not nonthreatening to those of us in church.
- Rethinking your personal and corporate definition of success. Unity is no longer just found when everyone is under the same roof at the same time doing the same thing as church. Unity is found in common core values and allowing these core values to be expressed in different ways and places and times to accommodate the diversity of people you are called to reach, disciple, and assimilate.
- Creating frequent intergenerational and assimilation experiences. These experiences are bridge-builders and places of developing relationships and ministry friendships along with mentoring relationships. Intentionality is essential here. Create the opportunities and value the sharing and building of such relationships. (For example: holidays, birthdays, and rites of passage are great opportunities. Valentine's Day is a great time to share stories of first loves, first kisses, how you first understood love, and tips you would give the next generation, etc.)

God is always in the birthing business, creating the best out of chaos. When a church changes, it takes some risks and may experience some chaos along the way. Some intergenerational planning meetings may be filled with tension; but through that tension and with that desire to grow the kingdom, God can make the church new and dynamic again.

The struggle gets even more intense for some. Do Christians seek to engage and influence the culture we are in, or do we batten down the hatches and resist and protect ourselves from the culture around us? Some suggest that what one resists, persists. Others suggest that engaging the culture is compromising the mandates of the church. We'll explore this in the next chapters.

COACHING QUESTIONS

- What do you resonate with most in this chapter?
- What are the disconnects for you as you read the chapter?
- How can you deal with these disconnects?
- Who can help you?

5

When Cultural Realities Impose on Church Traditions

There's little question in 2015, while revising this book, that the culture in North America is shifting. The diversity of our country continues to call for rethinking, reframing, and refocusing. The change includes diversity of people groups, family systems, multicultural relationships, and a growing acceptance of the gay community. Many individuals, families, and congregations are deeply challenged by these new realities. A cultural image from the past for diversity in the United States was "the melting pot." The image was one of people coming from different nations to blend into some sort of homogeneous whole called America. Of course, even with their differences, most of those people were white, European, and Christian. The idea of the melting pot could be compared to a big pot of stew with cultural, lifestyle, and ethnic differences added to give a little spice and flavor.

The image of the melting pot is a thing of the past. In the United States today, the mix of cultures and ethnicities, languages and religions is far more diverse than in the past. While all of these people may, or may not, be American citizens, their goal is not necessarily to blend in. Their goal is to honor and maintain their heritage while bringing their distinct gifts and talents to the diversity that characterizes the United States today. How can we maintain distinctives and create community? The Body of Christ is a viable model.

To continue the food analogy, have you noticed how few cafeterias are still in business? People don't go to one place to seek variety, especially where that variety is pretty bland and flavorless. On any day in almost any small to midsize city or town in the United States, you choose whether you'd like to go to a restaurant that features Mexican, Thai, Chinese, Korean, Italian, French,

Ethiopian, Middle Eastern, Indian, Spanish, Japanese, or any number of other kinds of food. Such diversity was once unheard of in the United States except in the largest cities. The diversity doesn't end with restaurants that typify food from other countries. Restaurants in general specialize in other ways: diners, sub shops, pizza parlors, coffee shops, smoothie bars, soup and salad shops, bakeries, seafood places.

We live in a world that is not marked by blending into one large group but by many small niche groups living in close proximity. One image of America from the past that still persists is that the United States is a country of rugged individualism. And individuals we remain. People in America today struggle with relationships. In an age when people spend more time communicating via their smartphones and computers than face-to-face, social groups are on the decline. People don't join Civitan, Masons, or Kiwanis the way they once did. They may come together to work for a particular cause that interests them, but they aren't joiners.

Churches are another institution people often decline to join. Relationships are hard to form in most churches. Those looking for a church or going to church regularly have as distinct differences about church preferences as they do for the restaurant they choose. Some change churches about as often as they do restaurants, going to the one that suits them on any given Sunday.

The cultural reality in America today is that people don't form relationships; they don't join organizations just to identify with a group; they say they are spiritual and that they pray but they don't necessarily go to church; and they have individual preferences that in some areas of life, such as eating, are pretty easy to satisfy. In this mix, the church is trying not only to survive but also to thrive, to draw into the body of Christ all the people Jesus died to save.

An article in the online *Baptist News Global* states that the unchurching of the church, already well underway, is not a trend to be reversed or a problem to be solved. Rather, the unchurching of the church is a Christendom-shaking revolution.

> The nearly two-millennia paradigm of sacred edifices operated by salaried clerics is crumbling. While the model of church buildings and full-time clergy will not entirely crash to the ground in the future, it will at best serve in a supporting role to the unchurched church, and at worst take the form of isolated enclaves lacking relevance in the outer world.
>
> The good news, however, is that the early Baptists were, in a manner of speaking, the original Millennials. Like today's young generations, our Baptist forebears walked away from established religious institutions in a quest for 'authentic' community. They emerged from the 16th- and 17th-century institutional, doctrinally certain church and scandalized Christendom by creating local communities of faith based on freedom of individual conscience. Despite two centuries of

establishment church effort to marginalize or co-opt Baptists, including the use of violence, the movement survived and attracted persons seeking authentic, voluntary faith.[1]

Yes, we live in a changing world, and the church will either change to continue to spread the changeless truth of the gospel or it will die. Ed Stetzer's research suggests that some of these trends can be frightening. Four now-evident trends will only become more important in days to come:[2]
1. The word 'Christian' will become less used and more clear.
2. The nominals will increasingly become nones.
3. Christians will increasingly change cultural tactics.
More robust churches will result from the death of nominalism.

Three broad categories make up the approximately 75 percent of Americans who refer to themselves as Christians, with about an equal number in each group: Cultural Christians, Congregational Christians, and Convictional Christians.[3]

Individuals do not use the word *Christian* in the same way. Cultural Christians tend to say they are Christian rather than say atheist or Jewish. They are Christian for no other reason than they are from America and don't consider themselves something else.

Congregational Christians do not really have a deep commitment, but will refer to themselves as a Christian because they have some loose connection to a church—perhaps through a neighborhood, family member, or some holiday attendance.

Convictional Christians' lives revolve around their faith in Christ.

So the word *Christian* encompasses a wide range of self-identity and practice—not just evangelicals, for example.

Stetzer says that *fewer people are calling themselves Christians and those who are take it more seriously.* In other words, cultural and congregational Christians, or the "squishy middle,"(as Stetzer calls it) is collapsing while convictional Christians are staying relatively steady.

"In the future, the word *Christian* will mean more to those who would be considered convictional Christians. However, it will mean—and will be used—less to those who were nominal Christians in the first place. The word will be less used and more clear," Stetzer says.[4]

A growing number of people are in name only Christians, claiming to be Christian for survey reasons, but in practice rarely participating in ritual or activity of a church.

Removing the Labels.

Many people who used to call themselves Christians are being more honest about their religious affiliation, or lack thereof. The "Nones" are those who check "none" on surveys, admitting they have no religious preference. They could make up half of the population in the next twenty to thirty years—it's already over 30 percent among college students (with a third of college students still being religious). Christians in the squishy middle (cultural and congregational Christians) are becoming the Nones.

As the number of Nones rises, Christian influence on culture will wane. As people no longer claim to be Christians, Christianity will be further marginalized.

The next twenty years convictional Christians and churches will be engaging in cultural conversations often as the minority we truly are. Those who aggressively fight this as a culture war will find it hard to reach people. Christians will be seen as an enemy. How we engage in ministry and causes is almost as important as the action of engagement.[5]

In response, we should look to two groups of people from the Bible. Ed Stetzer profiled these in "Creating an Assessment Culture By Being of Berea and Issachar"[6]:

We must hold the Word of God in high authority as the Berean Christians did in Acts 17:11. Christians must become seriously committed to Scripture and the gospel in every aspect of our lives. We should also wisely discern the present culture and strategize how to best glorify God. "Of Issachar, those who had understanding of the times, to know what Israel ought to do, two hundred chiefs, and all their kindred under their command" (1 Chr. 12:32).

The church and Christians must be examining the Scriptures daily to know the Word of God and also to know the times, the context, and the Spirit's wisdom to address the culture with the Good News.

Some Christians will go down fighting. Other Christians will go on loving. Convictional Christians will increasingly see they are not the moral majority and will advocate less for the legislation or traditional values and be more focused on protecting religious liberty.

It is beginning to cost something to be a Christian in America—not as much as in many places in the world or in much of history, but more than it used to.

Churches preaching the gospel and focusing on biblical truths are going to become more clearly distinct from the culture around them. The end result? Robust Christian communities are going to get stronger.

These gospel-preaching churches will have members who are more, not less, committed. Christianity will become more of a minority in culture, but more refined, more biblical, and more missional churches will be the result.

Where from Here?

The lasting effects of these shifts will force churches to make a critical decision. They will either become a cultural church that allows the societal trends to dictate their ever-changing beliefs. Or they will become a countercultural church that faithfully adheres to Scripture and proclaims the gospel in a carefully considered way. The countercultural church will offer real hope in the midst of an adversarial culture and is the only real future for the American church.[7]

The Implications of 'Dones' & 'Nones'

Thom Shultz and John Packard explore the "dones":

The Dones are fatigued with the Sunday routine of plop, pray and pay. They want to play. They want to participate. But they feel spurned at every turn.

Will the Dones return? Not likely, according to the research. They're done. Packard says it would be more fruitful if churches would focus on not losing these people in the first place. Preventing an exodus is far easier than attempting to convince refugees to return.[8]

Let's continue to look at the differences in age groups as a variety of mind-sets representative of the culture groups in America, their preferences and styles, and how they apply to the church. We'll also look at the differences in moderns and postmoderns and what that means for the church.

COACHING QUESTIONS

- Which of these trends are already evident in your church?
- What steps does your church need to take to ensure its ability to minister effectively in the years ahead?
- Which trend do you need to address first?
- Who can help you address the critical issues in your church now?

Where Are the Boomer Leaders?

Leaders are losing interest, burning out, or just evaporating in many churches across North America. There are many reasons for this, which churches are just beginning to explore seriously. Where are our church leaders for this and the next generation? The leaders of the Builder Generation have served and are serving us well in many situations. They continue to share their skills, dreams, and desires that keep the established church afloat. Many children of the Builder Generation are now established Boomers, and they are giving much less time, energy, and money to the established church than most of their parents or grandparents did. In fact, many of them and their children are not consistently active in church attendance, membership, or leadership. How can churches activate Boomers in the leadership circle? What's involved in engaging Boomers in ministry?

Many of the Baby Boomer Generation (those born 1946–64) are noticeably absent in many of our church leadership circles. Many of those "done with the church" are burned out, stressed out, and overly churched Boomers and some Busters. Our overly programmed churches focused more on competition with other community churches than they did on fulfilling the Great Commission. Now on the sidelines of church life, most are not even watching the game.

Consider some of their reasoning for not actively engaging in church leadership:

- *Prosperity*—Many have dual-career marriages, high-pressure careers, and more discretionary money, which buys weekend vacations, homes, etc.

- *Disappointment and disillusionment*—Many are disappointed with their churches being so inwardly focused. Others are disappointed because their churches are too *outwardly* focused and don't have enough ministries for "me and my family."
- *Spiritual apathy* runs rampant because this generation was not discipled in most church youth ministries. Most were entertained so that their spiritual maturity is lacking.
- *Spiritual maturity* also evidences itself among many of this generation. They want to be the scattered church and make a difference in the world. They look for a "hands-on approach" to missions and ministry rather than having to sit in meetings, serve on committees, and show up at church four or five times a week.
- *Irrelevant programming* keeps many away. Their church programs are more about doctrine and ecclesiastical and traditional preservation than about helping individuals with daily life issues in the family, workplace, and community.
- *Impact deficit*—Many Boomers are beginning to retire and want to spend the next part of their life making an impact. Many churches are not making much noticeable impact in their communities or membership. They are simply having programs and services to have programs and services. Little or no life or community transformation results.
- *Search for significance*—Many Boomers are moving from being success motivated to significance motivated. They are no longer willing to be part of committees, choirs, ensembles, teams, or to participate in programs that have little or no significance. This is one of the critical cutting edges of ministry for churches in the next decade or more. How do we engage, encourage, equip retiring Boomers?

The search for relevancy, authenticity, and impact provides real keys and opportunities for finding the answer to the leadership deficit! Churches can learn to birth Boomers into leaders in, through, and as the church. (I discuss this in greater detail in *Spiritual Leadership in a Secular Age.*) I use the birthing image here because this shift in many churches and leaders is likely to take time and intentional nurture. It could prove painful. So often we think of and value leaders who work in the church programs/services or through church organizations and mission endeavors. In the twenty-first–century world, we are having to learn to value and equip those whom God calls to work in the world. These Christians may not be as tightly connected to the established church, but may be committed and accountable to being the church in the world.

COACHING QUESTIONS

- How can churches retool programs and success standards to birth Boomer leaders into leadership AS the church?
- What would this retooled church look like?
- What shifts would be called for in your congregation? among your laity? among your staff and pastor?

- How can your church communicate equal and authentic value and account-ability of ministry for those who serve in, through, and as the church?
- How could you reframe church life around these three functions: in, through, and as the church?

These are heavy coaching questions that call for much dialogue, prayer, Bible study, and reflection. It's a clear example of needing to change values of the congregation, individuals, and leadership before you change structures. Remember, this will take time and intentionality. (My book *The Gathered and Scattered Church* can be another helpful resource in this effort.)

Now if your head is still spinning, and you are wondering what being the church in the world might actually look like, permit me to give you a couple of scenarios to consider as examples:

Churches cannot compete and win when it comes to extracurricular activities for children and communities. So how might we collaborate? A Little League ball coach feels called to reach and teach children through their Little League ball team. The problem is that the church member is a church leader/teacher/deacon/elder and needs to be at the church several times a week. The shift from "in" church to "as" church might be accomplished by the church commissioning this leader and releasing him from serving in the church to serving as the church as a Little League coach, even if the team has to play or meet on church meeting nights. The coach will then be accountable to the church for being an intentional minister to the team and their families. He enlists prayer for them, prays with his team when appropriate, becomes a mentor and maybe even a discipler of his team. He then shares his ministry report at the church business meetings. (After all, he is doing the business of the church, and I bet it will be more interesting than the budget report!)

A business leader/manager who is highly skilled in leadership has a burden for the relevancy of the church and is seeking ways to experience more significance. This person cannot or will not give time to fill an annual church committee or team position or other annual positions, but she might give her time to a short-term team that is working on a project she is passionate about. Another manager might catch the vision to exercise his shepherding/leadership gift among those he manages. Many workplace ministers are doing Bible studies, small-group discipleship groups, and other ministry experiences with those they work with and manage in the workplace.[9] These business leaders can also share their ministry needs, celebrations, and challenges during the church business meetings. What would happen if churches became an incubator of the new and attracted community entrepreneurs to make it happen? Think about it.

COACHING QUESTIONS _____

- What shifts do you see in these brief scenarios?
- What would need to happen in your church for these scenarios or something similar to be valued and experienced in your church?

- How would this leadership model impact your community? your members? your leaders? your pastor? your church?

Young Adults

David Kinnaman, a researcher of Barna Research Group since 1995 and now vice president, began a 2003 study of young adults, ages 20–29 and it continues today through many authors. According to that research, members of this age group struggle to find their place in the church today.[10] This is the age when young adults make a lot of decisions, often those that set the direction for their lives. They finish school, perhaps get married, and begin a career. With those decisions, they also determine where they will live, perhaps buying their first home. They may decide to have a child during this time period. All of these are significant, life-changing decisions. In the United States today they are uniquely individual. A few decades back, young adults were programmed to finish school, get a job, get married, buy a home, have children—pretty much in that order. But today everything seems to be an option. Each of these decisions young adults once made unquestioningly are today much more complex and customized. For example, at one time the decision was whom to marry. Today the decision is whether to marry, live together, remain single, or choose an alternative lifestyle. The dwelling decision may be to stay at one's parents' home, rent an apartment or a home, or buy a condo or a single-family home. The decision of where to live may be between staying where you are, across town, in another state, or around the world. Whatever decisions are made, they are based on the individual's personal choices—what the individual thinks will lead to prosperity, happiness, or an individual goal.

Where does church fit in all this decision-making? Often it's far down the list if it is even on the list at all. This age group more than any other in America today is likely to stay away from church. They are not likely to attend, join, give, read the Bible, or take a volunteer role. They are less likely to be involved in church than any other age group. When they do think about spirituality, they will not necessarily hold to Christian beliefs they may have been taught when they were younger (half attended church regularly when they were younger; more than 80 percent of those surveyed had attended a Christian church). Only three out of ten (31 percent) attend church in a typical week, compared to four out of ten of those in their thirties (42 percent), and nearly half of all adults age forty and older (49 percent).[11]

This low rate of church attendance can't be attributed just to the college years; only 22 percent of young adults age twenty-five to twenty-nine attend church in any given week. Still, young adults claim that spirituality is important to them and that they pray regularly. More than half claim that at some point they made a decision to become a Christian and that decision is still at least somewhat important to them.

The behavior of these young adults in many ways reflects their postmodern thinking. Kinnaman pointed out, "Since the postmodern viewpoint emphasizes that an individual's experience and personal insight are the prime sources of determining what's important in life, the decline in Bible usage is another sign that many twenty-somethings are trying to make sense of life without traditional sources of Christian input."[12]

Young adults are making their decisions about what to do with their lives and their schedules based on what makes them happy for the moment. Most often that doesn't include church. This group can be stubborn and bulletproof. Pain and suffering appear to be their universal teachers.

Kinnaman's study suggests a number of implications for the local church:

- Churches that target this age group need to know the challenge they face in attracting young adults and getting them to commit to Christianity, much less to one church.
- Churches seeking to reach this age group must realize their financial base may be precarious because on average this age group makes less money, has greater financial commitments than older generations, and chooses not to give to the church at all.
- Churches wanting to reach this age group will have to convince young adults that the Bible has relevance in their thinking in a postmodern world.
- Churches wanting to reach this age group will have to convince them of the exclusivity of Christianity.
- Churches wanting to reach this age group will have to be comfortable with young adults questioning everything that older Christians easily accept.

At the conclusion of his book *You Lost Me*, David Kinnaman offers fifty ideas to find the lost Millennial Generation.[13] The ideas come from Christian leaders—some well known and some unfamiliar—trying to inspire people to move from thinking and talking to doing and changing. What's unique about the list is that Kinnaman himself doesn't agree with all of the ideas. (And you may not either.) But he intentionally includes them because he believes we don't have to agree on every approach in order to fulfill God's mission. As of this writing I'm coaching an inner city congregation in Charlotte, North Carolina who is facing declining attendance and aging population, but now real estate developers and the city are revitalizing uptown Charlotte with high-end apartments and condos at the church's back door. The congregation has made a decision to retool, refocus, and reframe ministry to meet this new Millennial and Boomer population. I love churches with vision and am honored to work with them.

Here are just three key ideas for pastors, church leaders, and Christian organizations. Hopefully, these ideas will inspire (or incite) you to look at your approach in reaching Millennials:

1. Be intentionally intergenerational.

Some occasions may by nature require you to segment large bodies of people by age groups. Kara Powell—executive director of the Fuller Youth Institute and co-author of *Sticky Faith*—believes the church leans too hard this way. Her research shows that when younger generations are intentionally included and expected to engage in church activities, their faith becomes stronger. She suggests mixing and mingling older generations with younger generations as often as possible. Opportunities range from short-term service to hobby mentoring (e.g., cooking, gardening, art) to intentional small groups.

2. Tell on yourself.

Many of the struggles we face as believers are the same that nonbelievers confront. Gary Kinnaman—a pastor in Gilbert, Arizona—suggests, that's not always the image we convey to others. We try to look neat and put together. *You Lost Me* research indicates that Millennials know better than that. They've seen the conflict between the image and the reality and have grown weary of it. We need to start being honest with one another, to tear down our façades. Gary says we need to tell on ourselves like we see in the Psalms and Paul's letters. "Let people know what's causing you pain, what makes you angry, what's difficult for you to overcome in your life—and how God and your closest friends are helping you deal with it."[14]

3. Meet a need.

Look outside your church and into your surrounding neighborhoods. To Millennials, your community isn't made up of new members and financial donors. Your community represents an opportunity to serve and minister to people with concrete needs. Seek out tangible opportunities to create tangible change in your community (for example, cleaning vacant lots, repairing homes, providing food, etc.). Shane Claiborne—author of *The Irresistible Revolution: Living as an Ordinary Radical*, and founder of The Simple Way—describes how his church created a flag football game to engage with the fatherless youths in their area. Today, it's a flag-football league that serves nearly two hundred kids and allows the men in his church to witness through mentorship.[15]

What Questions Does This Raise for You Now?

All churches will soon, if they haven't already, realize that younger adults are largely missing from their leadership base. In fact, many younger adults and Boomers are part of the "dones" group. They have tried church and now decide they are done with it. In the average church in America today, most leaders are fifty or older. Adults in their twenties often are not asked to take leadership roles. When they are, older leaders who work alongside them generally don't approve of their new ideas or the thought processes that led to what they suggest.

Many young adults are in church. The church needs to nurture them, find ways to include them in leadership roles and the decision-making processes of the church, lead them to discover biblical truths, and give them handles for reaching their peers.

Church leaders need to listen to this postmodern generation. They criticize only because they care about the church. Their criticism has an element of truth. It reflects the thinking of that age group and should be taken seriously if the church is to reach and keep this generation. When older adults listen to them, the younger adults will most likely listen to the older adults. With a basis of mutual respect, younger adults can more easily hear the Good News, which does not change from generation to generation.

COACHING QUESTIONS

- Whom do you know in the twenty-something age group? What has shaped them?
- How do you typically respond to this age group?
- How could you improve this response to build bridges?
- What challenges do you see with this age group being an active part of your church?
- What are the gaps between what they value and desire and what your church currently offers?
- How might you go about closing this gap? Where will you start? What changes are you willing to make?
- How can you begin to include this age group in leadership roles or teams?
- Who can help you with this ministry challenge as you nurture the church and church leaders of the future?

Modern Versus Postmodern

We live in a postmodern world, reflecting a change of epochs, not generations. Postmodernism is a state of mind more than an age group. It is not generational, though it is often identified more with younger people. It is not something that affects only cutting-edge congregations; it affects everyone. Those over sixty may feel more comfortable in a modern world rather than a postmodern one, but the choice is not theirs—or ours—to make. Postmodernism is a present reality in all of Western society. Because change of epochs is gradual, the grand scale of change is harder to see. Some dislike the term *postmodern.* For simplicity let's say that things have changed and they will not return to what some call "the good old days!"

To understand postmodernism, let's begin with a little history.[16] Each group may have generational links, but the framework of each is more about a value system and a mind-set than an age group.

Western civilization can be divided into three epochs: premodernism, modernism, and postmodernism.

Premodernism

Premodernism lasted from the beginning of Western civilization until approximately 1500. After Constantine, the Western worldview became God centered. The church was the most powerful institution on earth. Communication was largely oral. Most people did not read and write. They had no need, for there was nothing to read. Written language was limited to handwritten documents. All books were reproduced by scribes. Depictions of biblical stories in stained-glass windows of cathedrals were not there for their beauty alone. They also told the stories of the Bible and reminded worshipers of the words of the sermons. The Bible was the authoritative source for all truth, yet few owned one, had access to one, or could read it. The preindustrial economy was based on agriculture, trade, and craftsmen.

Modernism

The modern period is generally viewed as from about 1500 to about 2000. The modern world became industrial and eventually technological. The Enlightenment was a time of progress, of optimism because of all that human beings were accomplishing. It was the end of the age of superstition and myth. With the invention of the printing press, people could learn to read. They no longer depended on the church's interpretation of the Bible. They could now read it and other books for themselves. Knowledge became powerful. People began to search for the truth rather than to accept what they were told. Scientific discoveries and inventions were changing the world. People believed they were making the world increasingly better and that they had the capacity to solve all problems.

Human reasoning, logic, and science formed the basis of understanding, even in helping to explain and interpret God. For many the certainty of science began to replace religion as the source of truth. Reason was more important than faith, giving rise to secular humanism.

Knowledge was empirical, certain, powerful, based on science. Knowledge was factual, objective, not based on values, and discernable by human beings. Truth was knowledge. It was not subjective but could be verified by science, by cause and effect. At another level came personal beliefs and conviction, which were subjective. At this level people dealt with issues of faith and spirituality, ethics, and morals.[17]

The dates for the modern and postmodern eras differ somewhat among writers. The date used, 1500, closely parallels the advent of the printing press, invented by Johannes Gutenberg in 1450. Others date the modern era from Descartes's famous statement, "I think, therefore I am" in the mid-1600s. It certainly represents and defines this age well.

Postmodernism

Likewise, the dates for ending the modern era and beginning the postmodern age vary somewhat. Some date the change in 1969 with Woodstock. Others equate the transition with the fall of the Berlin wall in 1989. Many use the date 2000, the beginning of a new millennium, a new age, and a new way of seeing the world.

The postmodern era marks the end of absolute truth from either the Bible or science. The age of reason, the Enlightenment, has ended. People are not inherently good. They are not becoming increasingly better, nor are they consistently solving problems and making the world a better place.

Each individual chooses what is truth at any particular time and place. Many of those "truths" may contradict and conflict with one another. Everything is based on personal experience rather than belief in any system outside oneself.

Communication is no longer limited to print or even television or radio. The Internet has made information, both good and bad, readily available around the world to all at the same time. It is up to the reader to determine how useful and accurate the information is.

Many people see the Bible as only one of several or many religious books. Like everything else, the Bible is subject to interpretation. All paths to truth are perceived as being valid and equal. Those who speak with authority are viewed suspiciously.

The postmodern era rejects reason, which dominated the modern age, as the *only* pathway to discover truth. Experience and intuition are equally valid. This is much of the basis for subjective truth. Truth that is discerned by experience or intuition comes from within rather than from an objective search based on scientific processes.

As is evident, postmodernism grew out of modernism. In many ways the new age is a reaction to the failures, or perceived failures, of the modern age. If the modern age claimed to have all the answers, the postmodern world doesn't have any. Some even declare culture is now moving beyond postmodernism.

Modern	Postmodern
romantic view of life	absurd view of life
purpose	play
design	chance
hierarchy	anarchy
word	silence
a completed work	a process
analysis from a distance	analysis through participation
creation/synthesis	deconstruction/antithesis
presence	absence
centering	dispersal
semantics/words	rhetoric/presentation
depth	surface
narrative/grande histoire	anti-narrative/petite histoire
metaphysics	irony

transcendence	immanence
Bible analyst	spiritual sage
broadcaster	listener
technician	spiritual friend
warrior/salesman	dancer
careerist	amateur
problem solver	coquester
apologist	apologizer
threat	includer
knower	seeker
solo act	team builder
respect, love, and wisdom	value, knowledge, and authority
stress "Does it work?"	stress getting the right answer
value leaders who ask the right questions	value leaders who give the right answers
lead by example	lead with information
value leaders for example	value leaders for knowledge and delivery
trust who, negotiate what	value what over who[9]

To further describe postmoderns, consider these characteristics regarding leaders and authority:

- Reject power of position but trust relationships
- Reject hierarchies but recognize earned authority
- See hierarchy as illusion of structural efficiency and as a carryover from the modern/technological world
- See people as one community rather than in dichotomies such as helper and helped

Most clergy face various leadership shifts if they are to work with postmoderns. These metaphors might help get a picture of the shifts needed if church leaders are to work effectively within a postmodern culture.

Preferences for Metaphors and Models

Leadership faces challenges when working effectively with postmoderns within a church atmosphere. For instance, look at these metaphors.

- Air traffic controller—An air traffic controller doesn't fly the plane, he just gives direction/assistance when needed for takeoffs and landings and to prevent in-air collisions. A leader of postmoderns does not have control or even give the indication of direct control, but he does have influence and direction at critical times in life.

- Conductor—A conductor doesn't play the instruments but listens to bring everyone together, assisting with the overall "feel" of the performance. Postmoderns desire a listening ear that is a safe place and authentic. They want to connect the dots of life. How life ties together and makes meaning is a significant contribution of life coaches and those who seek to influence postmoderns.
- Storyteller—Storytelling is key for ministering to and with postmoderns. They like stories. They see themselves as living a story; and they can and do connect with the many biblical stories as places of exploration, guidance, and instruction. They believe that narrative carries truth, and story allows for creativity instead of just carrying facts. Most stories offer a way to see
- God bringing order out of chaos.[18]

Let's try another approach to understand the difference between the modern age and the postmodern. Modern-age television shows focused on the ultimate good of people and their ability to reason and solve problems. Some of those shows include *Father Knows Best, Ozzie and Harriet, The Dick Van Dyke Show,* and *The Brady Bunch.* Postmodern shows make losers the stars. The plots often don't seem to go anywhere; there is no respect for truth and authority; and someone with a modern mind-set may wonder what the point is. Examples include *The Simpsons, Married with Children, Seinfeld,* and *South Park* (other illustrations are in chapter 6).

A quick review of the generational descriptions provided earlier makes clear that the numbers of people in each generation who are Christians and who support the church are declining. Chris Altrock notes:

> The postmodern era could also be called post-Christian or anti-Christian. The Boomers, . . . Busters, . . . and Next-Gens . . . are the transitional generations within this cultural shift. The highly publicized differences between these generations can thus be attributed to factors beyond simply generational differences. Their differences are largely the result of the varying degrees to which they have been raised in postmodernism.[19]

Altrock goes on to list seven "faces" of postmodernism, saying that postmoderns are uninformed about the basics of Christianity, interested in spiritual matters, anti-institutional, pluralistic, pragmatic, relational, and experimental. He points out that these characteristics may not be unique to postmoderns, but postmoderns display them altogether and with more intensity than people of the modern age.[20]

In *Postmodern Pilgrims,* Leonard Sweet provides an acronym for remembering the primary characteristics of postmoderns: EPIC—experiential, participatory, image-driven, connected.[21] These are the characteristics that the church must keep in mind as its leaders seek to reach those born into and influenced by the postmodern world. (Additional insights can be gleaned from *The Gospel According to Starbucks.*[22])

The writer of Hebrews assures us, "Jesus Christ is the same yesterday and today and forever" (13:8). The message is the same. How we communicate it needs to be packaged in ways for all generations to hear and respond. "For the LORD is good; / his steadfast love endures forever, / and his faithfulness to all generations" (Ps. 100:5).

The Sixty-Forty Split

Now that we have a better understanding of generational differences and the differences between those born into a modern and a postmodern world, what can we do about it in the church? Do we just want to keep the over-sixty crowd satisfied, or do we want to do some adapting and adjusting to reach a younger generation? It doesn't have to be an either/or; rather it should be both/and. But most churches function like it's an either/or. Since senior adults and the Builder Generation built the church buildings and invested deeply in shaping churches as they are—ministry and functional buildings—we don't want to make them mad. We need to honor them, and we do. We still love them, and we need them and their wisdom.

Each generation deserves the tools, language, and faith formation venues that fuel personal and corporate faith. Until each generation understands and embraces the needs of the others, gridlock is likely to occur. A couple of new thoughts are emerging here: (1) To be unified, all age groups need to worship together at the same time and in the same place. There's virtue in this position and extreme value *if* all are open and responsive to it. (2) Youth coming from "church culture" families and values will be at one extreme or the other on this "unified worship" issue. Some will vehemently resist it because "it doesn't work for me."

Others will say, "It works to be with others who share the same music, theology, and personal preferences that are rooted in our valued church traditions."

While this is a plus, it is also a warning. The youth with church culture values/roots are few in number compared to the large percentage of youth who are basically unchurched or part of the "nones" or "dones." That reality can't be ignored and sacrificed just so some can enjoy the church value culture in a "unified service" (that attracts all age groups worshiping basically the same way). An article in *Faith & Leadership* shows that Thanksgiving dinner offers a picture of this.

> That's the image that popped into Steve Jones' head five years ago when a search committee at First Presbyterian Church in San Mateo, California, asked him what intergenerational worship should look like.
>
> "It occurred to me that it should be like Thanksgiving dinner at grandma's house," Jones said. "There may be a dish that you may not like, but there will be something that everyone will like. The point is

not whether everyone likes all the food. The point is that everybody experiences the dinner together. . . . The goal, Jones said, is to help everyone pray, sing, study the Bible, receive the sacraments and enjoy fellowship in a way that all are drawn into a fulfilling experience of God's presence."

"To do that," he said, "everyone has to show up willing to give up a little of what they prefer in order to worship together. Not every day—not even every Sunday—is 'grandma's Thanksgiving dinner' yet at First Presbyterian, but the church has made great strides toward intergenerational worship."

Fueled in part by a Vital Worship Grant from the Calvin Institute of Christian Worship, they've boosted the participation of all ages at the Sunday service, launched a weeklong children's camp on worship, started a church-band mentoring program, published a pew booklet on worship and held a church-wide worship workshop.

Together, these and other measures are creating not just a culture of intergenerational worship at First Presbyterian San Mateo but an intergenerational church, said the Rev. Shannon Pappas, the pastor and head of staff.[23]

The answer is not knee-jerk change. It begins with looking at the generations already in the church, valuing all of them, and determining together how to reach out to a younger generation in a postmodern world.

A friend has a little plaque on her kitchen wall with these words, "Home is where we live for one another and all live for God." Those words seem fitting for those in the community of faith as well. As we live in relationship with one another and together for God, we will find ways to communicate the Good News and to love one another as Christ has first loved us—both to those over sixty and those under thirty.

Culture Clash or Culture Comfort?

We interviewed more than two hundred believers who declared they are losing interest in church for an article I wrote called "Why Some Believers Are Leaving the Church"[24] The top ten quotes really surprised us. Unrelated interviewees used almost these identical words

1. "Church adds little value to daily life experiences."
2. "We find it difficult to add value to and get involved in the church experience."
3. "Church is too inward focused in action, giving, and care!"
4. "Church talks about living by faith but rarely takes risks into the new and unknown."
5. "Church has little interest and active involvement in justice issues of our day."

6. "Churches preach love and practice hatred and judgment!"
7. "Churches are often dominated by a few people."
8. "Churches rarely make room for outsiders in their leadership base."
9. "Pastors preach at us rather than engaging us in the Scripture lesson."
10. "Churches typically use offerings for self-care rather than community engagement."

Granted, this is not scientific research, but the data gathered through interviews have extended over time and, for many, created opportunities for ongoing dialogue and relationships. Many were thrilled that a local church was really concerned about why so many believers were disinterested in church today. Most of those interviewed had at one time been faithful in attendance, active in leadership, and considered themselves believers. A few acknowledged they were through with church. "Been there done that!" was a familiar refrain, particularly from the Busters/Gen X sample.

An article in *the Washington Post* describes current church attendance:

While the number of religiously unaffiliated Americans has risen dramatically in recent years, measures like belief in God and church attendance have appeared remarkably stable. Researchers have hypothesized that people were turning away from religious institutions and taking more of a 'cafeteria approach' to belief. Michael Wear, a former adviser to President Obama, has defined this as the 'notion of "picking and choosing" what one wants to believe and follow from religious traditions while ignoring the rest.[25]

The article goes on to say that people are rejecting institutions and are choosing not to affiliate with them. While America is not yet at the point Western Europe is in terms of distancing itself from the church, we are becoming a more secular nation.

So how do churches reach a younger population today, even in light of these discouraging statistics? The Faith Communities Research project provides practical insights based on their research.

How are faith communities with a significant proportion of young adults distinctive? The Faith Communities Today research project has been studying congregations of all faiths across America that are doing an exceptional job of engaging young adults. A congregation is considered to have significant young adult participation if 21 percent or more of its participants are 18 to 34 years of age. Across all faiths, a total of only 16 percent of all congregations have such young adult involvement.

The findings identify some best practices for congregations that wish to attract and engage young adults. These can be summarized in a dozen 'do's' and four 'don'ts.'

What congregations should do:

1. Offer a high-quality worship experience that is contemporary in style or refashion traditional worship in new ways.
2. Start a new congregation or young-adult-only worship group within an existing congregation, or move an existing congregation to a new location.
3. Prioritize metropolitan areas and communities near university campuses.
4. Allow people to bring coffee to worship.
5. Provide food.
6. Be intentional about reaching out to young adults.
7. Form friendships with young adults.
8. Involve young adults in leadership.
9. Sponsor activities that mix socializing with theological reflection.
10. Apply theological principles to everyday-life issues that young adults face.
11. Figure out how to connect with the different types of young adults — whether they are still in school or starting careers, single or married, with or without children. These groups cannot just be lumped together without some facilitating rationale.
12. Figure out how to connect with young adults who are aging out of the category in their mid- to late-30s.

Congregations should NOT do the following:

1. Be theologically doctrinaire.
2. Insist that people wear dresses or suits and ties to worship.
3. Expect growth in the number of members or total giving.
4. Expect young adults to sign up for long-term committee work."[26]

Tobin Grant, in a blog for Religion News Service, telescopes American history from 1940 to the present to frame the state of religious life in contemporary America: From the turn of the millennium, religion has once again declined.

But this decline is much sharper than the decline of 1960s and 1970s.

Church attendance and prayer is less frequent. The number of people with no religion is growing. Fewer people say that religion is an important part of their lives. But the decline in religiosity was not as sharp as its 1950s rise.

Religiosity in the United States is in the midst of what might be called "The Great Decline." Previous declines in religion pale in comparison. [Since 2000], the drop in religiosity has been twice as great as the decline of the 1960s and 1970s. Overall, the hundreds of survey measures point to the same drop in religion: If the 1950s were another Great Awakening, this is the Great Decline.

The Great Decline may be a recent change, but our current level of religiosity isn't new. In 2005, the level of religiosity was about the same as it was in 1945. We have since continued to see lower and lower levels of religiosity, but we're not that much less religious than we were eight decades ago. The rise of religion in the 1950s has skewed our perception of the past — things have changed but not in a straight decline.

What next? There is nothing inherently cyclical about the change in religiosity; what goes down does not always go up again. The 1950s had some unique events that helped spur religiosity. The long-run trend should be toward less and less religiosity (because of increased wealth). That said, there's no reason that we cannot see another up-tick in religiosity in the future.[27]

Looking Inward, Looking Outward

If you walk into a church where most of the hair is gray, where the sanctuary is much too large for the congregation, and where those who sit in the pews are scattered all over the church, sitting where they have sat for many years, chances are that this church has an inward focus. If you're looking for a church where the people love and care for one another, this is it. They may even do some good ministries that care for people outside the walls of the church, but somehow they haven't learned to connect with people in the community—at least not enough to get them to come to church. The worship and Bible study meet the needs of the people in this church. The fellowship inside the church is warm and friendly, and guests who find their way inside the church are welcome, just not sought after or pursued.

In a day when the number of unchurched Americans has increased 92 percent between 1991 and 2014, we are confronted with church values and systems that are designed to be more inwardly focused than outwardly focused.[28] Today if you walk into a church that is vibrant and alive, with people talking with one another in crowded corridors, children filling the halls, and a mix of adults under thirty and over sixty, chances are this church has an outward focus and is reaching people and growing.

Thom Rainer provides provocative observations about the top eleven mistakes a church makes in today's culture.

1. *Failure to have an informative, easy-to-use website.* The website is the first place a prospective guest visits when he or she is thinking about attending a church. High-quality websites are incredibly affordable and should be updated at least weekly with good, accurate information for guests and members alike.

2. *Failure of pastors and staff to be actively involved in social media.* That is analogous to a missionary in another land failing to learn how to speak the language of the people.

3. Failure of pastors and staff to understand they represent the church on social media. . . . Church members read [blog posts]. The community reads them. . . .

4. *Failure to urge people to be a part of small groups in the church.* Groups are key to healthy assimilation, ministry involvement, evangelistic intentionality, biblical accountability, and community connections.

Church leaders should regularly encourage members and others to get involved in a small group, home group, Sunday school class, or some other ongoing group.

5. *Failure of leaders to be actively involved in influencing the content of groups.* Can you imagine a pastor asking a random person to preach on Sunday morning without any idea what that person would say? That's how many leaders treat their groups. . . .

6. *Failure of church members to be considerate of where they sit during a worship service.* [Guests do not want to climb over church members who arrived early, grabbed an aisle seat, and left no room for others because they used space for their coats, Bibles, smartphones, or other items.]

7. *Failure to have parking lot greeters.* This ministry is a church's opportunity to make a positive first impression. . . .

8. *Failure to have clearly marked guest parking.* Most churches have guest parking places. The problem is most guests can't find them.

9. *Failure to have clearly marked entrances to the worship center.* Ask a friend who has never attended your church to help you in an experiment. [Drive into your church parking lot and ask the friend to lead you to the worship center. Ask the friend how easy it was to find the worship center. Report the results to the responsible body in the church organization.] Because we know our own church so well, we too often don't comprehend the challenges a first time guest may have.

10. Failure to have clearly marked entrances to the church offices. Of course, this particular issue is more of a problem during weekdays.

11. *Failure to have adequate restroom facilities.* . . . Guests should see clearly marked signs that tell them how to find them.[29]

You might use these eleven points with members and leadership to do self-assessment as to how others might be experiencing church in your gatherings.

The difference isn't just about worship style, though that may be part of it. Eric Swanson and Rick Rusaw suggest four attributes of an externally focused church:

1. Externally focused churches are convinced that good deeds and good news cannot and should not be separated. Just as it takes two wings to lift an airplane off the ground, so externally focused churches couple good news with good deeds to make an impact in their communities. The good news explains the purpose of the good deeds.

2. Externally focused churches see themselves as vital to the health and well-being of their communities. They believe that their communities, with all of their aspirations and challenges, cannot be truly healthy without the church's involvement. Only when the church is mixed

into the very life and conversation of the city can it be an effective force for change.

3. Externally focused churches believe that ministering and serving are the normal expressions of Christian living. Christians grow best when they are serving and giving themselves away to others. These churches are convinced that Christians can learn through good instruction, but they really cannot grow if they remain uninvolved in ministry and service.

4. Externally focused churches are evangelistically effective. People are looking for places of authenticity where the walk matches the talk, where faith is making a difference. These words are carved in stone at the entrance of Vineyard Community Church in Cincinnati: "Small things done with great love will change the world.[30]

The Lewis Center for Church Leadership has also compiled a helpful list for externally focused churches - "50 Ways to Take Church to the Community." They provide tips in nine areas: (1) embrace an expansive concept of community; (2) prepare spiritually; (3) get to know the community surrounding your church; (4) listen and learn; (5) build authentic relationships; (6) turn your existing ministries outward; (7) reach out through community events; (8) extend your congregation's spiritual presence beyond the church walls; and (9) connect spiritual outreach to community service.[31]

COACHING QUESTIONS

- What are your takeaways from this chapter? What's ringing in your heart now?
- Whom else do you know who might identify with these same issues?
- How can you move forward in your understanding and practice in a way that will help your church move forward

6

Tips for Creating Community with People over Sixty and People under Thirty

A woman in her early sixties—let's call her Edna—called her best friend at church to tell her she wouldn't be seeing her on church the next Sunday or any other Sunday in the future. Alarmed, her friend asked what had happened. Here's Edna's story.

Edna had just moved into the oldest women's Sunday school class in a small suburban church a year or so ago. She was active in the church, loved her class, and wanted to see the church grow. The women's teacher moved away, and the women were told to go to the men's class, combining the classes for the first time. The women in this age group had never been in a coed class, and they didn't like it. So Edna made an appointment to talk with the pastor. She had some ideas about things the church could do, and she was thinking about volunteering to teach the women's class.

Edna began by telling the pastor how much she loved the church, appreciated him, and wanted to help. Then she started to share some of her ideas with him. She told him that the women weren't really happy having class with the men with a men's teacher and she didn't think the men liked it too well either. She had just started to tell the pastor that she would like to teach the class when he interrupted her.

He said, "We're really not targeting your age group at this church anymore. If you really want to help, you'll get out of that Sunday school class and teach a younger group. We're focusing on young families here. Let me know what you'd like to do for that age group."

His abrupt words ended the conversation. Some of her ideas did, in fact, focus on reaching a younger age group. But his dismissive tone communicated that she was really not wanted or needed. He didn't listen to her or talk with her about using her gifts in a specific way with the younger age group. He just told her the church wasn't interested in her or anyone else over sixty. Obviously this didn't work for Edna or for the "home church."

The next week Edna joined a neighboring church. She teaches a women's class on Sunday morning, participates in evangelistic visitation every week, leads a prayer ministry, and tithes. Though she misses seeing some of her old friends every week, she loves her new church. The pastor at her old church has moved on, but the church has forever lost a faithful member.

This true story is a great example of what's not working—just the opposite of win-win. What's more, the pastor's behavior was at best thoughtless and unkind, perhaps even destructive and cruel. He was focused more on the institution than the person. Targeting a younger group doesn't mean neglecting those over sixty.

Recently, I was invited to speak in a church. During the week before I spoke, I received a call from their deacon chairperson. He notified me that they had asked their pastor, who had been there five years, to resign immediately. As I listened carefully and explored with some open-ended coaching questions, it became clear that they were asking their pastor to resign because he was bringing in too many new younger people too fast. The longtime members and families were "uncomfortable and upset that the pastor was not paying as much attention to them." The deacon continued to explain that "they had talked with their pastor many times about their concerns, and he had not listened so the deacons felt they had no choice."

When I continued to explore, I asked, "What is the most important thing to your church now?" He quickly declared, "We want peace in the family and for our pastor to do what we ask him to do."

Well, I guess I heard that loud and clear. So many of our congregations are so concerned about "us" that we don't have room or desire to be concerned about "others." Somehow the members of the above church understood that the church and the pastor are to serve them. How sad!

Many things were not working for this pastor who was being asked to resign. Several things were not working for the church because of the mismatch of their leader and his philosophy of leadership with the church. I can hear many church members and leaders say, "But we need and deserve to be cared for." That is true, but Jesus died for the world and gave us a mission to reach the world. What do we do with that? Those churches who are more concerned about caregiving of each other than engaging to care for the broken and hurting in their community are destined to plateau and stagnate in faith, attendance, and impact.

People over sixty are not necessarily the barriers to growth. Sometimes, as in these cases, pastors, staff, and volunteer church leaders of any age can be their own worst enemies. Learning just an idea about church growth, such as targeting a certain age group, must be combined with a well-thought-out and prayed-over plan to reach people under thirty without losing or abusing those over sixty.

Here are some ideas that may help you formulate your own plan. The ideas and solutions presented are simply to help you evaluate your own situation and equip you to explore options to expand your church's ministry in its context.

Different Circumstances, Different Approaches

Times continue to change as a result of historic and catalytic sociological, economic, and/or political events and experiences. In 2012 Trayvon Martin was killed in Florida. As I work on this revision, a series of deaths of young African-American men/boys by white police officers continues to have an impact in the second half of 2015. In June 2015 in Charleston, SC at Emmanuel AME church 9 persons were senselessly murdered during their Bible Study. Such actions have brought people of all races and persuasions to the streets in protests seeking justice and acknowledging through signs and posters that Black Lives Matter and through chants of "I can't breathe"—the last words of Eric Garner, who died in a police confrontation. In a number of these cases the grand jury chose not to indict the police officers. The journey for community and justice continues even now, and the consequences will certainly impact the future of churches, schools, communities, and political agendas.

How many times have we heard since September 11, 2001, that we are now living in a different world? How many times have we heard our national leaders say we are fighting a different kind of war from any we have ever fought before, calling for different strategies and approaches? How many times have we heard from the FBI that their prior assumptions about investigation procedures are having to be rethought in these new days?

How many times have we heard the airlines say they are having to retool, rethink, retrain, and refocus their industry in light of September 11, 2001? Their very survival has been on the line. Passengers, frustrated with the ongoing hassles of security, are rethinking whether they have travel options that don't include flying.

How many times have we heard the postal service declare words of warning about receiving and opening our mail as they describe the challenges they face in security with the billions of pieces of mail that come through their hands each year?

We really are in a different world, facing circumstances most Americans have never known. The world that once felt safe and free feels at times to be at high risk of terrorism attacks, and our freedoms often feel as though they are slipping away. Our fear and anxiety levels are high. Our desire to go on with life is present in our minds and hearts, but somehow there's a lingering fear in most of us about what's next.

Many assumptions of the past are being rethought by those planning war strategies; new coalitions are being formed to sustain peaceful times and reduce international threats of terrorism. Schools and families are paying closer attention to caring for our children. Communities are filled with flying flags indicating our unity, the support for our nation and troops, and calling on God to bless America. My, how tragedy brings us together, while times of peace seem to breed all kind of controversy, diversity struggles, and threats. Such focus in times of peace seems to be a self-centered and selfish focus. Meanwhile, in times of war or being under the threat of losing our freedoms, the focus seems to be on unity, self-sacrifice for a common cause. What lessons can we as Christian leaders and churches glean and act on? Let's review some of the challenges leaders and churches face in light of changing circumstances in our world.

Identifying Barriers

In what often seems to be a deteriorating culture, why isn't your church growing? Perhaps growth is not a goal. Perhaps some members are even against growth because they or their family members might lose their historical status if the church grows. When in a small church one family controls the leadership and budget of the church, the pastor and other leaders must proceed carefully, seeking to enlist the support of the controlling family. This is just one example of the importance of identifying barriers to growth in your church at the beginning of your process. You can take many steps to growth, but if you ignore the barriers, your growth efforts may yield less than their potential.

As the pastor (who is usually the church's visionary leader) or other staff or volunteer leader begins to lead the church to grow, embrace a new direction, or expand its ministry, identifying barriers may help jump-start the process. The pastor or other leaders may see some of the barriers, but not all. Identifying barriers is much like personal confession. The sin must be named before it can be eliminated.

Here are some barriers or obstacles that individuals and congregations must grapple with if they are to grow or experience an expanded ministry. Do any of these exist in you or your church?

- Prejudice—against other racial/ethnic groups, old/young, secular adults with secular lifestyle issues, rich/poor and related occupations, anyone "not like us"
- Not knowing how to grow
- Wanting things to stay the same
- Fear of success and how to assimilate new members and minister to them
- Lack of a plan
- Lack of member involvement to work the plan
- Inadequate resources
- No clear understanding of need for change
- Satisfaction with the status quo
- Lack of spiritual foundation

- Fear of reaching "needy" people
- Believing change requires too much time, energy, and other resources
- Fear of losing some current members because of change
- Being comfortable with things as they are
- Fear of losing the close family feel and good relationships in church as it is
- Lack of agreement about new direction
- Discouragement because of previous, disappointing attempts to change or grow
- Resistance to learning a new language. Language is key for communicating with the generations under thirty years of age. Having the language and skill set to allow "heart issues" to serve as entry points for connection will be extremely important for building bridges to this age group.
- Lack of clearly defined goals
- No clear mission statement
- No value-added proposition for business plans
- Measuring effectiveness with inappropriate standards. How do you measure ROI (return on investment)? Is it captured in numbers and data or measured through personal life stories and transformation? Or both?
- Not understanding the postmodern culture

Early in any process, church leaders, or the entire church, may want to identify barriers. You can use a formal group setting or informal conversations to discover your personal barriers or your church's barriers. *By identifying them, you can formulate a plan to overcome them.* For example, if the plan lacks a biblical basis, the church can plan a Bible study and/or sermon series. If a lack of communication is a barrier, church leaders can plan a variety of ways to keep people apprised of the change process. *Church leaders might build into their personal spiritual growth plan shifts of attitudes, ways of measuring effectiveness, or ways of building bridges rather than barriers.* Creating some accountability with others to make and live into these shifts is a critical but necessary step in preparing an atmosphere and leadership base that moves the church forward in ministry to all generations.

Throughout any plan for change, church leaders may want to step back and consider whether barriers are impeding progress. Small-group and one-on-one conversations will keep both leaders and members informed. The congregation will follow their leaders. Where are the leaders leading the church—toward reaching one generation or multiple generations? What shifts in personal preference values or understandings are you needing to learn to live into? What will help you get there?

Cornell Thomas summarizes his journey that surfaces a number of factors that many individuals and churches face in these times of growing diversity and cultural shifts. He explains:

I first want to start off by saying that I am not an expert in the field of reaching and keeping the younger generation in the context of diversity. It just so happens that I'm surrounded by it all the time, and it's now become my DNA. My hope for you is that through my experience you will find some kind of insight on how to be the church amid growing diversity.

Early in life my experience was pretty stereotypical of most African-Americans. You hear the story all the time—victim of fatherlessness, single-parent household, older sibling incarcerated three-fourths of life, and neighborhood filled with drug activity, violence, and hopelessness. That was me. The neighborhood I grew up in in Cleveland, Ohio, wasn't diverse at all—100 percent African-American. The only time I saw diversity was when the cops were driving around. Like most, I quickly found an unnoticed way of escape from the difficulties of my living situation through athletics. Sports was a big part of my life, and not only would it keep me off the streets as a young adolescent but would afford me the opportunity to attend college.

I first attended a small junior college in Minnesota. If someone had told me I would spend the first two years of my college career in Ely, Minnesota, I would've laughed and told them, "I couldn't even point that out on a map." But Minnesota was amazing in my time there. I was exposed to a lot of cultural changes—for example, playing sports in a rural setting, learning in a rural setting, but most importantly living in a rural setting.

It was pretty much known that if you were an African-American living in Ely, Minnesota, you played one of two sports, basketball or football. I went from living in a culture where everybody looked like me race-wise to truly experiencing what it's like to be the minority. I excelled for the most part at this junior college even though some surprises caught me off guard along the way. One surprise was an athletic scholarship to play basketball at a school here in North Carolina, but I'll get into that later. The most important surprise that completely caught me off guard while attending this junior college was meeting my future wife, and I'm so glad I did. We are truly meant for each other. But I do want to use the time we spent together before we got married and after as an example of reaching people under thirty. During this time I was twenty-one, and she was twenty-four.

National Geographic says that by the year 2050, the average American will look "mixed," due to the African-American and Caucasian races integrating with each other.[1] And I am a proud contributor to this fact! My wife and I have three beautiful daughters. When asked on applications and forms, which have no "mixed" category, they check "other." But before we talk about that, from our experience I hope you can benefit from knowing how to reach and keep a mixed couple that walks into your congregation because I can assure you it will happen!

Before we got married, neither my wife nor I was a Christian. She grew up attending a Lutheran church that did a great job planting the seed, and I only attended the nearest church when Easter came around. Needless to say, before we were married, we didn't practice Christian values. This stage of our life was in between my first semester as an athlete on scholarship and after my last semester attending junior college, the summer of 2007, spent in beautiful Alexandria, Minnesota, where it's not much bigger than Ely but at least they had a Walmart and a McDonald's.

We totally experienced all the benefits of marriage before getting married, and as my wife's mother's statement constantly floated in her mind, "It's not right to live together," we continued living together, not having a clue what we were doing. Looking back today, I'm thankful her mother and father didn't shut us out completely and that both her mother and my mother were constantly praying for us.

From the first time I met them, they took me in and loved me as one of their own; and when Jamie and I cohabited, they spoke the truth in love, planting the seed. That truth spoken to us eventually weighed on us to the point we realized we needed to do something about it, and as a complete shock, I would say to my wife, 'Let's go to church.'

Though we didn't have a clue what to look for in a church, we knew the one when we found it. Sadly most churches we visited weren't prepared for us, an interracial unmarried couple searching for something but not knowing what we were searching for.

Here's what we came up with. The first church we visited was very liturgical. That's OK; it just wasn't for us. But again, we didn't know what to look for in a church so that probably would've been OK had someone greeted us. From the time we walked in the church to the time we left—I am not kidding when I say this—no one said hi to us, shook our hand, or told us good-bye or, most importantly, see you next week. I probably would've paid more attention to the sermon if I didn't feel like I didn't belong at the church. I felt as if during the whole service all eyes were on us and not in a good way.

Do you think we returned to that church? Absolutely not, and personally I don't think they cared if we did! Apparently our desire to find the thing that would satisfy the guilt we were experiencing from living together fueled our search for a church, and so the next Sunday we gave it another try. We walked in to this church that was noticeably larger, which made it easier for us to sit on the back row and hide, but at least we were there.

What was different with this church from the last? Other than size, it looked alive. People were genuinely talking with one another. As soon as we walked in, someone greeted us. This changes the game. Hospitality is a gift, and I would advise you not to place someone in the ministry of greeting people to make others feel welcome if they aren't gifted in it. We felt extremely welcome, and this is what kept us coming back.

We knew we wouldn't be there for much longer because of the basketball scholarship I accepted in North Carolina. (Note: This is true of most young adults. They are constantly in transition and can easily go unnoticed. But they will walk in our doors, and we have to be ready as the church to reach them.)

This church my wife and I attended for this season played its part in watering the seed.

Apparently God was working on us. Some tribes call this the theology of prevenient grace, the work God does before to draw us to Himself. As stimulated as my brain was to focus only on school and sports in order to make it to the pros to be able to make a lot of money because that was so important, sarcastically speaking, we still had it in us to fill the God-sized hole that only God can fill.

So the search continued, and luckily as an interracial couple fresh in the South—you can imagine the thoughts we had in our heads—we were able to find a church minutes from our apartment. How did we find it? We searched for it online, and the church's website reflected the ministry in person. We couldn't help but notice the pictures on the website of black and white people laughing together, which sold us. So we visited, and this first visit captured our hearts long-term.

"Here in Charlotte, North Carolina, big churches are everywhere so it's hard not to attend one, and that was true of the church my wife and I attended. Again we quickly noticed the hospitality when we got to the door. We also quickly noticed that we were overdressed because no one there dressed up. I take that back—people dressed up but not in a way that made us feel out of place.

Though there were so many positives to this church—not that we had a checklist because again we didn't know what to look for in a church—what really stood out to us was when one of the kids of an interracial couple with seven kids asked us if we wanted to come to their home and share a meal. I have got to tell you, for a couple that's new to the city with no family, who's searching for something, this was huge. Almost eight years later as I write this, my heart still wells up with joy and thanksgiving for that family that welcomed us and made us their own. Today, simply put, they are family!

In searching for a church—for us as an interracial, twenty-something couple—being connected was the first step. Some may argue it's the responsibility of the person to take the first step in finding connection, but in our experience it was the complete opposite! I guess it can be argued in our case that we took multiple steps toward connection, taking the time to find it online. At the time, as a skeptical couple of this faith called Christianity, we had to wake up on a Sunday and drive there, and go through the anxiety of being the sore thumb in a big church (close to twenty-five hundred every weekend). And now you want to make us find connection too?

This church would play a pivotal role in watering the seed, not just from the pulpit but also from the congregation, and eventually God caused the growth. My wife and I had a dramatic encounter with God because people spoke truth to us in love about our living situation. Coupled with hearing the gospel weekly, in only a few weeks we got married at this church, and during our ceremony my wife was baptized. I had been baptized the week before after attending what's called Discipleship Weekend, which is a class held at the church that invites any and all people to come and listen to the lead pastor teach on apologetics. But also the people are encouraged to ask any and all questions about the faith. This class is held on a Friday night and all day Saturday, and through this experience I met the Lord and was baptized that following Sunday.

Today—seven years later, married, three children, I minister in the inner city where I am attempting to pioneer urban ministry. I'm asked the question, "How do we reach and keep the younger generation in a growing, diverse community?"

When it comes to the importance of diversity in our church, my pastor states, 'When it comes to diversity, it's important to me because it's important to our Savior. And if it's important to him, I'll give everything I have to see his dream, his prayer in John 17, fulfilled.'

Since being a congregant earlier in my faith, in the stage of receiving ministry, then actually believing God can use me, I have faced some challenges in reaching the younger generation inside of our church. I believe it's because they're so transitional. I have seen our young adults ministry go up because college is out for break and go down because it started back up again. I've seen some of our young adults leave the country because they felt a calling to the mission field while others would get new jobs and have to stop coming to our young adults ministry. I still have not yet seen a consistent group of people in our young adults ministry faithfully commit to learning and growing together in our faith. This is something I am zealously committed to although the time I can invest in the church isn't much compared to the time I invest in pioneering urban ministry. The two in my eyes go hand in hand in reaching and keeping the younger generation amid a growing diverse community.

I absolutely love how God has strategically placed me today as a pastor/missionary with one foot in the church and one foot outside the church, though it is extremely challenging. But shouldn't it be this way for all churched people? The problem is, we either have both feet in the church and forget about the people outside or both feet outside pretending to be churched!

What does it take for someone who is churched to reach and keep the younger generation amid a growing generation? For starters, it takes all of you, the whole body. Hopefully the leadership is demonstrating transparency well enough so it becomes contagious and the laity are able to catch it.

We all have to be willing to let people in our homes. Again, this was a big part of our experience.

The next thing that needs to happen is what I call a "church detox." I wish I were smart enough to coin that term, but it came from a night at Magnolias in Charleston, South Carolina, during a staff conference, where I had a thought-provoking conversation with another pioneer. We talked about my confusion at why inner city ministry doesn't call itself a church. A lot came out of this conversation, but two things stuck out to me: Young Life, to use Eddie's [the author's] terminology, would be considered the "church on the go" because we don't invest in buildings but people. (Though I affirm buildings and there's nothing wrong with them, our camp has a more outward focus.)

The other thing that stuck out to me was that phrase "church detox." My colleague said people have a hard time reaching the unchurched because they have both feet in, or in other words they are too churchy. This brought me back to my initial reaction to being exposed to the inner city ministry. I was actually offended because of its approach to those that are disinterested in Christianity. My first exposure to this ministry was at an "all-city club." About four hundred to five hundred high school adolescents attended. The majority of students there did not act churched. I'm laughing now, but then that actually rubbed me the wrong way. I can understand why there are those who don't agree with the way some ministries do things, but I've met teachers in profound seminaries who met Christ through an inner city non-church based ministry.

Hear me clearly: I'm not saying a non-churched based ministry is the way but a way to introduce kids to Jesus and help them grow in their faith. Why was I initially upset with this ministry that gathered so many—what some would call "lost"? I can honestly say I was just too churchy, and I had to undergo a church detox. I am certain a few like me are sitting under you or next to you. It never crossed my mind to go outside the church (building) and sit with sinners; I always thought they would simply show up at the church (building). I heard someone say, "We (Christians) should be famous among sinners!" The church has got to leave the building!

My last point I'll make in reaching and keeping the younger generation amid a growing diverse generation is to have a community that fosters living on mission together. I once attended what's called "work week" held at one of the Christian camps close by. I brought a van full of young adults with me from our young adults ministry at the church. Work week is basically going to the camp for a few days to help prepare camp for the summer for the thousands of high schoolers who will attend.

I couldn't help but notice how many young adults were there. The pastor in me kicked in and asked myself, How can our young adults ministry look like this? During this time we did everything you would see at a local church—we served, received the teaching of the Word together, and worshiped through song. Except it wasn't in the church; it was at camp in the mountains.

How is it that hundreds of young adults here at this camp, though there were thousands across the nation participating in a work week, can come from all over to do church? I am convinced it is because they knew they were a part of and doing life with a community of like-minded individuals who live on mission. Everybody there, when they went back to their state, would be doing the same thing—introducing adolescents to Jesus Christ and helping them grow in their faith. This common mission attracted more than forty thousand young adults and older adults last year to give up their time to be a part of that mission.

Why did I, as a young adult, leave your church? You didn't give me anything to do. What generations were reflected when your mission statement was made? Are people actually living it out? So much so that if someone visited your church once, when they left your church, would they know what your community was about? Churchy people are difficult to move out of their seats, but it takes everybody to reach everybody. People have to decide which people group they want to do life with, churched or unchurched? This was the conversation on the way home from work week I had with the young adults (churched) I brought from our young adults ministry. I will not go into detail or give my opinion here, but I will say, one is in the church and one isn't!"

Challenge yourself to think outside the box. The only thing permanent in life is change. When trying to attract the younger generation and keep the older generation, don't simply assume the things you think they will enjoy and understand. Do some research. For example, many movies, books, and TV shows have great episodes and topics around spiritual formation and true-life issues/experiences. Let me give you some examples. Would you consider having a pizza party and movie night with your church members? This could be a great way to promote a family night and show a film that caters to multigenerational and multicultural families. Or have a special movie showing for your teenagers around serious teen topics that need to be addressed. Are you willing to discuss drug prevention and teen pregnancy in your church? Maybe this is an area where mentoring relationships with another generation can be helpful.

Many postmodern persons enjoy watching online shows at their leisure and on demand, often binge watching. Shows like Modern Family, Mad Men, Game of Thrones, West Wing, and Breaking Bad have a theme of communication, issues of the heart, and often challenges of the current norms. Such can become a springboard for spiritual conversations to explore what's missing, what works for them, and what does not work for them. Is this the end of the spiritual conversation? Certainly not, but it can be a comfortable entry point.

The territory of the heart can be a key connecting point and entry for building safe intergenerational relationships. The show might deal with anger, resentment, unresolved grief, sadness, grace, mystery, miracles, acceptance, suspense, diversity, secrets, the supernatural, etc. The key point I am trying to make here is that you have many ways to approach spiritual formation with the younger generation without starting with Scripture. Unfortunately, we have learned that starting with Scripture with the younger generation can be a barrier instead of a bridge. Did you ever think that the Bible could be a barrier? This is true evidence of our changing world.

COACHING QUESTIONS _____

- How does spiritual growth happen for the younger generation, the older generations? For people of other cultures or ethnicities?
- What are the places with which you identify? Or with which you have a disconnect?
- Whom else do you know that shares Cornell's family experiences?
- What might you do to support them in their journey of faith?

Think about your children, grandchildren, or friends who are not connecting with church at a deep level. Are there some bridge-building experiences you are hearing about here that you are willing to experiment with in order to build stronger relationships with the younger generation? Consider the words and behaviors of your children or grandchildren, "they are not giving God enough credit or using the 'right church language' to describe their experience of spiritual transformation." This is understandable, but such language is a characteristic of postmoderns, many of whom do not have the church background or come from another social or ethnic background. They find their own words to describe their spiritual renewal.

Now let's look at creating a win-win for the church. We begin with the individuals and move to the corporate gathering. (This leadership style and process are framed in the companion book, *Making Shifts without Making Waves: A Soulful Approach to Leadership*.

7

A Win-Win for Your Church?

Your church will follow your leaders. We've already taken a glimpse into finding a win-win situation for leaders and helping leaders identify the shifts God may be calling them to live into in order to move their church forward. Now we will shift to a more intense issue of finding a win-win for the church collectively so community can be experienced. Here we provide multiple practical examples and coaching questions to help you explore options, possibilities, and directions that will reach people under thirty while keeping people over sixty.

Clinging to the Past and Sabotaging the Future

Many of the barriers to growth in the church revolve around a congregation's love of the past. While the warm feeling individuals have for what the church has meant to them in the past should propel them to desire that relationship for those outside the church, too often clinging to the past has just the opposite effect. Whether members' affection for the church means they don't want to change their comfort level or they want to keep the church just as it was when their grandpas were deacons, their reticence to change actually sabotages the future of the church they love. Perhaps you can identify some of your church members in this section and discover some ideas about making those who love the church eager for change.

"Too much entrenched traditionalism here, I'm afraid. Just mostly people who want to be comfortable, come to a social club, pay their dues, and expect pastoral visitations all the time. Oh, and sing music they've known for years and that is within their acceptable boundaries. I know it must make God's heart long and yearn that we would find more than this." These words from a recent e-mail reflect the angst many of our clergy are living with during these days of transition for the church. Our culture has shifted many times over the last decades, while most churches have changed little. Somehow they believe that staying the same is being faithful. How can this be when who we are and what we are doing as the people of God has turned many of our churches into hotels for the saints rather than hospitals for sinners? Today, a church's culture is more important than its vision.

Now many churches are facing critical days. Membership and finances are decreasing, faithful church culture leaders are rapidly dying out, remaining leaders are increasingly afraid to take risks, while membership is increasingly self-absorbed and much more concerned about their comfort than about fulfilling the Great Commission or the Great Commandment. We say we believe the Bible from cover to cover, but in many churches our behavior and values certainly do not seem to reflect biblical teachings and practices. The church faces some severe and crippling consequences when most members and leaders decide to live in their comfort zones rather than seek to please the heavenly Father.

Now, I understand wanting to live inside my comfort zones. I, too, have personal preferences I enjoy. Where does a person's need for personal comfort end and a person's commitment to the costliness of the gospel begin? Where does one leave personal comfort and personal preferences about worship styles, hymns, pastoral visitation expectations, and the way we prefer to do church to embrace the biblical mandates given to all believers "to go into all the world," "to take up our cross [no comfort there] daily" and follow Jesus? For me, that is the real question. *Until our leaders and church members get to that point, I'm not sure many of our churches will reach the new generation.* Many of our churches across this country are and will continue to close their doors and become recycled churches turned into bookstores, restaurants, or community service centers.

Has it happened in your neighborhood? In one city suburb an evangelistic group started a church and built a building. They had chosen a wonderful location near the interstate and several other major highways. After a short time in the facility, the congregation didn't have the membership or financial resources to keep the doors open. The building stood vacant. Thousands of cars drove by every day, watching the weeds grow on the once beautifully landscaped property. Then one day the parking lot was full, and a sign near the main entrance caused passersby to go home to their computers to look up the unfamiliar name on the sign. This evangelistic church building had been converted into a Hindu temple, right in the middle of the Bible Belt. Who would have ever thought such a thing could happen? Unfortunately, such transitions are happening more and more in this country.

- The United States is beginning to see doors close in churches much as has happened in European churches in decades past. Church buildings have been repurposed, turned into museums, torn down, or left empty. The term for such facilities is "recycled churches." Will churches become recycled in this country because of members' unwillingness to change? It is already happening! More than 10,000 churches close their doors each year across the United States. Will your church be one of these in the next few years? What are some consequences for a church that decides to live in comfort rather than on mission in the world?

- Will our current leaders and membership decide to preserve their comfort so much and for so long that they will sabotage the future of their churches? Now, God will use his church to accomplish his purpose, but unfortunately not every church with a steeple and a pastor is functioning as his church.
- Communities and family units become more and more diverse while many congregation want to stay homogenous in multiethnic neighborhoods. We sing the great old hymn "Just as I Am," but mean "Just become like we are."
- The spiritually thirsty who might visit or need a church will not likely find help or a place that is open to them. We take communion but practice exclusion.
- We really expect people to get it together and become "like us" before they come to our churches. This is not new. In the early church Jewish believers wanted Gentiles to become Jews first before they could become Christians. They wanted the men to be circumcised and everyone to follow Jewish dietary laws. For the sake of the Great Commission, the church decided that Gentiles did not need to become Jews first.
- They will lull their pastors into becoming a chaplain whose primary duty is to care for the members, particularly those who are active and faithful contributors to the budget. This job description doesn't have roots in the biblical call for the "equippers of the saints."
- Many pastors/clergy will become depressed, disillusioned, and weary of calling their people to go on mission while the people expect pastors to become caregivers. These clergy are now leaving the church-based ministry for ministries in secular careers.
- Our leaders will make decisions to stay comfortable in their church life, but their example will lead many to stay immature in their faith life.
- The church will expect their clergy/ministers to become caregivers rather than equippers. The membership will create unhealthy dependencies on their clergy, ignoring the doctrine of the priesthood of all believers for their church.
- They will talk about outreach and "come grow with us," but their inward focused behaviors will call members to "come slow down with us.
- Their expectations of one another and clergy will sound good to insiders but will prevent those outside the active membership from feeling welcomed and invited.
- Many of those churches are living in their comfort zone. They will simply die out after the generation of current members die.
- Many churches haven't been reaching people under thirty for decades. Now most of those congregations are filled with senior adults who desire living in comfort zones that continue to prevent their churches from reaching a new generation.

- The lost go unreached, and our churches become museums for our saints rather than mission outposts for the gospel.
- Many leaders and churches want to do better at fulfilling the biblical commission for the church. They don't want to face the steep learning curve, take risks, make anyone mad, or lead into the future. Most just don't want to rock the boat.

A once large and lively church had been slowly declining for years while doing everything the way they had always done it and wondering why it no longer worked. The much-loved pastor of more than two decades announced his retirement. When members were asked what they would like to see change under new leadership, the almost unanimous response was, "Nothing!"

But enough of the challenging situations. Here are some win-wins of churches I've experienced over the last decade. You can review their websites to see the current directions, but as of this writing they are doing super.

Mission Baptist Church in rural Locust, North Carolina (www.missionchurch.org). Over the last decades they have moved from a plateaued one-service church to having two campuses, with two services at one of the sites, and with about 70 percent of their membership involved in mission-focused small group experiences.

A couple of "First Church inner city" situations. These faith communities are dealing most effectively with transitioning facilities, staffing, and reaching people under thirty while keeping people over sixty as they also broaden their leadership base to include newcomers and established members alike.

First Baptist Church, Goldsboro, North Carolina, once a struggling inner-city, county-seat-town church, has not only created powerful partnerships with the community to feed the hungry and provide care for the poor, but they created ways to mobilize intergenerational groups of leaders to carry out these significant ministries and community partnerships.

Westwood Church in Cary, North Carolina, is seeking to develop vision for service from church to the outside world. They have already helped their church see the importance of "people over program." Their ministry is one of transitioning a program-based church to a mobilized partnering congregation that impacts people and groups outside and inside the walls of their church facilities.

Cindy Bolden, minister, Love Abiding Ministries, Apex, North Carolina, is a church leader, academic, and creative soul who meshes all facets of her life with her calling. Currently Cindy is an adjunct professor at Campbell Divinity School, working on her doctor of ministry degree, and director of the nonprofit Love Abiding. The focus of Love Abiding is a community ministries named Coffeehouse Conversation, Tavern Talks, and Soul Yoga. Cindy is a member of Westwood Baptist Church, Cary, North Carolina.

Grace United Methodist Church in LaSalle, Indiana, has designed a church around ministering to men and their families. Not only have they reached men for membership, but also they are experiencing transformation of men and family units.

First Baptist Church, Waynesville, North Carolina, is located in a county-seat town. This declining congregation decided they wanted to discern God's future for their church and make the needed alignments. Not only have they turned around attitudes and participation, but their leadership base has also grown. Their presence in their community is more visible, and they are restructuring staff, budget, and organization to keep the momentum focused and moving forward.

Intergenerational churches have strengths and challenges just like any other church model. Consider these comments about "vital and engaging worship":

> For worship to be vital and engaging and significant in a healthy church, it's best that it be inclusive of all generations," said the Rev. Kathy Smith, the associate director and program manager for grants programs at the Calvin Institute.
>
> Church has always included people of all ages with a wide variety of gifts, Smith said. Intergenerational worship is about including the gifts of all in leading and participating in worship.
>
> Beyond the programs that the Vital Worship Grants make possible, there is another benefit that many recipients don't anticipate, Smith said.
>
> "We're told all the time that the money helps but that it was the accountability that made a difference," she said. The grants force recipients to think deeply about their projects and what they are trying to achieve. . . .
>
> Those benefits became even clearer . . . when the [First Presbyterian Church San Mateo] held an all-church worship workshop to evaluate how the grant has impacted services and the congregation's understanding of worship.
>
> Robert Nordling, a former music director at the church and a former professor at Calvin College, led the workshop. About 60 people, from age 11 to 82, attended. If feedback from the participants is any indication, members have learned much about both worship and themselves.[1]

Immanuel Baptist in Greenville, North Carolina, in some ways typifies this model as they take an aging, struggling congregation into a college community. They are using their music ministry and the college's music degrees as a place of intersection and celebrating the diversity of the skills, talents, ethnicities, and lifestyles. I think God is up to something powerful with them.

A final illustration in that same town, Oakmont Baptist Church, has experienced amazing growth and partnerships due to their deep roots in spiritual formation and in their local community and college. Not only did God lead them to buy and restore an apartment complex for intergenerational and multiethnic tenants, but they have also restored an area facility into a nonprofit medical clinic.

God is up to something in Greenville, North Carolina, through the people of God at work inside and outside the walls of the churches.

These churches and many others listed in our resource listing at the end of this book have ventured into uncomfortable waters to move forward in ministry. Jesus said we should cast our nets on the other side (a very uncomfortable thing for some) if we are not catching fish by the way we are currently fishing. I think there's great wisdom in this teaching of Jesus. What about you? What legacy do you want to leave? Will you be seen as one who contributed to the death of your church or one who took risks, moved from your comfort zone, and helped birth the future of your church?

What about Sunday Night Church?

Just to be specific about an example of something that's worked in the past but isn't necessarily working today, let's consider the issue of Sunday night church. Recently I have been asked by several pastors and lay leaders, "What about Sunday night church?" Many churches are wrestling with the realities of declining Sunday night attendance and the traditional expectations that churches should gather on Sunday morning and Sunday night. Some believe the traditional format for Sunday night church is the greatest obstacle we have in making disciples today. The church wants to be faithful but also to be good stewards of time and power and provide busy families family time. What's a church to do about Sunday night?

For many, Sunday night church still works and that's great. Church history tells us that the beginning of Sunday night church evolved from those who worked hard on their farms early on Sunday to be able to travel by horse and buggy or by foot to get to church by about ten or eleven for church. They had traveled so far to church, and they hadn't seen their friends all week, so they decided to have dinner on the grounds and stay around for evening fellowship, prayer, Bible study, and worship. They were trying to maximize their time too. Ronny Russell, author of *Can a Church Live Again?*, explains, "I read somewhere years ago that Sunday evening services began in England (the good folks who gave us Sunday school) when gas lights became widely used in businesses and factories. Churches couldn't stand the thought of people going out on Sunday nights (it was still the Sabbath), and so they decided to install gas lights and open their churches for Sunday night services."[2]

The pinch many feel today around these issues is not unfamiliar to history. Those of one generation grew up with certain expectations, and those of the emerging generation have other needs, and often the two sets of needs and expectations clash.

The New Testament talks much more about the functions of the church than the forms of the church. However, most of the time the debate about Sunday night programming ignores the issue of function and focuses on "we've always done it that way." Most of the emotional charge is around preserving the forms of Sunday night church, while little energy is going to discussions around being good stewards of time, energy, and resources—or what tangible fruit is coming from the scheduled events. All too often the decision-makers want to maintain the programming, but they rarely participate. Still, they expect the preacher to open up the church for those who want to come. Is that really good stewardship and decision-making?

Consider what you are really trying to accomplish by Sunday night programming. How is it really working? What other options are available to help you more effectively accomplish the biblical functions of the church? What adjustments could be made in programming and scheduling to fulfill the biblical functions of the church in today's culture?

Today's new realities include busy people, multiple venues of competition for our time and attention in our communities, a seven-day workweek for many, the challenge to find family time and at-home time, increasing numbers of single-parent families, dual-career marriages, and economic challenges to families, communities, churches. The list could easily continue.

The new challenge is how to grow believers, reach the unchurched, and grow churches in the face of these new realities. A question many are wrestling with is this: Does downsizing of programs or number of times we meet at the church necessarily mean we are less effective or less faithful in our mission? Families and individuals have a declining amount of discretionary time and money, and they are deciding to give less of that to church programs and church meetings, especially if these traditions are not meeting their life needs. All too often we struggle to preserve our forms without ensuring that we are accomplishing our desired functions.

New opportunities are evolving for many churches out of the new cultural realities and challenges. Many churches have dismissed their Sunday night worship to meet in small discipleship or life groups. Sometimes these meet at church; other times they meet in communities in homes to save travel time and expense. Still other congregations are designing intergenerational and multiethnic and multifaith groups to increase understanding and deepening of relationships with one another, the church, and the community through their faith walk.

Other churches have prayer and Bible study for those who want that. These meetings are led by deacons or other lay leaders. The pastor and staff are cultivating and discipling new members, new prospects, etc., in their homes. Others in the membership meet in small groups in homes throughout the week as their discipling ministry.

Other churches use Sunday nights as a time of ministry and mission as the scattered community of faith instead of gathering again to repeat basically what was done on Sunday morning. Ministry projects for the family and community transformation events are planned. In other venues, mission experiences with other cultures and other people groups are engaged in on Sunday evenings.

Some churches use the Sunday night time for an alternative worship service or a second or third worship service for a specific target group, such as people who work on Sunday morning or people who would rather sleep in on Sunday morning. Deciding about your Sunday night must evolve around some critical questions that only you can answer for your congregation and community.

Leadership Crunch

Another challenge faced by many congregations is the leadership crunch, with not enough capable and committed leaders to operate the church programs and ministries. While I sympathize with this and hear it often, I have seen numerous churches respond creatively to this challenge:

A large suburban church in North Carolina is downsizing its organization and streamlining its structures and need for multiple levels of leaders (often the same leaders pulled in many ways) to follow ideas for a more simple church as presented by Thom Rainer.[3]

An inner city church in Virginia is intentional about growing new leaders by discipling those who are ready for leadership. Among this church's tools are gift discovery and mentoring by an experienced leader who is serving effectively in a ministry the new leader believes God is calling him or her to serve in. How fun and effective. The old teaching the young—now that works! Transferring the wisdom of experience and years to a new generation of leaders.

Partnerships

Still another challenge facing many churches is the influx of transplants into established churches and communities. People are mobile these days, and many look for churches open to their values, traditions, beliefs, and so on. Often the "natives" of the church do not respond well. However, one church in western North Carolina has handled this beautifully by creating parallel structures and programs to meet the needs of everyone. It does work.

A dying congregation in the Atlanta metro area realized their membership was aging, but their facility maintenance needs were outgrowing the budget receipts. This harsh reality led them to prayer triplets, dialogues with other community churches in similar situations, community nonprofits, and businesses seeking next steps. The dialogues generated a number of partnership possibilities that were win-win experiences for the church and area businesses. This congregation is partnering with a local assisted-living center that needed more space but had people and finances. Now they share the "church facilities" for lodging, fellowship, and a corporate weekly worship experience. They share staff, facility, and maintenance expenses. Now that's a win-win!

COACHING QUESTIONS

- What function, if any, does Sunday night play in the big picture of your church's mission?

- What is working and what is not working about your Sunday night schedule/program or any other programs in light of your church's mission?
- What evidences can you identify that prove you are bearing fruit, making disciples, and transforming lives rather than just having meetings to be having meetings?
- What other options might be available that would help you be more effective and fruit-bearing?
- How does your current structure and programming facilitate multicultural relationships? How might these structures create barriers to deepening the multicultural relationships?
- What prevents you from exploring other options for disciple-making? Tradition or effectiveness? Familiarity or fear of the unknown?
- How could you meet the needs of those who prefer Sunday night and those who prefer other times?
- How much of your key leaders' and pastor's time and energy goes to shepherding the membership rather than growing the membership?
- What shifts are needed in expectations of pastor, staff, and lay leaders to ensure a more effective, more fruit-bearing ministry?

Church Organization

The church organization most people over sixty know is based on a business model. It's logical, linear, has leaders, and a place to put everyone. But folks under thirty often rebel, ignore, or opt out of this structure, which they see as inflexible, impersonal, and impossible to change. As you rethink the structure you need, consider the following ideas.

Form and function are key concepts. The function of the church is unchanging; it is based on the Great Commission and the Great Commandment. The form (new wineskins) is the place we need new organization and reflection. We must rethink how we function through our man-made forms/structures. That means churches must make an accurate and honest assessment of the function of all aspects of the church organization. What is the real—not perceived or desired—function of each committee, team, class, organization, task force group, etc.?

Invite others into this assessment via surveys, dialogues, inventories, testimonies, etc. If your church is mostly people over sixty, you may need to search out some younger people who attend irregularly or people who have visited and shown some interest in your church to also participate in this evaluation. Senior adults are loyalists, and they may perceive this process as being critical of the church. They will need reassurance that the goal is to improve, not destroy. Key senior adults will have to be involved in the planning process as will key under-thirties.

Share hard and soft data about this assessment, and point out the gaps and values this reality adds to the vision and function of church.

Find the remnant who have the passion to fill the gaps and begin to align the organization for more effective ministry.

Celebrate the successes of the new creations and ministry groups and the ministries of the existing groups.

Key functions of the New Testament church always include disciple-making, outreach, missions, and evangelism. In your evaluation, ask:

- What are the disciple-making functions of our committees? teams? classes? groups? organizations? music ministry? sports ministry?
- What classes, groups, committees, teams, or organizations do we have already bearing disciple-making fruit? How can we bless them? resource them? celebrate with them?

Rather than trying to align all groups, committees, teams, and organizations to perform all of the vital functions, instead build on the groups' strengths and create new groups to fill the recognized gaps in your structure and organization. Most churches' major organizational problem is that much or most of their function is maintenance-oriented or caregiving–oriented while the disciple-making or evangelism functions are ignored or desired but not formally functional. (My books *Recovering Hope for Your Church* and *Making the Church Work* are designed as workbooks to help leaders through these shifts and decisions.) A significant issue in many churches is who makes the decisions and how decisions are made that direct the church.

The older church culture generation's experience is that decisions go through "proper" channels—usually an array of committees, sessions, etc. The younger generation resists "jumping through all those hoops." When they get an idea, they are ready to run with it. How are decisions made in your church? What changes need to be made? What type of culture does your church value most?

A rural struggling congregation in western North Carolina discovered that they were losing momentum and focus far too often because their organization was way out of date. They were living by the same organization of leaders and programs they had twenty years ago when they had more members. They explored their mission and asked, What do we need to make this happen? Such reflection led them to experiment with new structures, times and work teams for designated projects. It worked! The leadership circle grew, effectiveness improved, and newcomers of all ages got involved.

Church Decision-making

Who makes the decisions in your church? How are they made? Are only a few making decisions for the many, pretending that this is a congregational form of church government? Are you finding fewer persons, particularly from the younger generations, coming to your church business meetings? Do you sometimes feel that the way your church makes decisions clogs the system rather than empowers it to move forward? I'm hearing and observing this frequently these days. What are some of the issues to consider that might make your decision-making more empowering and more effective as you seek to reach people under thirty while keeping those over sixty?

Let's explore a variety of issues on a continuum and do an evaluation of your congregation's decision-making in light of these areas that I think are significant for twenty-first–century churches. On the continuums below place a mark on the continuum that best describes the reality of decision-making in your church.

Control_____Empowerment
Doctrinal Purity_____Community Building
Following Traditional Protocol_____Engagement of Others
Leader Dominated_____Need Dominated
Leader Appeasement_____Ministry Development

In today's culture, many churches are caught between pleasing those in current leadership, who are usually from the church culture, and trying to make decisions that will engage and empower those from the postmodern culture. Far too many church leaders spend too much time placating members rather than making progress in their mission. It seems that if you please one group you alienate the other. This often translates to another dichotomy of those over sixty with those under thirty.

The time has come in many churches that want to reach and mobilize a new generation of believers to pay more attention to permission-giving and empowerment than polity and control. Maybe the time has come when streamlining decision-making in your church will expedite decision-making and push it from those who are in positions to those who are filled with passion for ministry. Streamlining will move toward birthing the new rather than just managing the present or past. Maybe decisions will be made by empowered teams rather than employed clergy. Maybe we will learn to concern ourselves more with birthing than preserving.

Streamlining decision making to move things along is needed and embraced by many churches these days. Quick decisions, without going through multiple hoops of permission getting, attract the younger generation and often scare the older generation. I know of two inner city churches who did streamlining effectively and immediately broadened the leadership.

Other churches use an administrative board to make decisions. Still others use deacons and elders in the decision-making circle. Some, usually larger congregations, are directed more by staff. Options to consider experimenting with to improve efficiency will vary depending on your polity, but many models stand available as you streamline.

Churches struggle with decision-making with most clinging to their constitution and bylaws far tighter than they do the mandates and guidance of Scriptures. Much of the challenge is tied to loyalty to former members or memories more than ministries that ensure forward movement in faith and function. Most churches will create the new, but they never want to bury the ineffective programs or groups. A Facebook friend shared a great process to help congregations self-assess and reach discernment through processing the move of the Spirit and the collective thinking and consensus of the congregation. The process idea originally came from an industrial engineer who brought his management skills to bear on this kind of challenge (thanks James Jarrett!):

> The formula was this: SSC (Start, Stop, Continue). During the fall of each year, ask these questions:
>
> What do we need to START doing because a new need has arisen?
>
> What do we need to STOP doing because an action/task/committee no longer fills a need in our changing times?
>
> Meanwhile, what do we need to CONTINUE doing because it does meet needs and fosters the mission of the church?
>
> From there, we looked at meaningful ways to STOP things, marking an ending with actions and/or a ritual that recognized an entity's usefulness "once upon a time," while acknowledging that ecclesiastical "time to stop." As we realized a new need had arisen, we'd form an ad hoc task force to study that need and make recommendations as to how that need should be addressed. Finally, continuing things was easy. But the challenge: most churches just keep doing everything without evaluation. I know, for instance, churches that still do weeknight visitation for prospects. Perhaps that was a great way to grow a church in the 70s, but it's totally ineffective today. Social media is the new way. I think one of the reasons churches never evaluate their work at this higher level is fear of hurting people's feelings, but once a congregation has the theological/biblical understanding that change is essential for meaningful work, they more readily embrace this kind of SSC work.

COACHING QUESTIONS

- What is working about your decision-making process in your church?
- What is not working about your decision-making process in your church?
- How effective is your church at engaging persons, both new and established members, in ministry?
- How does your church's decision-making honor or value intergenerational and multicultural dialogue?
- What adjustments need to be made in your decision-making process to facilitate a broader base of leaders engaged in new and established ministries?
- Whom do you need to talk with about these issues?
- When will you have these conversations?

Communicating in a Postmodern Culture

Whatever route your church chooses to take, whether small shifts in ministry focus or radical redirection with a totally redesigned and refocused worship service, good communication will make a huge difference in how change is perceived and accepted.

Basic understanding of communication is essential if you want to build a church for all generations. Leaders must realize what Jesus realized in his ministry, that true communication hasn't occurred until a message has been sent, received, and examined to make sure the message received is the same as the one sent. In recent years we've learned more about how people learn. This influences how they receive communications as well. Some people won't receive any message unless they read it. Others can be bombarded with written communication, but unless they also hear the communication, all other communication attempts are futile. Some people need an interactive presentation at churches; others will do best with a one-on-one phone call or visit. The bottom line is, we know that not everyone receives and processes information the same way, so the church needs to communicate in a variety of ways to reach most of the people with what's going on in a changing church.

Not only does the church need to remember the different ways people learn, but they must also remember the different audiences in the church. The same message is likely to be perceived differently by Builders, Boomers, and Busters, Gen X, and Millennials. What's clear to one group may not be to another. While one group responds to change announcements with, "Finally!" or "Whatever," another group is thinking, "That's just one more indication that the church no longer cares about me."

Let's also be careful about our preconceived ideas. One of mine was recently shattered while visiting my grandmother in the nursing home. Her roommate was eighty-nine years of age and was visiting with her grandchildren, daughter, and her priest via a Webcam connected to her personal laptop computer! I saw it with my own eyes. We talked about this. I discovered she loved the computer and the Webcam visits from her family and her priest. What a lesson for me about communication and my preconceived ideas.

Even the method of communication can alienate people. For example, many churches have decided to save the time and expense of printing and mailing a newsletter by putting it online and sending it electronically as an e-mail alert or attachment. Yet far more people under thirty than over sixty use the Internet regularly and prefer online communication. A wise church will let members choose whether they want a print or electronic newsletter. Now we live in a time where many get their Bible study, sermons, pastoral care, leadership training, and friendship connections on the go via iPads or some type of personal digital device. Churches and leaders are using multiple delivery systems to get their information in real time and an on demand.

If you're really trying to reach other people in your community, you may need to consider in your communication the education level and even the language of the people you are trying to reach.

There was a day when any communication from the church was top priority. People who received a written communication of any kind—letter, newsletter, or meeting reminder—from the church sat down and read it word for word. Some seniors may still do that. But most of those under thirty will scan printed materials, especially those not personalized, to see if anything is relevant to them or especially interesting. One person may look to see what's being served for Wednesday night dinner while another checks the names of folks on the prayer list. A student parent may look at the youth schedule. All these folks may overlook information intended for them because they sought and read only the parts they thought they needed. The pastor's column with news about vision and new directions may go unread by most of the congregation.

Bottom line—folks are busy. You've got to get their attention for them to spend their time reading written communications.

Wonder what your members are reading? Try a test on Sunday morning. On one Sunday simply ask them, in writing, to check off the listed parts of the newsletter that they read. The next week give a written quiz to adults on Sunday morning based on last's week's newsletter. You'll quickly see that some excitement needs to be generated about the written communications to get people to read them.

- Try "watch for" posters and announcements at church about upcoming news in the newsletter or online. Get folks in the habit of watching for and valuing information from the church.
- Ask members how they'd like to receive information and what kinds of information they'd like to receive. If they're more interested in ministry opportunities than nickels and noses reporting, make sure your newsletter gives them opportunities to get involved.
- Remember that the most successful periodicals today are targeted to small groups of people. You can do the same at church. Especially with electronic options, you can target students, senior adults, and Boomers with information just for them. If some people don't have or want to use the Internet, just print the same message, put it in an envelope, and mail it to that dwindling group.
- Trying to reach Hispanics in your community? Develop a simple English-Spanish newsletter. They'll read it to develop their English skills as well as to connect with the church.
- Try online chats about Bible study or for a discipleship group.
- Text message teenagers, host a podcast or YouTube channel, engage through Twitter, Snapchat, Periscope, or whatever the latest social media tools are.
- Phone senior adults.
- Identify influential persons or groups in your church, those whose opinions matters to other members of the congregation. Keeping these people informed is worth extra effort. It may mean a quick phone call, personal

e-mail, or even an occasional lunch meeting. When influential people have good information and support what the church and its leaders are doing, other people will also be informed and supportive.

- Support comes not just from sharing a vision and promoting what the church is going to do, but also from telling what the church has done. Never fail to tell about mission trips and ministry projects. Show video before worship services or during the offertory of ministry taking place. Include live or videotaped interviews of people who give and receive ministry. Showing changed lives demonstrates the reason you do what you do.
- Don't neglect your website. A good website is essential today. People will often check out your website before they ever visit your church. The look of your website, as well as the words, tells a lot about your church. Make sure the website is current. Promoting Easter services in July tells Internet visitors that not much happens at your church between Easter and Christmas.
- To draw people to your church, try online help for singles or parents of school-age kids or leadership coaching online. Offer both in-person and electronic chat assistance. This might be anything from a job board to a prayer line. (Additional help is available in my *Reframing Spiritual Formation* and *Spiritual Leadership in a Secular Age*.)

The Role of Meetings in the Church Today

Business meetings, committee meetings, deacons' meetings, even team meetings can quickly consume church leaders, both vocational and volunteer. These meetings can be productive, consensus building, and provide direction; or they may be time wasters, held only because the group is scheduled to meet on a regular basis. Business-as-usual meetings today may cause quality leaders to say no to responsibilities.

"All too often deacons' and elders' meetings are fruitless, unfulfilling, if not futile," explained a well-seasoned deacon of a church in which I was consulting. After hearing his story, I found myself asking, How many times have I sat in or heard about such meetings. How sad when these are the primary descriptors of the meetings for the spiritual leaders of a congregation! How can a result-focused agenda be put in place? What are the ingredients of a fruit-bearing deacons' meeting? Seems to me that spiritual leaders have for too long focused on how to be faithful without a commitment to be fruitful in living out the Great Commission and the Great Commandment.

If leaders of a congregation have in mind the vision and ministry of the church when they meet, how is it possible that their meetings are lifeless, dull, boring, and/or filled with tension, conflict, or personal agendas? Seems to me churches have to face reality. How can you have meetings that make leaders want to be involved?

Building a meeting agenda is crucial to having a productive meeting. Most meetings I hear about have one of the following:

- no agenda
- an agenda of maintenance rather than mission
- an agenda that's more about placating the pew than penetrating the world with the good news

How can such agenda issues be avoided? How can a good agenda turn around a meeting to equip leaders to produce fruit and move the church forward in its God-appointed mission? Let me share my suggestions.

Commit to planning meetings that matter. Make a commitment as a leadership team to having meetings that matter. Work collaboratively to determine what this type of meeting would look like. What would be the qualities of a result-focused meeting? Your list might include the following:

- opening up the meeting to celebrate God at work in your church/community
- prayer, thanking God for his presence and work in your midst
- exploring the next steps God is leading you to take now
- identifying needs in the church and community and ways to respond
- creating a passion or burden for these needs
- assessing the resources available from the church to address these needs (This might include a quick look at budget, human resources, program updates, etc.; otherwise these maintenance issues should be addressed by other appointed and empowered committees.)

These meetings should be planned at the most suitable time for those involved and planned with a starting and ending time. Having a time to end keeps the meeting moving. Unless announced ahead of time, no meeting should go over one and a half hours without renegotiating with the group.

Lead fruitful meetings. The team leader or chairperson is often seen as the natural leader of the meeting. In some churches the pastor or a staff member is seen as the natural leader. Let me suggest that the best leader for a result-oriented meeting is the best leader in the group. Who can coach the church leaders through an agenda best? Who can keep the meeting focused best? Maybe different segments need to be facilitated by different persons in an act of shared leadership? I'm learning that the coach approach to leadership keeps a meeting moving and helps make meetings more fruitful.

Basically, a coach approach is built around the group's agenda, not the leader's agenda. The leader (coach) asks powerful questions (as illustrated in each chapter) to keep the group focused and moving forward. The coach, through asking questions, clarifies the tasks of the group, helps the group discover who is best suited to do the tasks, and discovers how they will know when the tasks have been successfully accomplished. Good coaches move you from where you are to where you want to be, and from talking to action. Sounds like a great objective for most church team meetings. What do you think?

Move from wandering to walking. Moving to action is a worthy objective for a group of spiritual leaders. Congregations are looking for role models—how to minister effectively in an ever-changing and challenging world. Seeking to move a group from wandering in the wilderness, getting nowhere fast, to walking with intentionality can make a significant difference in people. Recall, if you will, the last chapter of Deuteronomy and the first chapter of Joshua. It is clear that under Moses' leadership the people of Israel were wandering. Under Joshua's leadership, after the death of Moses, God promised them that he would be with them every step they would take. They moved from wandering to walking and made it into the promised land.

An Assembly of God pastor I've been coaching declared that "since learning to coach the church rather than carry the church" he feels lighter, more hopeful, and more encouraged. He has noticed that staff and lay leadership respond more effectively. Sometimes a change in leadership style of the pastor or staff has direct empowering impact on a church that needs to make some shifts.

COACHING QUESTIONS

- What can you do to make the shift needed in your church meetings?
- What options are available to you to make the shifts needed?
- What are you willing to do now?
- Who can help you?

What would happen if your regular church meetings become more fruitful and fulfilling? What would happen if you maximized the giftedness in your leadership team to bring forth the best fruit? What if you focused on God's mission for the church rather than personal agenda items that often consume so much energy and time?

Let me encourage you to make a commitment to meetings that matter, to pleasing the heavenly Father by keeping your focus on his mission for the church and maximizing the gifted leaders he has planted in your midst.

What are your next steps?

Volunteer Leaders' Roles in Transitioning Churches

In the New Testament, servant leaders were involved in introducing and managing change in the church. Some people were being ignored, and some needs were going unmet. This was the case in Acts 6. Church leaders were being called upon to introduce and model change. Church leaders today—deacons, elders, and others—are being called upon in many churches to help transition churches to a more effective ministry in a rapidly changing world. What are the changes many are being called upon to address, and what are the implications of this for the role and function of lay leaders?

Churches are different, and so are needs; but my observations are that the following are more often than not challenges where churches are looking to their lay leaders for help:

- Demographic shifts in the community. People moving in are not like the people in the membership, and there's a cultural clash.

- Plateaued church and consequences. Over 85-90 percent of the churches in this country are now considered plateaued or declining in attendance. Subsequently, there's a growing leadership and economic crisis on the horizon.
- Complex pastoral care and family life issues challenge the best-trained clergy and certainly the typical lay leader. Family structures and personal challenges abound, and the care needed usually overwhelms most; yet most churches still expect pastors to do all the pastoral care. This is burning out our clergy and causing deacons to flee from nominations and service. Can lay leaders with specific gifts for ministry be enlisted to meet these needs? Are some in your church just waiting to be asked?
- Economic challenges generated by national economic realities, unemployment in a community, the dying out of a generation loyal to the institutional church, and the decrease of young adults trained as leaders and tithers demand a plan of action and lay leader support in most churches.
- Learning to live into a secular culture challenges all church culture leaders. Many live out of fear and cling to the past. They miss walking into the future as the people of God on mission in the world. Learning to be salt, light, and leaven in this world is overwhelming to many.
- Spiritual immaturity of the membership and the seeming inability of the existing church to keep people over sixty while reaching people under thirty demands lay leaders who care about one another—all generations—get involved and grow disciples inside the church while reaching out to the community around the church.

Lay leaders, such as deacons, teachers, team leaders, elders, and others are called to be spiritual leaders during this age of change and transition. Churches will never go beyond their spiritual leadership, and lay leaders are certainly part of that spiritual leadership team. What then are the implications for volunteer leaders in this age of transition?

Gene Wilkes outlines eight realities that speak to the role of lay leaders:

1. Call—What are lay church leaders called to do in your church? How has God gifted them? What are the issues he has planted you in the midst of?
2 Preparation—What are the pains, struggles, and experiences of your leaders, and where and how do they interface with needs in the congregation and community?
3. Vision—What is God calling the church to be and do? What is God's plan for the church?
4 Character—What are the virtues and strengths of the body of Christ and its leaders in your church?
5. Sending—Where is God calling the church to be and live out her ministry?
6. Conflict—How can the church deal with the conflict created between what is and what God is calling us toward?

7. Shared leadership—How do spiritual leaders model shared leadership with one another and those in the pew?
8. Unending story—What are the next steps for the church, and how can lay leaders help lead the church forward?[4]

I had an energizing coaching conversation with a client about creating a "compliant church" versus a "creative church," and the lay leader's role in this scenario. Here are some of our thoughts. I think they are worth considering for the church that is attempting to rethink whom they are trying to reach in today's culture.[5]

Compliant Church Values	Creative Church Values
Complies with historic constitution and bylaws	Recognizes constitutions can be changed in order to allow more relevant ministry
Complies with the way we have always done things	Understands that cultures change, people change, needs change, and structures and programs must change
Works to keep everyone happy in the church family	Understands that conflict is not bad and that a few dissatisfied persons might be necessary in order to become more relevant and reach the community for Christ
Preserving and maintaining actions takes precedence in leadership meetings	Mission and ministry are always first on leadership groups' meeting agendas
Focuses on membership preferences as church focus	Focuses on needs and preferences of those outside the church as church focus

What about *your* leadership meetings? Are they nurturing a compliant church or a creative church value system and priority? I fear that all too often our leaders work to maintain a compliant church. Until church leaders change priorities, focus, and behaviors, many of our churches will remain stuck and become increasingly irrelevant in a rapidly changing culture.

COACHING QUESTIONS

- What insights surface as you review the previous chart?
- What challenges do you see for your leaders and leadership groups or teams?
- Who in the church shares your concerns?
- Who will disagree with your concerns?
- What bridges of communication or learning might be built to nurture forward movement among your leaders?

• What are you willing to do and by when?

The whole concept of team leadership is one transitioning churches should consider. Team leadership can maximize everyone's strengths in a consensus-building environment rather than a more traditional top-down business model of management that churches have used in the past.

In 1989, Dave Ferguson, along with some friends, started Community Christian Church in Naperville, Illinois, a church that now has thirteen locations. Community Christian Church began with the concept of team leadership and has continued to practice that style of leadership throughout its growth. When Dave talks about team leadership, he's talking about pastor and staff ministers working together in a leadership team. His advice offers principles and values the staff leadership team can use when coaching volunteer leaders and groups in the church. He offers four secrets of team leadership. In 2015 most of the numerical growth in churches of all denominations are in multisite/campus congregations.

1. The secret about the cause: "We are committed to the cause first and each other second." Great leadership teams are always clear about the cause. The model at Community Christian is that leaders don't have job descriptions or rules about office hours, dress, or vacation days. The organization is pretty fluid and unstructured. This doesn't mean they don't get the job done; they do all that needs to be done because they are all committed to the cause. You may not want to do away with your church policies and structure; people over sixty often find comfort in the structures, while people under thirty are more comfortable with the lack of rules. But a more dynamic environment without a list of who's doing what and when will only work if everyone is committed to getting the job done—not to having a position, being in charge, doing only what's assigned, spending lots of time on administrative details. The cause at Community Christian is to "help people find their way back to God." That's the basis of their mission statement: "Helping people find their way back to God by reproducing congregations, campuses and churches that celebrate, connect and contribute to the dream of God."

This mission statement and the commitment of the individual ministers to it is what keeps them together and on track, not their love for one another. Yes, they care about the members of the team, but the mission, the cause, comes first.

COACHING QUESTIONS

• Does your church have a mission statement?
• Is that mission statement evident in what the church does?
• Do church leaders know the mission statement? Are they committed to it?
• If not, what needs to change?

The book of Acts clearly shows that the early church thrived because leaders worked together for a clear cause. Those leaders may or may not have been willing to die for one another, but all were willing to die for the cause—and many did.

2. The secret about community: "We don't know when we are working and when we are playing." Team leaders find so much joy in what they are doing at Christian Community that they stay excited about their work. They're not clock watchers. They don't count the days until vacation. They don't look forward to a break. They are energized by doing what they're doing and by doing it together. The leadership team has expanded as the church has grown. When adding ministers, the team at Christian Community has three "Cs" in mind—character, competency, and chemistry. Chemistry is the most important for them. Many members of the church leadership team are hired from inside the church. The existing leadership team is able to test chemistry with a candidate before inviting a new team minister to join them; and they usually already know about character and competency. A fourth C—commitment—is a given because that's secret number one.

Chemistry means that team members enjoy being together, but it goes beyond that. They look for complementary gifts; the team needs a gift mix, not everyone with the same gifts. Ultimately, team members must want to be on that team rather than anywhere else, feeling that they are all going in the same direction—together.

COACHING QUESTIONS

- How does your team measure up in regards to chemistry?
- Does your team have a good mix of gifts? What's lacking? How can you fill this void?
- What steps can you take to maintain or improve the level of community in your leadership team?

3. The secret about characteristics: "We may look crazy or chaotic to you, but there is a method to our madness." People who have observed the leadership team at Christian Community at work have found it chaotic. Dave Ferguson says that the very characteristics of team members that might offend are also the reason they have succeeded. He says the characteristics are often paradoxical.

- Team members are both collaborative and competitive; they want to win at everything but realize that the only way to reach their part of the world for Christ is to do it together.
- Team members are both compassionate and comfortable with conflict. They care about one another, but they care more about the cause. That care will inevitably mean conflict. Working through different opinions about the direction to take usually leads to the best solutions.
- They are both spontaneous and accountable. They'll go with new ideas, but they are also accountable for goals they set, for the ministries they lead, for budgets. Still, team members are more likely to hear and say yes than no.

COACHING QUESTIONS _____

- How comfortable is your team with conflict?
- Is your team a yes or a no team?
- Can such contrasting characteristics exist on your team? Or is the need to be polite, to not hurt feelings, to stay in your ministry area and not cross any lines more important?
- Which characteristics of your team help, and which hinder, your team's doing what they are called to do? What needs to change? How will you make the changes?

4. The secret about creating culture: "We really are going to change the world." The leadership team sets the standard for the church—in enthusiasm, commitment, attitude, and concern for the cause and for one another.[6]

COACHING QUESTIONS _____

- What standards does your team set for the church?
- In what ways do you see the attitudes, commitment, and values of the team reflected in the congregation?
- Do you like what you see? If not, what needs to change?

Not all leadership teams include only full-time ministry employees. That is another paradigm shift in the way churches are changing to reach a new generation. The team may be a mixture of full-time, bivocational, part-time, retired, and volunteer leaders. More important than how they are compensated is that they are all on the team because of their commitment to the cause.

Carey Nieuwhof offers some powerful observations about why churches are losing leaders. At least 6 reasons explain why high capacity volunteers never join a team or leave it early.

1. The challenge isn't big enough.

It's really quite simple. People with significant leadership gifting respond best to significant challenges. Under challenge them, and they won't stay engaged for long. So many church staff and non-profit staff I talk to are worried about giving their volunteers too much responsibility. Newsflash: that might be exactly why you don't have enough high capacity volunteers (not to mention a thousand other problems on your team.)

2. Your vision, mission, and strategy are fuzzy.

People want to serve a cause bigger than themselves. That's what the church (and most non-profits) are all about: causes bigger than ourselves. But often our mission, vision and strategy are fuzzy.

Mission is the what.

Vision is the why.

Strategy is the how.

Even if these three elements are written on a piece of paper, most people functionally can't tell you what they are. That's a tragedy. The motivation for volunteers IS the vision. It's the why behind the what. And—get this—the church has the best vision and mission on planet earth. So why on earth do we hide it?

Quite seriously, helping people discover the God who created them and the Saviour who died for them is the most rewarding work volunteers will do in their lives, regardless of what they get paid to do their day jobs.

3. You're disorganized.

Few things are more demotivating than giving up your time as a volunteer only to discover the staff person responsible didn't set you up to succeed.

The tools they need to do the job are missing or incomplete. The rest of the team is late.

Or maybe—worse—they're not even 100% sure what they are supposed to do or how they are supposed to do it.

You can always find people who will put up with disorganization, but many more will simply give up. High capacity people will make a beeline for the door.

4. You let people off the hook too easily.

I know I know. They're *volunteers*. You can't hold a volunteer accountable can you?

Wrong. You most certainly can. And should. For everyone's sake.

If a volunteer is late, it's really no different than if a staff member is late. Sure, you want to address it kindly, but you need to address it.

Again, few things are more disheartening for a motivated volunteer than doing their homework and showing up early only to find that others didn't, and then to top it all off, a staff person excuses the behavior of the people who didn't pull their weight with lines like "it's okay, we're just glad you're here."

The high capacity leader dies a thousand deaths every time he or she hears a staff person utter those words. Almost 100% of the time, the organized, highly motivated exactly-the-kind-of-leader-you-were-hoping-to-keep will leave, and the slackers will stay.

5. You're not giving them enough personal attention.

Another big challenge for church leaders and non-profit staff is the innate desire most of us feel to treat all people 'equally'.

You don't want to play favorites, so everyone should be treated the same. Again, wrong.

The church should always be a loving organization. Certain people require more of your time and attention.

Unless you're intentional, you'll end up spending most of your time with your most problematic people and the least amount of time with your highest performing people. Flip that.

Cut ties with the low performers, and spend most of your time walking alongside and developing your best leaders.

Before you think that's completely unfair, just know your entire team will thank you for it because you'll end up with a strong team.

By the way, Jesus did this too. He had crowds of disciples, but then a group of 72, an inner group of 12, an inner circle of 3 and placed his greatest investment in 1 (Peter).

6. You don't have enough other high capacity volunteers around them.

It's never fun to lead alone.

As soon as you find a high capacity volunteer, your next step should be to recruit more and move others alongside them.

Nurture this team. Build into them. Take them for lunch. Take them with you when you travel. Do life with them (again, I think Jesus modeled this pattern). Sadly, many leaders don't do this, and high capacity leaders once again walk away, demotivated.[7]

Your church should decide what needs to be done to reach people under thirty without losing those over sixty and determine the kinds of leaders required for those ministries. Then the church can explore options about how those positions are to be filled. People with a passion will find a way that doesn't always mean another paid staff member.[8]

Building a paid and volunteer staff is a challenge for many established churches who have lived by "church culture" staffing values. Now, we have many options as we learn to maximize the callings, gifts, and talents of all members. Let me simply introduce some ideas that might attract and effectively minister to persons of all generations, but would call on the church to make some value shifts to make it happen.

Reinventing Staff for Today's and Tomorrow's Churches

More often than not church leadership takes on the priorities and personality of those guiding their spiritual formation. If the clergy are maintaining programs and only sustaining an institution, you can expect the leaders and congregation to move in that direction. In a secular and pagan world it is vital that the spiritual leaders have, at their heart, making and reproducing healthy disciples.

As the world around our churches and the population inside our churches change, pressure increases to reinvent staff to ensure effectiveness in discipleship, outreach, and inreach ministries. Dual-career marriages, diversity of family structures and people groups, shifting demographics, early retirements, economic shifts, home-based businesses, and the impact of technology on daily life seem to be creating an atmosphere that calls forth new directions in staffing churches. While some churches are already experimenting with new configurations, new ministry descriptions, titles, and compensation packages, many others continue to work from titles, descriptions, and packages from the 1950s and 1960s. By so doing, they are fueling the burnout rate among ministers.

Burnout's Connections to Outdated Staffing

Over the past twenty years I've noted an increasing number of excellent, committed, and called clergy who are struggling with or have been consumed by burnout. That burnout often shows a connection with out-of-date staffing issues. Many clergy. . .

- are overworked because the needs and demands in their parish are intensifying and multiplying due to the rapid changes around them.
- suffer because of a lack of continuing education. While the pace of life is rapid, many churches do not encourage or support ongoing education so the clergy can stay current.
- have families who are faced with personal struggles like all other families, and yet many clergy are not given permission or encouragement to take care of their families. They are almost affirmed for sacrificing their family's health so they can take care of others.
- struggle with their physical health because the demands and expectations of most congregations are so great. Again, they are expected to sacrifice their health to "take care of others' needs."
- are underpaid when compared to other professionals with similar education and experience in their communities. Therefore financial pressures are intense. Sometimes second jobs are required for financial stability, and this creates more stress in family and congregation.
- have a growing dissatisfaction with their ministries and their ability to find fulfillment and effectiveness in ministry.
- are locked into "job descriptions" designed to maintain the institution, rather than freed by "ministry descriptions" designed to empower them to work from their calling and gifting.

Other Indicators of Ineffectiveness of Current Staffing Issues

While burnout is one indicator of the need to rethink and reframe staffing, other issues point to the increasing ineffectiveness of our current models of staffing our churches.

- Increasing number of mismatches between clergy and congregations create tensions for both parties.

- Most churches and most church leaders (including clergy) continue to function from values, mind-sets and traditions from a modern world, a church culture, when the reality is we are now in a postmodern, unchurched culture. Consequently, most of our energies and priorities reflect a modern culture. The unchurched have no advocate in our midst, and the postmodern world is not addressed.
- The definitions of our success/effectiveness for our staff and churches are still based on modern and churched culture standards. Such only creates more tensions and ineffectiveness. (A rethinking of these standards can be found in my books *The Gathered and Scattered Church, Spiritual Leadership in a Secular Age,* and *Recovering Hope for Your Church.*)
- Dysfunction seems to have deep roots in many of our existing congregations, leadership cores, and clergy. Such has created a real sense of control and dysfunctional, neurotic organizations we call churches. Until we have healthy leaders, we are not likely to have healthy churches.
- Some of the best clergy, pulpiteers, and pastors I know are leaving the professional ministry and entering vocations in the business world. Their bottom line reason is, "I just can't fight this system any longer. My people want to play power games; they don't want to do and be church!"
- We've lost balance in ministry, focusing too much on institutional maintenance and survival rather than perpetuation of mission and ministry to the hurting, lost, spiritually thirsty, and broken of our world.

Models to Consider When Reinventing Staff

Staffing for churches and denominational groups are in a rapid state of transition driven by economics, culture shifts, and a growing diversity of issues. Current models for staffing churches seem to be focused more on institutional maintenance and caring for the flock than activating the people of God on mission. We have pastors who are "hired to lead in worship, marry the engaged, bury the dead, visit the sick and lonely, administrate the variety of church based meetings, and raise the money for institutional programming" rather than pastors who are called to equip the laity to do the work of ministry. We expect and hire our pastors to do the work of ministry.

Many of our churches cling to this care-giving model, while the Ephesians 4 model of staffing is that of an "equipper of the saints for the work of ministry." Seems this biblical model of equipping of the saints (the people in the pew—the believers and members of the congregation) has given way to a pastoral-care, pastor-driven model to "take care of us at all costs" and "perform for us upon demand." Such a model that we've embraced and practiced for decades has created a vast number of spectator congregations, a host of God's frozen chosen, and generated not an active army of the people of God on mission but an apathetic, self-absorbed congregation that has lost sight of the biblical mandate of "going into all the world" with the mission of God, as his missionaries.

Churches do have other staff positions—minister of education, youth, children, families, senior adults, administration, etc. Believe it or not, some poor souls have all of these people groups in their title! In most situations the "job descriptions" again revolve more around "taking care of us and performing for us" rather than "equipping us to reach and disciple them." How did we ever get into such a narcissistic place with our staffing? What would have happened if Jesus had come to earth just to take care of the twelve or the inner circle of three? He did spend much time with this remnant but for the purpose of equipping them to carry his message into all the world. Such a focus ensured that his mission would reach us. If he had only been on a pastoral care mission, our generation would have never known his message.

I'm certain that some of you are now either feeling defensive or ecstatic. Some readers will say the church minister should "take care of us," and others will say, "It's about time someone pointed out the church's narcissistic tendencies in its staff!" If you're not too upset, let's explore some of the emerging models of staffing built on equipping and discipling rather than just institutional maintenance.

Emerging models for staffing churches involve a struggle only the brave, courageous, and faithful are willing to face today, for staffing issues touch personal comfort zones, institutional and personal identities, and self-image—as well as one's theological assumptions about church and ministers. So, as we outline some emerging models, keep in mind these struggles in yourself and among your leaders and congregation. Remember, too, that more often than not the congregation takes on the personality and focus of its lay leaders and clergy.

Mission/Ministry Focus—When mission and ministry become the focus of the professional staff, the typical congregation faces the realities that their staff no longer exist to serve them, but rather exist to send them on mission and ministry. The model of the book of Acts comes into play. The mission is found in the reality that, because of the presence of the Holy Spirit, believers have more power to do greater things than Christ and that he "sends his followers into the world."

Equipping Focus—Takes seriously that the real ministers and missionaries are those believers in the pews who stand in need of "equipping for the work of ministry" in the church and in the world. The Ephesians 4 equipping model comes from the image of "mending nets." The skills and ministry of the laity are to restore brokenness, pain, hurt, and alienation from God. The professional clergy are the "equippers" to help heal the hurt and brokenness among the lay ministers and to empower, unleash, and equip them to "comfort others and minister to others in need of comfort and ministry."

Discipleship Focus—Takes seriously the only mandate the church has—"to go and make disciples"—found in the Great Commission. The staff here seeks to help believers and nonbelievers who are spiritually thirsty inside and outside the church to move toward greater maturity in their knowledge of and experience with God through Christ. Again, the staff here invest in a few—the remnant—and seek to grow them in Christ and to lead them to reproduce healthy believers through their callings, giftings, and ministries.

Team Focus—This team acknowledges the diversity of callings, giftings, and ministries of the body of Christ, but also acknowledges the common mission and function. Through their diversity and learning to work in harmony with one another, the mission of Christ in the church and the world can be accomplished. This staff functions as team, does what needs to be done in a crises (whether in their ministry description or not), but more often than not they work from their calling and unique gifting, in cooperation with others who are uniquely gifted, on a common project or mission. The model of this staff focus then births lay ministry teams following the same model.

New Configurations: Part-time, Bi-vocational, Multi-Career, Volunteer, Church-grown, Adjuncts, Partnerships on Multiple Sites

The changing landscape of our world and church seems to allow new configuration for staffing churches. Part-time staff are emerging from churches of all sizes. People who are retiring early offer alternative staffing options for many churches. Retired, they are still looking for a way to invest their lives. These laypersons, who are professionally trained in a variety of disciplines and have a deep faith, are candidates for part-time positions. These people have an opportunity for a ministry of significance in the second half of life, and the church benefits from their skills without having to pay full benefits. The church then provides for training at teaching churches, specialized classes, and coaching by pastor or full-time staff. These part-time staff can be custodial, ministry assistants (who can even work from their home offices rather than the church having to prepare office space on-site).

Bi-vocational and multi-career staff have been around for a long time, but they are finding a greater place of significance in kingdom work these days. Because church life and Christianity have been bashed in the media, we are having to earn the respect of those in the world before we can share our message. Bi-vocational staff help build this bridge by creating a ministry for the church through their vocation in the world. For instance, if your church wants to reach children and youth, maybe your minister to youth and families can be a person from the public school system or the community recreation leagues. Or if you want to reach senior adults or people with aging parents, then maybe your part-time, bi-vocational staff person can spearhead this and also work within the field of gerontology, nursing homes, social services, etc.

Volunteer staff are an increasing group in churches of all sizes. These are usually retirees or persons who work from home or who are seeking opportunities to share their gifts. This is akin to the ministry of elders in some churches where these volunteer, called, gifted believers are commissioned to shepherd, care for, and give pastoral leadership to a segment of the congregation. For instance, a volunteer staff person might be your minister of small groups or to families of preschoolers or to school teachers/administrators or to the medical community or to the business population in your area.

Yes, these are new ministry designations emerging among volunteers, but are sometimes full-time positions as well. See the outward, mission focus? It is important to ask for believers to consider this calling in their lives and to prepare the church organization to resource and accept such a ministry. Certainly these staff need to be affirmed, recognized, resourced, and celebrated as often as, or maybe even more frequently than, other full-time staff.

Church-grown staff, rather than seminary-trained staff, are increasing as well. Churches with well-defined core values, targeting effective ministry in an unchurched culture, find that persons groomed in their own church life make the best leaders. Most seminary-trained persons, while having a good theological education, can be greatly deficient in practical ministry skills that are effective in an unchurched culture. Most seminaries are still training clergy as if we were living and ministering in a modern and church culture.

In most situations I know of, this new church-growth staff model works effectively, but it does offer unique challenges and needs for personal coaching and for theological education on concepts needed for ministry. Adjunct staff are emerging in situations in which a unique skill set is needed over an extended yet short-term time to help move staff or church forward in a given specialized area of ministry. Usually this is a contractual agreement between a church consultant, congregational coach, seminary professor, author, coach, or other skilled professional. This agreement allows for specialized coaching of leaders without the full economic or management responsibilities over a long period of time. The success is that you get expert leadership from a reputable person from the outside who can challenge and work the system to move forward. The existing leaders don't have to catch the flack usually encountered during change.

Partnerships are growing between groups of local churches (of same or different denominations) who employ a full- or part-time clergy person to target a particular group and to facilitate a partnership ministry within rural or suburban communities. Usually these are small, single-staff churches. They discover that they can network to find guidance for their ministries and not have to face the full economic or supervisory requirements alone. This usually works best with a cooperative leadership team working with and for this partnership.

Accountability: Evaluating Success and Effectiveness in a Postmodern World

To put any staff in place and ensure effectiveness, new standards of success, accountability, and evaluation must be fashioned in light of the postmodern world in which we live. In days gone by we made everyone accountable to the pastor, a deacon or elder group, or a personnel committee. The staff they supervised were usually evaluated by church culture standards:

- how many came to the programs
- how much money was collected or sent to missions
- how big the church buildings were

• how many new members were gained? or baptized?

These were not very effective in a church culture, and they are certainly not effective in this secular, postmodern world. Let me make a few suggestions for you to consider:

1. Evaluation and standards should be built from the primary focus of the staff, not the traditions of days gone by. For instance, if the focus is disciple-making, then staff ministers should give account for the number of persons they consistently disciple and give evidence of the progress those persons are making in following Christ.

2. Evaluation should certainly acknowledge the secular, busy world we are in rather than condemn it. For instance, rather than condemning leaders who will not serve all year in a church program, staff can give account of the number of persons (new and established leaders) they involve in short-term, project-focused teams to help the church accomplish its objectives. This helps with assimilation and development of the leadership pool and acknowledges the real challenges of people in a busy world. It also opens the possibility of including nonchurched, community persons in some short-term projects as an entry point for them into relationships with church leaders. See the difference!

3 Accountability should also involve persons, other than immediate supervisors, giving evidence of the discipling, mission, or leadership skills of the staff persons. In other words, how does the target audience/ constituency evaluate his or her effectiveness? For instance, let's say the focus is discipleship. Could the immediate supervisor have a fellowship time for all those in the discipleship group and dialogue about how they have grown in Christ, fruit of the Spirit, discovering gifts, callings, etc. This is a great time of celebration, affirmation, and planning for next steps. (There are several instruments out there to help frame this dialogue and assessment of one's spiritual journey. See *Spiritual Leadership in a Secular Age.*)

4. Provide opportunities for the body of Christ to speak, to assess, and to celebrate. These might even replace or become part of your regular business meeting. Focus on the mission by letting those who have been discipled, been on mission, or discovered their ministries share their stories. Let this be a tool of accountability, celebration, evaluation, and affirmation for the staff and the other ministers God is using in your midst.

All of this really can be—should be—fun, fulfilling, and challenging! Let me encourage you to consider your staff, your mission, your church's mission and calling. How can you and others in your church be most effective? fulfilled? accountable?

Another way of attracting and effectively ministering to all generations is caught up in a movement that is multiplying across the country and across denominational lines. Multisite and multicampus ministry is here and growing in impact, number, and significance. Let's review the basics of having one church in multiple settings. Yes, a value shift. Unity of the one church is not in being under the same roof at the same time, but in building the church unity around common core values that are often expressed differently in different settings to attract different generations.

Multisite/Multicampus Churches

One way Community Christian Church in Naperville, Illinois, is attempting to fulfill its cause, its mission, is by having more than one church site. This church isn't the only one doing that. It's a phenomenon that seems to be growing—and working. Sometimes it comes about from the beginning of a church start. Church planters begin several cell groups, and sometimes more than one thrives and becomes a church—multiple sites of the same church.

Sometimes an existing church—often of people mostly over sixty—may not want to change their style of worship and risk alienating the older group to reach the younger, but they still want to reach people under thirty. So they start a new ministry with a seeker feel and a contemporary style. Often they meet in a school, a shopping center, or even a warehouse—a place where nonchurched young people are comfortable. Both campuses can work fine, but they are both parts of the same church. They may have the same preaching pastor, and the contemporary church may have its primary worship time on Saturday night.

Or perhaps the older church—those over sixty—may be in a neighborhood that is aging. The community around the church may be filled mostly with senior adults. To reach younger people, the church may begin a ministry in a new, rapidly growing area filled with younger adults but underserved by churches. A few years ago that new start might have been on the suburban fringe of the city as people continued to move out from town. In many urban areas today, the new starts are needed in the city center. Years ago many churches fled to the suburbs with their congregations. If churches stayed downtown at all, their congregations have often dwindled to the senior adults who have been members there all their lives. Today young people are returning to the cities. They live in skyscraper condos, and they have few choices of places to worship. So the new ministry might be a seeker/contemporary setting right downtown.

Sometimes legal restrictions ignite the new start. In one southern city a historical church was badly damaged by a tornado. The thriving church wanted to rebuild with a larger facility, but zoning codes wouldn't allow it. The ratio of required parking to seating couldn't be reached. That was just the beginning of the restrictions for restoring the older building. Beginning a new campus offered one solution—one church in two locations.

A suburban church on the edge of town had filled its space but didn't have the financial resources to build a larger facility. The church was able to partner with another church, joining ministries to have a multisite church and a more economical financial plan for both churches.

A church may also have multiple campuses because it is establishing congregations to reach different ethnic or language groups.

Multisite/multicampus churches have unique staff situations. If you are considering multiple sites for your church, here are some questions you may want to think about:

- Will you have one preacher for all sites? Will worship times be staggered so that the preacher can move from place to place? Or will preaching be video-driven, at least for one service on Sunday morning? If the choice is a "live" sermon on multiple campuses, how will one person hold up with the demand of preaching multiple times each week? Will a "preaching team" be needed?
- What about the music and other aspects of worship at the multiple sites? Will one leader be responsible for worship at all campuses? Or will volunteer leaders be used to direct praise teams, choirs, drama, etc.
- If a team approach is used, will they plan together so that congregations are going in the same direction thematically in worship? Will the same person be at the same site regularly, or will team members rotate?
- Who will each site call "pastor"? Who will be the lead person with whom a congregation identifies? Can one person do this for multiple sites? What plans can ensure that people connect with the pastor or the leadership team?
- When, if ever, will members from the different sites come together to feel that they are part of one congregation?
- If team members are assigned to the same churches regularly, when will leaders come together? What will keep the multisites unified as one church with a single mission or vision?

Having multiple campuses is a growing, working way to do church in a twenty-first–century world. The previous questions will simply help you begin to think about this option. Leadership Network and Warren Bird have recently published research on multicampus churches and their various distinctives. See www.leadnet.org.

Discipleship Shifts

Another issue to consider is the vital ministry of discipleship. For decades the church created programs designed to meet the needs of many people all at once; everyone studied pretty much the same thing. If you went to Sunday school, on any given Sunday the Methodists and the Baptists and lots of other people studied the same thing. You could talk with your neighbor about what you studied in church when you got home on Sunday afternoon. But one-size-fits-all programs like this are no longer meeting needs. People want something that more specifically meets their needs.

Most churches need to rethink the Bible study and discipleship to meet people's needs. Consider the following examples.

Shift from focusing on program preservation to person development—More is needed than changing the age group numbers on classroom and department signs. Take a survey. Ask adults what their needs and desires are for spiritual development. Give them choices of what they study and when. Offer a curriculum plan that includes several books. Pair new Christians with spiritually mature people for mentoring. Facilitate prayer partners or accountability groups. Plan retreats that focus on a discipleship need. Redirect your planning to look for options rather than focus on new promotion plans, outreach, or a guilt-inducing attempt to increase numbers in the same old programs.

Shift from limited time frames for education to equipping that is convenient and user-friendly—Libraries in many churches have closed their doors. Some have shifted to bookstores. If this is true in your church, does it close another avenue or option for discipleship? Are all your Bible study and discipleship options small-group settings at the church on Sunday and Wednesday? If so, whose needs are going unmet in your congregation? How can you discover other ways to meet people's needs by offering a greater variety of times and places for discipleship?

Shift from developing a cognitive knowledge base to a community building experience—Many adults won't show up for a small-group study of the Old Testament kings and kingdoms, but they will sign on for an opportunity to repair a home for a widow, to teach inner-city kids how to play basketball, or to feed disaster victims. As they experience ministry in Jesus' name, they may also want to know more about what the Bible says about how we should love one another. Adults today are often more interested in doing than in listening, more interested in learning from examples and experience than in serving on a committee, more interested in ministry outside the church than maintaining the power structure inside the church.

Shift from church development to penetrating and engaging culture by integrating faith and life issues—Christ followers today want answers to help them live their lives with integrity. They want Christian answers in a complex culture. They want their church to make a difference in the quality of life in the community. Hope Community Church in Manitowoc, Wisconsin, is a great example of this (see www.hopechurchalive.org). Another super example is The Open Door, a PCUSA church in Pittsburgh, Pennsylvania (see www.pghopendoor.org)

Shift from church growth to spiritual formation and integration—The church totals of nickels and noses are less important to individual believers than whether the church is meeting needs and changing lives, including their own. Spiritual formation and development are more difficult to measure than church budgets and baptisms. How can your church know if individuals are growing in Christlikeness?

Such shifts in how churches do discipleship are essential because enrollment and attendance in traditional Bible study/Sunday school have been declining for years. Here are some additional thoughts about needed shifts, with a specific focus on small-group Bible study/Sunday school.

1. Focus on learning and community, not teaching and inreach/outreach.
2. Move beyond traditional hours and places for Bible teaching.
3. Enlist good facilitators and people of passion for various people groups, not necessarily good teachers.
4. Build curricula off of life passages and life challenges of your people and those you are trying to reach, rather than using standard curricula. Use a spiritual formation team to design these learning experiences.
5. Understand that shifts have occurred in culture that impact the way we do church. The modern/traditional church values a believe-behave-belong cycle for newcomers, whereas the postmodern culture values and demands a belong-behave-believe cycle if they are to be attracted to your church.
6. Use technology (e-mail, social media, periscopes, websites, telephone) to involve pupils in building class topics/agendas.
7. Create a dual or multiple track for Bible teaching/learning based on needs and expectations of your membership and those you desire to reach.
8. Understand that most people will not participate in all activities/programs of the church, but they will connect in places that meet them where they are.
9. Most folks under thirty are spiritually thirsty but don't value committing to traditional church expectations as much as they enjoy connecting heart-to-heart with people.[9]

If you're wondering how you will go about discovering a new way to do Bible study, consider trying a coach approach to transforming Bible study in your church. Bible study found its start on the streets of England among the outcasts of the community and the traditional church. The risk that Robert Raikes, the founder of Sunday school, took was trying to connect persons in his culture to life-transforming truths from Scripture. Today the coach approach to Bible study might lead us back to our roots and facilitate movement from where we are—running a program for people who want fellowship and to be faithful to a program—to where most churches desire to be—engaging persons in life-transforming Bible study. (See chapter 8 for more details.)

Intentional Ministry

Ideas for intentional ministry have been suggested as integral for a new model of church that reaches people under thirty because hands-on, experiential worship and discipleship are essential for them. Intentional ministry can also include celebration with and ministry to those inside as well as those outside the church. For example, in the church today, developing a plan for celebrating holidays with the unchurched can meet the needs of people both in the church and in the community. Older adults have focused holiday attention on family, but many senior adults are now alone. Holiday ministry will also appeal to many of them. This ministry is truly a way to have an intergenerational appeal to one area of need in the church.

How can church members come together to minister to those outside the church during holidays, while at the same time caring for one another? Consider the ministries of two very different churches with similar ministries that impact their churches and the unchurched postmodern culture: see www. reallifeministries.com and www.fbs.org.

Since most people are now unchurched, what are the intentional avenues of ministry for building bridges instead of barriers with those who do not celebrate holidays with Christian traditions? Here are some ideas to help you develop your own plan.

- Educate yourself about the holidays of various cultures and people groups who are your work associates, neighbors, friends, etc.
- Invite them to join you in nonthreatening holiday events related to your traditions—family caroling, singing, Christmas tree, or other such programs at your church.
- Express your interest in their traditions and customs. If invited to join them, go with eager interest, without a judgmental or argumentative attitude. Go to build bridges of understanding and relationship, not competition.
- Ask questions to clarify what's happening in their traditions. Hopefully this will encourage them to ask questions about your traditions and beliefs. Telling them is not as effective as answering their questions.
- Invite them to join you for holiday activities—holiday movies, musical programs, parties, festivals, or educational events that are not designed for just the purpose of converting them, but for building relationships. God will do the rest in his time.
- Create groups and support services for single-parent families, blended families, single adults, and senior adults during the holidays. Many need extra relationships, opportunities to fellowship and meet neighbors, and assistance in managing extra financial and parenting challenges during the holidays.
- Offer "Surviving the Holidays" seminars and support groups for all those who have lost loved ones and pets during the year. Offering a community-wide seminar, publicized through the secular press and other media, can provide persons with grief support and relational support during the holidays. This is a much-needed and much-valued ministry. This can be a collaborative effort between funeral homes, hospice workers, social workers, churches of various denominations, and hospital chaplains.

COACHING QUESTIONS _____

- What might work for you?
- What are you willing to do to build bridges with the unchurched and offer ministry services during the holidays?
- What other ideas for intentional, intergenerational ministry does this idea suggest for your church and community?

Of course, not all the church's intentional ministry will be celebrations. Churches must be aware of the needs of church members and of people in the community. Not only will actions to meet needs help those in need, but ministry actions also give an experiential generation of Christians opportunities to put feet to their faith. And the needs are great.

Often a church that helps the community also helps itself in the long run. Loren Mead, author of *Financial Meltdown in the Mainline,* declared, "We are in bad trouble in the churches, and we won't be out of it in your lifetime or mine."[10] People are giving less to churches and denominations today. The statistics are frightening and present a growing challenge to church leaders.[11] Many of our churches either continue to ignore these harsh realities or are simply just tightening their economic belts. What can we do to turn the trend around rather than just work off of survival strategies? Let me make some suggestions for you to consider in the area of helping people in economic hardship or crisis.

- Design opportunities for retooling and retraining the unemployed workforce. Such an investment by the church can create strong partnerships and new avenues for giving.
- Build partnerships with community organizations and leaders and other churches to establish emotional, financial management, and spiritual guidance for families who are touched by economic hardship.
- Provide spiritual companions for each member of the family or business experiencing financial crisis. Having someone to walk with and someone to share concern with offers a safe haven and often diffuses tension within the family system.
- Provide forums for family members and business owners to share their stories of recovery and faith formation in the "refiners fire."

Note that these ideas in one area of community need speak to both the physical and the spiritual needs of those facing economic hardships. Although the motive in helping those in need shouldn't have the goal of economic benefit for the church, such benefits often happen. Not only is it possible that those helped will in turn give to the church when they are back on their feet financially, but church members engaged in such ministry also see the ways the church is helping others. They become more generous in their church giving. All areas of intentional ministry should be included as part of the church's stewardship education and appeal. Demonstration of that ministry should frequently be shown to the church in more ways than statistics—through testimonies and technology: websites, videos, etc. Churches today are also looking for other sources of funding, such as grants, foundations, and alliances with faith-based ministry groups. Intentional ministry opens the door for this kind of funding. Stewardship focus is shifting to encourage believers, churches, and denominations to live out of generosity rather than scarcity values. Ruben Swint and The Columbia Partnership are pioneering in this significant strategy to provide financial and human asset for innovative ministry. See www.generosityguy.com and www.TheColumbiaPartnership.org.

Evangelism

In looking at what's working and what's not in churches that are reaching all age groups, we have looked at four of the five functions of the church—worship, discipleship, fellowship, and missions/ministry—though we haven't neatly labeled them as we've moved through this look at the effective church in the twenty-first century. The fifth function, evangelism, is equally important. A church that doesn't include all five functions really is out of balance. Some churches seem to be great at outreach while neglecting other functions. Some churches ignore evangelism altogether, focusing more on the other functions. Either approach is out of balance.

Sharing the Good News often becomes bad news for the evangelist and the evangelized. Sometimes the evangelist is trying to use a 1950s model of evangelism in a twenty-first–century world. Other times the person being evangelized is from a postmodern and unchurched culture with little or no understanding of or appreciation for Christianity or the "language of Zion" the evangelist uses. Chaos or embarrassment erupts, and more damage than benefit is done to both parties. Such experiences are not Good News for anyone. Nevertheless, *evangelism* is not a dirty word. In a postmodern, secular culture, we just have to retool, as we see in the model of Jesus in John 4 and the model of the early church in Acts 17. What lessons might be learned?

Consider the following as you learn to be more culturally sensitive in reaching others for Christ. Review Acts 17, which tells how Paul changed the way he shared the Good News because he found himself in a culture different from that in which he grew up. The reality is most churches continue to function and believe we are still in a church and Christian culture. Unfortunately neither is true today. So we are asking new questions and finding new responses.

- Are the people you are seeking to reach churched or unchurched in orientation?
- Are they from a modern or a postmodern mind-set and value system?
- What are the family background issues that might impact sharing the Good News?

- Do they come from a rural, urban, suburban, or metropolitan mind-set?

Consider the following as you learn from John 4 and the model of Christ as to how to share the Good News without jeopardizing the integrity of the gospel.

- What language will best communicate the Good News to those you encounter?
- What will redemption look like, and how might it be experienced and understood by those you encounter and with whom you share?
- How might the Spirit empower and unleash them from their bondage and imprisonment and into new life?

A great illustration of this type of church is First Baptist Church, Spartanburg, South Carolina (www.fbs.org). They have a very traditional church in many ways but have mastered creating nonthreatening entry points for the churched and the unchurched of every generation. They baptize frequently because their evangelism is so real and so effective.

COACHING QUESTIONS

- What are the places where your life naturally intersects with persons in need of Good News?
- What might it look like to practice "walking with" those you encounter?
- What language will help you effectively "talk with" and be authentic in this relationship as you pray for and seek opportunities to share the Good News?
- What are the teachable moments or divine appointments as you practice "life on life" ministry?

As one who has been actively involved in and seen the fruit of door-to-door visitation, bus ministry, "Evangelism Explosion," and the "Roman Road to Salvation" during the years of my adolescent ministry, I now see little fruit from the same or similar investments and strategies. The changing of our culture is creating a shift in the way we reach out and connect with the unchurched in our communities. Many churches are still calling for members to do door-to-door visitation and challenging leaders and members to be faithful to Tuesday night visitation. Some are responding to the challenge, and God is blessing some of the contacts made. In more cases than we like to admit, however, we seem to harvest little, if any, fruit for the amount of energy put into visitation. Furthermore, most of our church members and even most of our leaders do not participate. The guilt trips and challenges are not working anymore.

I would like to invite you to consider that the new culture, which is riddled with fear, skepticism, distrust, and secularism, requires a new approach. What does effective visitation look like in a postmodern, post-Christian world? How do we connect with unchurched people in today's world? Let me suggest, in more cases than not, that visitation is out and connection is in.

Visitation in a Postmodern World

Visitation is out and connection is in when it comes to reaching people under thirty and those who are of a postmodern mind-set, as well as most of those who live in suburban and metro areas. In some rural and agrarian cultures, visitation is still expected and, in some cases, effective. However, those who live in the community as transplants do not often share the expectation by the natives of the community for home visitation and pastoral visits. They do not want to be visited or interrupted.

Postmoderns (many believe we are beyond postmodernism, but for our purposes think of those outside the traditional church values) and those in the unchurched culture often do not trust or respect churches, church leaders, or the motivations of church people. The moral crises found in many churches and denominations these days and the high visibility given to these by the media have fueled cynicism, fear, and distrust by many inside and outside the church. Because of this and other reasons, "cold calling" or confrontational visitation often creates barriers to evangelism rather than creating bridges that lead people to Christ.

Postmoderns do not want to be visited as an initial contact; they want to connect. They aren't interested in hearing a cognitive approach to Christianity that hinges on Scriptures or formulas.

Postmoderns desire to connect heart-to-heart, not head-to-head. They are looking for authenticity and a genuineness of spirit. They want to hear your story of finding and growing in Christ. They don't want to hear a memorized set of Scriptures, nor do they respond to guilt trips or a list of shoulds or musts. They want a casual and comfortable environment to kick back and share spiritual journeys and life challenges and discoveries.

When church and leaders insist on using those "proven" visitation strategies from the past and choose not to learn new ways to connect in a new culture to postmodern people, the postmoderns feel the church doesn't genuinely care about them. They think the church only wants their pocketbook or their services. When leaders continue to promote a visitation strategy that is not bearing genuine fruit, then the church loses energy, and apathy results.

Often churches pursue old strategies because that is what they are most comfortable with, rather than being what they have experienced as most effective in the current culture. Churches like the familiar. They like to live in comfort zones. Often churches and their leaders greatly fear even the simplest of changes. If they change anything or any strategy that their parents or grandparents embraced, they would be "leaving the faith" or "compromising the message" or "leaving biblical teachings."

Jesus faced a similar challenge with his disciples in John 21 when he challenged the fishing disciples to leave their comfort zones and cast out their nets on the other side of the boat. When they followed his counsel, they caught more fish than they had caught in some time. My experience is that most church members are guided by their feelings, and few have a clear understanding of biblical teachings. More often they depend on their family's or their own church history. Do we want to maintain our local church history and our comfort, or do we want to please our heavenly Father and fulfill the Great Commission?

Creating Connection

Our concern should be about how we create connections with the unchurched in ways that move them forward in their spiritual journey, rather than sustaining comfort zones for established church members. How then can we create effective connections with the unchurched who are on a spiritual journey but often are not in church?

Learning to create connections that matter and move people forward in their spiritual journey, often demands that we let go of our bias, our comfort zone, and learn to walk through our fears and learn to walk by faith and not by sight. What a challenge for church-culture people! We don't want to let go of our comfort before we can grasp the new. Jesus called people to be people of faith and to walk by faith not by the known. God called Abraham and Sarah, in their senior years, to leave their place of comfort and to go to a new place, a place God didn't reveal until they proved their obedience and moved away from familiarity (Gen. 12).

Jesus modeled beautifully, making meaningful connections with persons outside his culture. He modeled gracefully and consistently that he was willing to take risks and to leave his comfort zone and even his friends to build these meaningful connections to unchurched persons. Remember the woman at the well (John 4)? He met her while on his journey. He stopped, changed plans, listened, used language she could relate to, and met her on her turf at the well.

In Jesus' story of the shepherd leaving the ninety-nine to find the one, the shepherd left the familiar to search for the rebel, the lost one, the one who didn't fit with the group. Wonder how the ninety-nine felt when the shepherd left them to find the one? (Matt. 18 and Luke 15)

Relationships are vitally important in a postmodern, increasingly unchurched world. Individual leaders who make these shifts will model for and lead their congregations to make and value similar shifts. Helping secular people learn to trust Christians, their institutions and teachings, takes time, energy, and consistency. What does building bridges look like in a postmodern, post-Christian, post-church culture? Consider these possibilities.

- Make a choice to leave comfort and take risks. Jesus often called his disciples to leave their fathers and mothers or their careers or their personal preferences to follow him.
- Meet people where they are, rather than where we would like them to be. Jesus was a master at breaking through social barriers and personal comfort zones to reach others with his love and mercy. In fact, he moved from his personal preference and "while we still were sinners Christ died for us" (Rom. 5:8).

- Take the initiative and be consistent. Building trust takes time and consistency. According to the Scriptures, Jesus spent more time in fellowship with sinners at weddings, parties, and social gatherings than he spent in the synagogue. He understood the value of consistent fellowship. When he left, his commands for his followers were and are clear: he left us *in* the world but not to be *of* the world (John 17:15–20).

- Learn to listen for understanding rather than judgment. Jesus spent much of his time trying to convince Pharisees and Sadducees not to be so judgmental in the way they treated others. Much of the reason unchurched people keep their distance from church people and churches is that while we sing "Just as I Am," we tell them verbally and nonverbally to clean up their acts before they come to our church or, at least, to learn to put on their "religious masks," as many church people do, when they attend our services.

- Learn to listen to understand rather than to talk/respond. So often we listen only to talk and to respond. We need to follow the model of Jesus to listen for understanding. A good shepherd observes and listens, then guides.

- Learn what they mean by their language/words. Language is powerful. In today's diverse and pluralistic culture, words have many different meanings and connotations to different people in different contexts. It is crucial to ask those we seek to reach to help us understand what they mean by their images and words. Unchurched people do not necessarily have biblical or church language to define their spiritual journey; however, they often use metaphors or other language to describe or define their spiritual journey and their religious questions or connections. We need to be able to listen and understand rather than worry about teaching them *our* language, which we often do just to make us comfortable and put us in a teacher/leader role. The journey can be authentic and valued even if they don't or can't use our church language. Jesus knew this when he dealt with Nicodemus, the woman at the well, and the woman with the issue of blood.

- Listen for life pinches/struggles and how the unchurched interpret them. As we listen and observe, we can identify the life pinches they are experiencing. Usually, at the point of a life pinch (divorce, unemployment, aging, caring for aging adults) or moving into a life passage (new career, marriage, empty nest, etc.), people are open to help and are seeking meaning in the midst of the life challenge.

- Learn to tell your story in words and concepts they can relate to. Jesus used images of water when he talked to the woman at the well. He used images of money when he talked with Matthew, a tax collector. He used images of farming and flowers when talking to farmers. Finding the common right language is a clear pathway to building bridges of relationship and connecting with people at their point of need and communicating heart-to-heart rather than head-to-head.

- Learn to ask open-ended, nonthreatening questions that connect with heart and not just the head. Begin conversations with open-ended questions such as, "What do you think about . . . ?" Another way to build bridges of conversation is to respond with, "Help me understand what you mean by . . ." or "Do you have an example of what you mean by . . . ?" Jesus certainly knew the power of questions in his ministry, and we should value nothing less as we build bridges to the unchurched.

- Find common interests. Jesus spent much of his time fishing, sharing meals with others, attending social gatherings, and engaging others at their point of common interest. We should do no less.

- Once trusted, learn to connect faith stories and biblical stories/concepts. As the trust is being built, life issues and passages are shared, and meaning is pursued, find ways to connect faith and biblical stories to daily life events and challenges. It might be that a struggling businessman might connect with Nehemiah as he "gave the people a mind to work," or one who is feeling the pain of a shattered life might connect with the story of Job, or someone caught in an adulterous relationship might learn something from the story of David.

Instead of door-to-door visitation or community census, maybe we would build more bridges and connections by creating some nonthreatening, comfortable entry points around life passages and life needs. Consider:

- What if those who have experienced broken families and broken marriages and have experienced some healing were to create some support groups for others caught in these painful life experiences?

- What if school administrators and faculty were invited to attend a support group or a seminar that offered support, encouragement, nurture, and love?

- What if the church, in partnership with community funeral homes and/or hospitals were to offer a "Surviving the Holidays" community-wide grief workshop with small support groups across the city from November through January?

- What if the church were to partner with the community to offer a seminar and support system for "caring for the caregivers" in the medical, social services, government, and police systems in town?

- What if the church were to invite persons into coaching relationships? Often people will continue the bridge-building in a coaching relationship that helps them move through their pinches or the gaps in their life—career, marriage, parenting, finances, etc.—when they may not be ready for church. Their thirsts keep them open to guidance. Maybe life coaches will supplement Bible study teachers.

On and on the possibilities go. These are issues of the heart. They are issues that many unchurched and churched people wrestle with and share in common. The challenge of these entry points is to read your culture and determine the best place and time to offer these or other entry points. Sometimes these groups need to meet in places other than the church, for many unchurched are intimidated by our massive churches. Maybe we need to meet on their turf instead of expecting them to meet us on our turf, or our schedule.

COACHING QUESTIONS

- What might your next steps be for connecting with the unchurched and the churched who are seeking more meaning in life and more connection with God and others?
- What strategies or ideas might work in your situation?
- Who are the core believers who share this vision? Might they become a planning team and core people to become intentional about building bridges and relationships with the unchurched? How can our church stop holding on to our comfort zones or traditions that have worked for us in the past but that might not be as effective today?

Membership Policies and Practices

Following the model of Jesus offers great guidelines for evangelism and visitation in today's postmodern and post-Christian culture. A final hot button for many, but an essential issue in reaching persons from the postmodern world and from our pluralistic and diverse culture, includes membership policies and practices.

Along with evangelism approaches, churches in many denominations today are rethinking their policies and practices about what it means to be a member. Membership is not a biblical concept. In an age when membership is declining, who becomes a member and how are important issues in the church. Many churches hold widely divided opinions on this issue. Some churches are more intent on whom they will keep out of their churches rather than whom they will welcome in. Receiving members and keeping members faithful and effective in the church's mission doesn't really come up very often in discussions about church membership. Perhaps it's time to review this area of your church's constitution and bylaws.

Some churches struggle to know how to accept and activate members who join from other faith traditions, other parts of the country, or from blended faith families where baptism becomes an issue. Persons already baptized in another faith tradition often do not want to be rebaptized by immersion, for it would seemingly invalidate their initial baptism. Others don't want to join a church due to expectations for leadership, tithing, or service; but they want to attend. Still others don't choose to join one church today because they and their family choose to participate in many churches due to their search for and need/desire for multiple programs, variety in worship styles, and/or ministry expertise.

Here are some of the issues making this such an important issue in the church today:

- Multicultural families—people marrying from different religious backgrounds and cultural heritages.
- Decline in denominational affiliation as an important piece of decision-making about church membership.
- High mobility in our culture—people move frequently and are less likely to join a church. They might visit or participate in a variety of churches rather than one church.
- "Membership is meaningless" is an attitude among many young adults who are cynical at best about church membership practices of the past generation. If they join a church, they want their membership to mean something more than just serving on committees or giving a little money. Wanda Kidd, a colleague, provides great insight about Membership and Millennials in a blog entry, http://cbfblog.com/2015/07/22/millennials-and-the-local-church-membership-or-belonging/ .

How are churches changing in this area? What are some of the shifts taking place as churches rethink baptism and membership policies and practices?

- Some churches are adopting open baptism in policy and practice. This opens the door for membership by those who were previously baptized by whatever means. Immersion is no longer the required mode for baptism.
- Participation is viewed as valid membership. Some churches are creating a membership status that validates those who attend regularly but choose for whatever reason not to be baptized. This opens some leadership areas to them and gives them a voice and role in church life as validated members.
- Graduated membership is created that offers some "attending membership status"; others choose "leading membership"; still others choose to be "giving members"; others choose the membership category "members on mission." This brings validity and lengthens the cords to create an inclusive congregation that shows its openness to seekers and searchers.

Dr. Will McRaney shares some significant shifts that those with a postmodern worldview are looking for in membership and their faith journey. Note the shifts we are facing as we rethink membership and faith commitments of a new generation.[12]

- Multiple encounters rather than single ones
- Listener centered rather than witness centered
- Dialogical rather than monological
- Gospel story rather than presentation of gospel principles
- Story then proposition
- Asking good questions rather than giving information

- Community integration
- Softer
- Consideration rather than argumentation
- Guided tour approach rather than ticket sale approach
- More supernatural
- More earthly benefits
- More relational validation than evidentiary validation
- More percent of time spent planting seeds rather than harvesting them.

COACHING QUESTIONS

- What are the implications of these shifts on the way you evangelize?
- What are the implications for how your church seeks to attract and assimilate new members?
- How do your current practices engage the new generation's value system about faith formation and church life?
- What is working in your church in light of these shifts, and what is not working in light of these shifts?
- What adjustments need to be made?
- When will you make the needed adjustments?

Stewardship

We mentioned stewardship earlier—ultimately all areas of the church tie together in inextricable ways—but we couldn't end this chapter without looking, at least briefly, at what's going on in this area in churches today. The seniors over sixty who have supported the church in every way, including financial, often don't have the same financial basis for tithing in their retirement years. As this generation ages and dies, the financial security of the church is also eroding. Adults under thirty just don't put the church first in their list of priorities; often the church is nowhere near the top, even in priorities for charitable gifting.

I had the opportunity to speak to the Stewardship Development Association (http://stewardshipdevelopment.org/ Document5) with my theme as "Creating an Appetite to Grow, Give, and Go." Permit me to share some observations and some challenges that might help move us forward in being more effective in stewardship development in a postmodern (mostly people under thirty) world.

1. Postmoderns respond to issues of the heart rather than institutional maintenance or survival.
2. Postmoderns are primarily Web or multimedia people rather than print people.
3 Most churches/agencies spend most of their resources addressing the Builder Generation's interests and needs, hoping it will reach the next generation too.
4. Telling our life-transformation stories is more significant than calling for commitment and loyalty to denominational agencies/issues.

This is what's going on. Here are the challenges:

1. Retooling our resources so they address the unique needs and learning styles of various generations. E-giving is rapidly becoming a major way of giving via smartphones. Research tells us it usually increases tithes and offerings.
2. Creating databases of transformed lives and life passage issues that become stewardship resources and channels for sharing of resources.
3. Balancing our personnel, resources, energies that effectively communicate management and stewardship issues among all generations.
4. Create channels for telling stories of life transformation and for connecting faith and daily life.
5. Finding and using language and concepts that communicate stewardship principles to persons not familiar with biblical stewardship language.
6. Building and managing networks between the passions and the resources of postmodern generation.

8

Bible Study for
Twenty-first–Century Adults?

Creating community for individuals and churches issues forth from a meaningful encounter with others and with God through relevant Bible study. The question of the role of Sunday school and Bible study continues to surface from persons who have read my books. Facing the issue of retooling and reframing structures and focus begins by examining the following questions. What is the role of Sunday school for adults? How will adults benefit from and participate in Bible study in the next decades? Will twenty-first century people want Bible study? How and when will they engage in Bible study?

Bible study will continue to flourish, but will radically change from just a church-based study to a variety of situations designed to accommodate a growing diversity, people with different belief systems, busy lives, and changing families with different needs for individual and community reflection. To trap or limit Bible study to a Sunday classroom experience will likely strangle the growing spiritual thirst in our country. Bible study lessons will be designed to release lay teachers in the world and serve as a catalyst for the face-to-face classroom Sunday school experiences that will function primarily as pastoral care center and community builder. The new function of the face-to-face group will be more about connection and community than Bible study and outreach. The primary place of life-transforming Bible study will increasingly be outside of the church facilities and Sunday morning, and such settings will serve as a catalyst for deeper relationships and accountability through community. The characteristics of effective Bible study for adults in the next decades will become more and more personalized/individualized, decentralized, digitized, customized, and improvised.

Personalized/Individualized

Bible study will be important to and embraced by many. I am confident that the rampant spiritual thirst in our country will continue to generate various venues of groups looking for truth, wholeness, healing, and hope. Scripture certainly provides these, but the groups will likely explore a variety of belief systems and resources in addition to the Bible. Postmoderns particularly like to explore a variety of tools.

Bible study will be highly relational. Relationships are critically important and will serve as a catalyst for significant Bible study. America is filled with people who are lonely in the midst of a crowd. More people than ever are living alone in this country, and many who are not living alone are lonely and searching for authentic, fulfilling, and life-energizing relationships. How can the church community maximize community and make entry points to the faith easy to access for the masses? What would happen if churches designed Bible study and membership around various preferred delivery systems and values? For instance, some members might value community and fellowship over Bible study; others might value Bible study over mission engagement; others might prefer face-to-face study/connections while others prefer online or streaming classroom studies and connections.

Let me give you an example. Linn, a realtor friend of mine, has created a significant community through her business connections. She markets herself with "buy a house, join a family." Her business is flourishing. She tracks carefully all her buyers and celebrates their anniversary dates—marriage, purchase date, move anniversary, new babies, and so on. Each year she invites all buyers to a mass gathering where she tells her faith story as part of the celebration of life and hope she has found. She invites them to join small groups and provides them Christ-centered resources to move them from pain to purpose or from loneliness to community, etc. She had more than 1,500 people at the last event, and now more than 400 are in groups. She is learning to how to do Bible study beyond the walls of the church.

For many, life coaches will replace or complement their Bible study and help maximize their search for truth, wholeness, and healing. Christian leadership coaching is a powerful discipling tool for postmoderns. Many postmoderns and many who are not connected to the church or faith are much more responsive to the "asking questions" model of coaching than the "telling" posture of traditional teaching. For additional information about coaching, review *Spiritual Leadership in a Secular Age* by Edward Hammett, *Christ-Centered Coaching* by Jane Creswell and *Coaching for Christian Leaders* by Linda Miller and Chad Hall.[1]

Bible study will be designed and taught based on the place the student is in his or her own personal faith journey, not necessarily on age. Age-graded Bible study works for some, but for many unchurched or seekers it is often a barrier. Also with the family structures changing, life stages are diverse.

How can churches provide faith stage groupings? How do we assess faith formation for adults? I would invite you to explore a variety of tools for assessment that can be found in the coaching page of my website (www. transformingsolutions.org). It's possible that life stage might be a better grouping than age, and the stage challenges become the hook or entry point for adults seeking help with life challenges.

We are living in an age where pre- and post-conversion discipleship is critical. Today we are told that more than 70 percent of our population is considered unchurched by missiologists. We are increasingly a secular nation, but many are looking for truth. The example of Jesus was to meet people where they are, not necessarily where we want them to be. I discuss this in detail in *Spiritual Leadership for a Secular Age* as I review John 4 and other texts. It is increasingly critical that we look at the salvation experience as a journey, not just a destination. Helping the nonbeliever move step by step toward Christ is pre-conversion discipleship. This is discussed in detail in my book *Reframing Spiritual Formation: Discipleship for an Unchurched Culture*.

Decentralized

Bible study will be at the student's convenience. I think one thing here is certain. Adults learn when they have time and need to learn. The busyness of most adults will increasingly necessitate that Bible study is on their agenda at their convenience and in their lives' pathways, or they will not likely be consistently engaged.

Bible study will be done for some adults through traditional Sunday school, but most will be done in other venues and at other times. The church culture generation will likely continue to do Sunday and Wednesday night Bible studies, but for others who were not raised with this habit or custom, their search for truth will be done online, in chat rooms, by podcasts, in small groups at work or en route to work, in coffee shops, in bookstores, or in community-based groups, with persons who share common interests and questions. You will note that Starbucks often has coffee shops close together and occasionally across the street from each other to capture persons in their daily traffic patterns and make stopping for a cup of coffee convenient for their customers. The church could do no less in making Bible study available and convenient for our students. Learn other such lessons from *The Gospel According to Starbucks* by Leonard Sweet. Such Bible study groups will likely be more conversational than taught. Coaching skills will be used more than telling/teaching skills. Christian coaching skills and facilitator skills are the emerging tools for Christian educators. For example, today there are vast numbers of Bible studies conducted during break time and lunch at workplaces across the country (see www.worklife.org).

Digitized

Bible study will be designed for individuals and communities via iPhones, Google circles, Skype, interactive learning experiences, Web-based learning opportunities, and who knows what else. Experiences will include a range of opportunities from pocket worship via podcasts (see www.podpoint.net) to online learning. Discovering and growing in how to validate and design digital educational and worship experiences is the challenge for twenty-first–century educators, pastors, and church leaders. The younger generations are visual learners for the most part. They learn through interaction, research, dialogue, and challenges via the computer. What are the implications and challenges for you? for your church?

Use of Webcams, online streaming and digital learning will flourish. They are opportunities for individualized learning and community-building experiences. Bible studies will be done using the phone and a www.gotomeeting. org-type tool. Learning experience design teams will become a key group at churches who are effective at reaching the younger generation. Many churches already have media teams for their worship, but that will grow into the Bible study experiences. Church, convention, and judicatory websites will include chat rooms as well as teleclasses around topics of interest. "A Pastor's Guide to Digital Outreach" by Andrea Bailey is a very helpful resource.[2]

Learning to use time-saving, cost-saving digital tools will be embraced by many, as church meetings are held on telephone conference lines, webcams or online real time dialogues. Does your church's website provide for these time-saving methods and resources? I think this would increase participation, maximize time, and deepen relationships as they are "jump-started" via the Web or phone and then nurtured in face-to-face experiences. Who are the technical "geeks" in your church who could help you design and facilitate such experiences?

Customized

Bible study will be done through a variety of ways, depending on the learning style of the student. As people have different dress preferences, so do they have differing learning styles. Most of the over fifty crowd learn through auditory means and in groups. Those under fifty prefer online learning, individual learning, and small group experiences. Providing something for everyone's learning style will continue to challenge our curricula designers and Christian educators.

Bible study will be based on life issues and life questions and challenges rather than expository or historical lessons. The group over sixty learn best in linear teaching styles and in classroom settings with a class instructor. Those under thirty learn best via computer online learning, small groups with a group facilitator, or a personal life coach. The older generation likes expository teaching and preaching. The younger generation tends to respond more to life issue and topical preaching/teaching that is driven by visual means and small group dialogue.

Bible study is attractive to many adults who are seeking truth, answers to life struggles, and relationship challenges. Many of today's and tomorrow's adults are not from the church culture, who value and understand biblical concepts or language, but they are asking significant spiritual questions about life challenges. To introduce and grow today's and tomorrow's adults into believers we must learn to build curricula off of life issues and needs. Utilizing the concepts of adult learning (andragogy) rather than concepts of basic learning for children/youth (pedagogy) is a challenge for curricula writers and facilitators of small groups of young and middle-age adults. Lifeway has an excellent ministry targeting twentysomethings at youngadults.lifeway.com.[3]

Effective Bible study is designed at the points of intersection, where life intersects biblical truths. This creates the teachable moment and divine opportunity for moving forward in one's faith journey. Designing and maximizing teachable moments "as we go" is the challenge of the Great Commission and Christian education in today's fast-paced culture. Effective Bible teaching and transformational learning will become connected more and more to "as life happens" than to "as Sunday school begins." Adults learn when life dictates that we learn, not always as classes are planned. Consequently the challenge is to design learning experiences for adults on the go. Designing and using podcasts, online learning, and workplace dialogue groups are critical for reaching and keeping the next generation.

I have friends under thirty who, when a life challenge comes, search the Web for relevant teachings or groups and download what they find. That download then becomes the entry point for their Bible study and/or worship experience to get them through the crisis or challenge of the moment. The downloads are not limited to a certain denomination or church or pastor/teacher. They learn from the resources of the world. Truly spiritual formation is a global economy these days for those who know how to use technology. We need to help them select wisely and deepen their learnings in community.

Training churches, leaders, and teachers about this challenge and teaching them to customize for their students is critical. Teacher training will be "on the go" too.[4] The skill of customization becomes critical for adult educators and for those who train teachers and facilitators of adults. Learning to use various forms of media, learning styles, and group experiences will heighten interest and availability for meaningful and "in the moment" Bible study.

For instance, several groups do Bible study and life lessons on a regular basis through podcasts that are downloaded from popular websites from well-known churches, pastors, and teachers. They share what's working for them and what's not via I-messages to friends or through text messaging. When they find something that speaks to them, they share it and celebrate it with their friends.

Does your church or judicatory website have a place for posting of helpful podcasts or digital learning opportunities? What about a real-time chat room for dialogue and collaborative studies? Some churches are beginning to have staff who design and post these Bible study resources. I foresee the role of the minister of education shifting to a designer of Bible study media and follow-up groups.

Maybe churches will have "spiritual formation engineers" instead of ministers of education. This is discussed in more detail in *Reframing Spiritual Formation*.

Bible study design and curricula may need to be regionalized in ways that address regional issues, cultural distinctions, and social issues. Learning to design and build curricula for adults around life issues calls for regionalization of curricula that can be done via Internet by educators who collaborate to design such experiences to address immediate community needs/crises, etc. Every church needs to have a curricula design team to assist the Sunday school director or Christian educator, who may or may not be on staff. Learning to customize and deliver Bible study through a variety of learning means, even simultaneously, is critical for today's busy adults. Adult learning is going to be done at the adult's teachable moment and at his or her convenience, often on a mobile device. Therefore churches are going to have to build multiple learning environments for adults, and gather groups through a variety of modes—phone, face-to-face, online, workplace, and Sunday or weekday groups that meet in the church or as the church in a variety of places and times.

Improvised

Capturing and maximizing the teachable moment of persons will be a challenge, but essential. Today's adults are busy and searching. The tasks of good Bible study leaders are to look for and maximize teachable moments in the lives of adults in their shepherding. Also, learning to provide some rich Bible study instruction through various media that can be accessed in the moment will be a great catalyst for face-to-face dialogue and follow-up from life's challenges.

Those believers with mature knowledge become the improvisational teachers in the moment where life and truth-seeking intersect. Those who have a deep faith and rich walk with God will be released and connected with those who are seeking answers and truth. Learning to make these formation connections is another vital tool for Bible study facilitators. Mobilizing the Body of Christ becomes imperative in the outreach and discipling challenge in this highly mobile and busy world. Churches are being called to decide if they are an engaged church (connecting persons to community needs) or are they primarily a self-serving church (inward focused on membership's needs and preferences). Those who know teach others. Helping persons discover truth for themselves and coaching them to make powerful connections in life for themselves are powerful tools for the postmodern generation. When persons discover the connection between the biblical narrative and the struggle of life, momentum is gained and transformation occurs. Pat Springle has written a super article about the vulnerability and authenticity of leaders (for the full download, see http://media. leadnet.org/blog-content/leadnet/advance/may07s2a.htm).

Bible study will be more in life's wake as it happens rather than localized to a time and place. Increasingly Bible study will occur more outside the walls of the church than inside the walls of the church. This is a challenge with deep

Great Commission roots. You might have noticed that the national news, local newscasts, and popular television shows are following this tenet. You can view their material at your leisure through whatever means you have—TiVo, DVD, online streaming, mobile device, podcasts, etc. You can do this on your timetable at your convenience from wherever you choose. You can then, in many cases, connect with others who watched the same show and talk with the actors or the writers via chat rooms or e-mail. Now isn't it time Bible study accessed this same learning pattern for postmodern people?

Bible study lessons will need to be counted, validated, and tested outside the classroom as well as inside the classroom. It will be increasingly critical that churches recognize, validate, and count Bible study that is happening beyond their church base. This will certainly be a leap for many. Also, studies and students will need to be assessed, since we are facing a steep learning curve in what is working and what is not transforming lives. In far too many of our traditional, church-based classes, we've met for years without the lives of many of the students being transformed, and the Bible knowledge is minimal in most cases. Surely there's room for experimenting with other means that might "bear more fruit."

Bible study will be more about asking the right questions at the right time than telling information in a didactic manner. I have been engaged in Christian coaching as a coach and a coach trainer for the last eight years. I wish I had had these skills twenty-five years ago. Coaching bears more fruit more quickly than anything I've ever been trained to do! (See www.ca-ministries, www.TransformingSolutions.org, or www.cbfnc.org.) Coaching is about self-discovery and helping clients or students connect the dots of their experience, knowledge, and questions. Coaching is about action, not just about knowledge. Coaching is about movement and empowerment. Coaching is more about asking than telling. Learning to ask the right questions and discerning the Holy Spirit's timing and work in someone's life are basic skills of coaches and for adult Bible study instructors for the next decades.

Bible study will be more concerned about relevancy to life than doctrinal purity or position. While doctrinal purity is important, it is not an entry point for most persons seeking help from Scripture or churches. The entry point to exciting, life-transforming Bible study begins with relevancy to life. Doctrine clarifies as students learn and experience the movement of the Spirit in life and connect life with God's design and plans.

Bible study will be more popular with adults in the next decades than in recent years. Many adults who have never had access to good Bible study options will start to have such choices as churches and Christian leaders create multiple learning experiences that are easily accessible, communicated around life issues, and in language that is in keeping with the student's faith stage. The best and most effective improvisational teachers of Scripture need a new set of skills, accountability, training, and affirmations to reach out and go to the deeper depths and higher heights of the Word of God. Learning to allow the "Word to become flesh" (John 1:14) through the lives we live and the lessons we embody and share are critical for adults in this and the next decades.

COACHING QUESTIONS

- What are your takeaways from reading this chapter?
- What ideas are you willing to work on now?
- Who could help you?
- How could you design an effective podcast?
- What reframing of your role and function in adult education and spiritual formation might need to happen?
- What would interactive online learning opportunities through your church website look like?
- Who in your church are your technicians that could help you?
- Who is involved in a weekday decentralized Bible study or online Bible study now?
- Who might be interested in online learning in the future?
- How could you make Bible study more effective in your church and for your community?

Consider the following questions with those leading your Bible study:

- What are the evidences that our Bible studies are life-transforming for the participants?
- What is happening that makes these Bible study experiences life-transforming experiences for the participants?
- What are we doing that contributes to the minimization of life-transforming Bible study?
- What are we doing that values life-transforming Bible study among our leaders and members?
- How can these learnings be shared and replicated among other persons or groups?
- How can we evaluate the life-transforming experiences of our Bible studies?
- How can these life-transforming experiences be shared with others?
- Who are the persons most passionate about ensuring that Bible study is life transforming?
- How could we prioritize these questions to help us focus in our dialogue group?
- What other questions need to be discussed?
- How can we dialogue with and learn from this group?
- When will we do this, and who will be the lead person for the dialogue?

Attracting and Discipling Twenty-first–Century Adults

Spiritual Formation Opportunities	Sacred/ Church Culture	Seekers	Skeptics	Spiritually Curious
BIBLE STUDY	Centralized; teacher led; age graded; designated time and place; curricula designed by national offices	Topical studies; Life-centered issues; small groups; home groups; crowd breakers; reflective questions and narrative Bible studies around stories, character studies, and life needs	Question driven; life pinches and challenges; decentralized and online selective listening and study at their leisure and around their issues; teachable moment focused; connecting	Dialogue; online and life coaching; question focused; around life and global issues and challenges; resolving disconnects they encounter; maximizing and recognizing divine appointments and teachable moments
WORSHIP	Centralized; pastor led; designated time and place; Bible centered; expository preaching; hymns and choir central	Celebration; convenient; comfortable; team led; creative; open; visual messages including drama/music lay led	Via Internet; "pocket worship"; challenging and encouraging messages helping them experience wholeness and relationship; learning to trust Scripture and others through mentoring relationships over time	"Pocket worship"; experiencing benefits of trustworthy community of peers; learning to be open to God's Spirit and removing blocks; discovering intersections between life and God's Word

Spiritual Formation Opportunities	Sacred/ Church Culture	Seekers	Skeptics	Spiritually Curious
GATHERING	For fellowship with like-minded believers; worship; bible study; mission support	For fellowship and exploration; community; seeking answers; seeking to trust others and church	Online; face to face; small groups; decentralized; at their convenience, comfort; non-judgmental; open; relaxed and focused on helping them move from pain to purpose	Online; face to face in comfortable nonthreatening places; decentralized; on their schedule; connecting with others
EVANGELISM	Telling the story; confrontational; reaping the harvest; "bring them in"; Four Spiritual Laws; Roman Road to Salvation	Confrontation to dialogue and community; joining us; being with others on the journey	Conversation; asking powerful questions; discovering for themselves answers and strength to take next steps in a journey of building trust and relationship with God	Dialogue around life issues/pinches and opportunities; moving toward wholeness and freedom from pain; growing into new relationship with loving God; life coaching
MISSIONS	Funding mission activity and personnel through church; hear reports; conversion growth	Hands-on missions; go with money; be missionary; impact on world	Hands-on; onsite with missionaries; cultural distinctives; social impact	Build partnerships; creative funding; work done by churched and unchurched

9

Win-Win Options for Your Multicultural Ministry

Letting go of the familiar or preconceived concepts or ideas—particularly when they have worked for you—is challenging at best. Joshua and the people of Israel encountered this. Picture yourself with Joshua as he looks over into the promised land. Moses has died, and now Joshua is the leader. What must he have thought? He had the vision. He knew the people could enter the promised land and prosper there because God had clearly directed them to go there. But Joshua had to wonder if the people would follow. An entire generation had died wandering in the wilderness and waiting to enter the promised land.

He had to remember what had happened forty years ago. As two of the twelve representatives of the twelve tribes, only he and Caleb gave favorable reports to Moses, affirming that the people should enter the promised land immediately. They would be following God's plan and receiving his ongoing blessing. Two voices spoke in favor of proceeding, but ten voices spoke against such action (Num. 13—14).

Surely Joshua saw the challenge before him. Perhaps that's why in the first few verses of Joshua, God tells him three times to have courage, not to be afraid:

> After the death of Moses the servant of the LORD, the LORD spoke to Joshua son of Nun, Moses' assistant, saying, "My servant Moses is dead. Now proceed to cross the Jordan, you and all this people, into the land that I am giving to them, to the Israelites. . . . As I was with Moses, so I will be with you; I will not fail you or forsake you. Be strong and courageous; for you shall put this people in possession of the land that I swore to their ancestors to give them. Only be strong and very courageous, being careful to act in accordance with all the law that my servant Moses commanded you; do not turn from it to the right hand

or to the left, so that you may be successful wherever you go. This book of the law shall not depart out of your mouth; you shall meditate on it day and night, so that you may be careful to act in accordance with all that is written in it. For then you shall make your way prosperous, and then you shall be successful. I hereby command you: Be strong and courageous; do not be frightened or dismayed, for the LORD your God is with you wherever you go." (Josh. 1:1–2,5b–9, NIV)

You've spent time in God's Word. You're committed to being a missional church led by the Great Commission and focused on reaching people and growing disciples. You have a vision for what your church can become. The question is, can you meet the needs of those under thirty without losing those over sixty? Yes, you can! This chapter is filled with ideas to help you do just that. What will it take to stop wandering and start walking? Maybe these suggestions will offer you some next steps to explore. Hopefully, they will give everyone a win-win. How can you provide everyone with what they need and still maintain the identity and function of one church? Here are ways to do this, but it takes work and commitment. Are you willing?

Win-Win Approaches

Churches really can keep those over sixty while reaching those under thirty. No magic formula, however, no prescription, no secret set of steps will ensure success. Some general principles will help. Let's look at some of them.

Allocate limited resources to target those over sixty and those under thirty.

You'll win the support of those over sixty in reaching those under thirty if they don't feel the church is turning its back on them. Make sure the church budget reflects their interests—foreign missions giving, senior adult fellowships and trips, church traditions. What honors and includes senior adults may differ in every church. The important thing is that the budget reflects their interests. Be sure to give prayerful and serious reflection and planning for those ten thousand Boomers retiring each day. They will certainly provide a level of expertise and significant discretionary time and money that church programs have known in the current generation of builders. Watch for a series of podcasts and articles on this subject on www.TransformingSolutions.org website over the next few years.

Staff time should also respect and honor those over sixty. Volunteers can be enlisted to help. Ensure you have a plan in place to visit them when they are sick, in the hospital, and when they can no longer come to church. Deacons or a deacon ministry team may want to take this responsibility. Call them. Send them notes. Take them gifts at Christmas. Honor them as if they were your parents.

Respect them. Ask their opinion. Not all of them have to have their own way. They may just want to be included, to know that they are not forgotten or ignored. Their wisdom is valuable. They have learned some lessons through the years; encourage them to pass on what they have learned.

This doesn't mean those over sixty need the lion's share of time and budget. It doesn't even mean it needs to be fifty-fifty. Determine a percentage and stick with it. Perhaps 30 percent of the budget will be allocated to those over sixty, and 70 percent to those under thirty and for reaching younger people outside the church. What would that look like in your setting? with your staff, deacons, and pastor?

The same is true for staff time. Church maintenance can consume all the time if given the opportunity. Limit the amount of time for those over sixty. That might mean that the staff won't attend every committee meeting or every fellowship. It may mean deacons and others do much of the hospital visitation. Existing ministries will crowd out new ventures unless that time is protected, so guard it well. This type of shift of pastor and staff focus is critical as churches posture themselves to break various growth barriers. *Making the shift of focus and priority of staff and pastor is tough for every church.* When your church average attendance is at about one hundred, two hundred, three hundred, etc., shifts in focus and time allocation are needed if the church is to move forward. How will your church learn about this and act to ensure these steps are taken?

Look for creative ways to meet the needs of those over sixty so that they don't require all the staff time and budget. Plan a covered-dish fellowship instead of a catered meal. Find volunteers over sixty to lead in ministries both in their own age group as well as with those who are younger.

Plan a mixture of "go" strategies and "come" strategies.

Make good use of your church building; these are "come" strategies. Offer ministries that interest those under thirty that might attract them to the church such as financial planning, divorce recovery, college planning for students. Plan parallel opportunities at the church for seniors—planning for retirement or living with grandchildren. I'm in the planning stages , with a cluster of churches in my community, to design an Institute to Maximize Meaning and Mission for Early Retirees (focus on Boomers). I'll be sharing updates of this journey on my website.

Balance "come" strategies with "go" strategies.

Ideas are limited only by your creativity and the needs and interests of those in the community—a safety seminar and contest for skateboarders and their families at a local park, English classes and Bible study at a secondhand store, Bible studies at the ballpark, one-on-one discipling at a local coffee shop. Over time, some go strategies will draw new people into the church, leading to a greater variety of come strategies. (Visit www.transformingsolutions.org and see *Recovering Hope for Your Church* and *The Gathered and Scattered Church* book for additional ideas.)

To illustrate this concept, consider a couple, empty nesters, in Colorado with a nice big home. They considered ways to use their time and their home for ministry and finally decided to open their home to unwed mothers. They did not stipulate that the girls had to go to church with them, but in many ways every day, they modeled practical skills as well as what it means to be a Christian—prayers at mealtime, a loving relationship in a healthy marriage, meal planning, a clean and orderly home, daily devotions, regular church attendance. This is an example of a go strategy that individual church members can do.

Most churches are filled with people over sixty who are looking for ways to do something meaningful with an eternal impact. They are looking for ideas for ministry. Helping those over sixty find or create or join community ministry opportunities are go strategies. They will enrich and, over time, grow your church. Retiring Boomers expect experiences that help them deepen meaning, faith, and purpose, not necessarily just recreational or social gatherings as has been valued by many in the Builder generation.

Change values before changing structure.

One reason those over sixty leave churches that suddenly retool to reach those under thirty is that a small group of leaders, usually staff and perhaps a few lay leaders, decide to reformat the worship service radically. They seem to think an announcement about this change is all that is needed.

A concrete plan of action that includes good communication can make a huge difference. The pastor can preach a series of sermons on the patriarchs about passing faith from one generation to another, including statistics on how churchgoers and active Christianity are declining in the United States. Such impassioned sermons will leave those over sixty wanting to know what they can do to reach those under thirty. (An example of such a sermon is "Can Our Kind of Church Save Our Kind of World?" found in my book, *The Gathered and Scattered Church*.)

Get church leaders over sixty involved in doing surveys and research to discover unmet needs, desired worship styles, and ways to reach those under thirty. Although the resulting styles may not appeal to those over sixty, they will be excited about the changes because of the purpose for the change and because of their involvement in creating the change.

Their values will have changed before the actual ministries change. They will be enthusiastic about being involved. One reason changing worship styles doesn't work in some churches is because worship leaders think that simply changing the way they do worship will show that people under thirty are welcome. If they do nothing in the church to change values, their net numbers may well be negative. Those over sixty will leave, and those under thirty in the neighborhood may not even know that the church is trying to appeal to them.

Changing values will add excitement. People will be talking about the church in the community. Those over sixty will be looking for folks under thirty at work, on the golf course, at the garage or grocery to invite to church. So many of our church leadership and membership have children, grandchildren, and great-grandchildren who have become church dropouts or have no interest in church. These efforts to reach persons with other needs and preferences include reaching their children and grandchildren. These are true heart issues and will be motivators for them to use.

Changing values turns hearts to God and changes the culture of the church. In addition to reaching those under thirty, a church will see those over sixty grow as disciples and valued mentors and missionaries as they see their church become more mission minded. As more people are focused on mission, and as they experience the self-fulfillment and joy of personally following the Great Commission, they will be less concerned about focusing on maintenance issues or complaining about perceived personal neglect from leaders. The culture of the church will gradually change from maintenance to disciple-making. (*Recovering Hope for Your Church, Making the Church Work* and *Making Shifts Without Making Waves* are designed to help leaders and congregations with this change process.)

Know the trends.

Learning what is happening in other churches and what those who observe and analyze church trends say is happening in churches today can help church leaders explore ideas and possibilities and consider what will work in their church. Knowing what others are doing in their churches shouldn't dictate what you do in yours, but examining trends can give you ideas for investigating what is going on in your own community. You might send out a research team of your leaders, including some of your skeptics. Encourage them to visit with the staff and lay leaders and ask questions about their transitions or journey. Then bring your research team back to debrief with the staff and other church leaders. This can be a real education for everyone. Remember, whatever you learn from trends and from what others are doing, you should formulate your *own* plan of action. Don't let others determine your plan. Develop one that is best suited to your situation.

Consider the following trends and see if they reflect your own sense of what is happening in your church and community.

1. Denominations are not important when people are choosing a church.
2. The term "home church" has no relevance.
3. Cell churches are changing.
4. People are involved in the church without attending every Sunday and often without joining.
5. High spirituality and low organized religion are characteristics of church congregations reaching postmodern young adults.
6. Worship service days and times vary.
7. Worship structures are changing.
8. Worship styles are changing.
9. Evangelism takes place in both seeker-sensitive and more blatant forms.
10. Revival comes in different forms.
11. The church develops, rather than trains, leaders.
12. Education for the church is moving from teaching to learning.

13. Leadership teams replace individual leaders.
14. Decisions are made by consensus rather than by a vote.
15. Church governments are changing.
16. The church is being forced to rethink sexuality.
17. The demand for excellence continues to increase.
18. Church leaders are being held to stricter requirements.
19. Immigrants seek a vision and a purpose-driven church.
20. Discipline in the church is expected and implemented.
21. Relevancy is demanded.
22. Immigrants stress effectiveness and measurable benchmarks in the church.
23. Family time is a premium consideration.
24. Pastoral care has higher and more complex demands.
25. "Future churches" recognize and respond to single-parent homes.
26. The number of younger retirees continues to grow.
27. Recovery programs dealing with addiction and abuse, self-help groups, and group discussions of moving from pain to purpose are forming in many churches now reaching the under-thirty crowd.
28. Church hopping is at an all-time high.
29. Technology allows people to worship and connect at their convenience and preference.

In light of these and other trends, you might see glimpses into ways a church can maximize its potential and opportunity.

Maximize potential and opportunity.

Three ideas adapted from Tom Bandy's material [1] can help a church make the most of its assets:

1. Make sure the leader and the teams are anchored in a "heartburst" and not a task. This is passion, yes, but specifically passion for a people or a microculture and not a program or a project. Celebrate the heartburst, but shape your public relations around the people being blessed and not a project being accomplished.
2. Equip teams with many possibilities and few limitations. Provide all the resources possible for those dreaming new ways to reach people. Don't allow limited resources to control ideation. Dreaming big doesn't mean lack of accountability. Publicly model how you use those as a vehicle for accountability. This will build more trust.
3. Continue to invest heavily in skills development, and market stories of praise or success like crazy.

Moving forward takes intentionality, effort, skills, and commitment. The challenge for many is to manage the present (satisfying existing needs) while you birth the future.

Manage the present while birthing the future.

A final tip for transforming a congregation is developing the skills for birthing the new while managing the present. This is a challenge for leaders and organizations; however, unless we reinvent the methods and reinvest in the unchanging message, Christianity becomes only a generation away from extinction.

These are some tips for leaders as they accept the challenge to transform.

Change your approach for outreach.

If going out on Monday night to visit your Sunday guests works for you, that's great. Unfortunately, many churches today don't have enough guests on Sunday to visit on Monday. Often, if they have the guests, they don't have enough members to make the visits. Why? They have made those visits before and found no one at home, people hiding behind the door because they weren't prepared for guests, or perhaps folks irritated that their evening has been interrupted by a social call they weren't prepared for.

So, if that type visitation isn't working for you, keep these ideas in mind for outreach in a secular age. Those under thirty prefer a more relational, less confrontational approach. They'd love a visit if it's planned in advance and focuses on their needs and interests. They do not welcome a lecture about what they ought to be doing or a litany of what the church has to offer them, especially when the visitor recites these without knowing what the ones they visit want and need. Focus on the person rather than the program—the slot where you think he or she should fit in.

Look for ways to connect outside the church. Plan to meet for breakfast or lunch. Invite them to a church event (other than a worship service or Bible study) that might interest them—a church concert or a ball game, or ask them to help with an international ministry.

Watch your language! Unchurched adults rarely understand the language of Zion. That doesn't just mean *sanctification, justification*, and *premillennialism*. It may also mean *Sunday school, born again, saved*, and *hymn*. (I offer practical guidance for visitation in a postmodern world and for this challenge with language in *Spiritual Leadership in a Secular Age*.)

Now, while it is important to do your research and be aware of the new trends outside your church, it is equally important to be aware of what is going on inside your own church and the makeup of your leadership team. Where is your team's passion? What fuels the team's excitement and dedication? What makes a good team? You can't have all leaders or all followers. That would not be productive. An exceptional team needs all work styles. What are your church leaders' strengths and weaknesses? Who has talent at birthing the new? Who has a passion for mission? for maintenance? All are extremely important and needed.

Think of your church leaders as "hunters," "nurturers, and gatherers," and/or "stallions." These are critical groups to identify and empower while forming your transforming strategies. This is not to be misunderstood that men are always hunters and women are always gatherers. Both sexes easily fall into all the categories below.

Hunters are true pioneers that embrace change. Birthing the new for all age groups is their mission. Hunters are eager to explore the unknown and search for new programs and opportunities. As a leadership team, you will need to define your new finds. What are you looking for? What new finds are needed to move you toward your goals? The hunters are willing to take some risks and "rock the boat" a bit.

You need to know your hunters. Will they assist or sabotage your goals? What are their motives? For example, if a hunter in your church wants to start a recovery group concerning drug addiction but that unnerves everyone else, then much more dialogue and communication are needed to decide how best to move forward. Also, if another hunter suggests that Wednesday night Bible study is no longer effective, but others want to keep it, then that issue needs to be discussed. Or, better yet, perhaps this is a perfect example of both programs needing to be done to create parallel structures that involve multiple generations.

Hunters demonstrate one type of leadership work style. Another style is nurturers and gatherers who take care of the new finds from the hunters. Nurturers and gatherers tend to be more soft spoken at times and can be better listeners. This is not always true, but certainly can be the case. They enjoy the fine-tuning and the maintenance of programs/events and getting into all the details. What is working well that you want to keep?

Some staff may be good workers; however, they still need mentoring from the more experienced members. These are your stallions. Stallions are important because they are your future. Your seasoned leaders mentor as you groom your leaders and workers of tomorrow. Communication and understanding are key here. How do you properly pair your students with mentors?

Are you beginning to see the breakdown now of work style and passion?

Using the chart on the next page, work to identify all the hunters, gatherers and nurturers, and stallions that you are aware of in your classes, choirs, congregation, etc. Write their names in the appropriate category. Then look for the common threads of shared passions and interests that can be explored in and outside your church.

Create parallel structures.

If I had to declare a secret of reaching people under thirty and keeping people over sixty, this is it! This is a certain way to keep those over sixty years of age and reach those under thirty years of age. Keep ministries to those over sixty while you begin to create nonthreatening, comfortable entry points for persons under thirty in the appropriate groupings for your community. A nonthreatening, comfortable entry point is modeled after the "come and see" phase of Jesus' disciple-making. This is a place that is comfortable for them, not for you as a church person.

Leader's Function	People under 30	People 30 to 60	People over 60
HUNTERS Take charge, birth the new; can be excellent public speakers; hunting for new programs, new partnerships, new alliances; thinking outside the box to serve as a strategic catalyst for change and renewal			
NURTURER/GATHERERS Can be more soft-spoken, caretaker persona; often better listeners; good at conflict resolution; often less stubborn—peacekeeper and peacemaker with a backbone			
STALLIONS Leaders in training, can be hunters or nurturers and gatherers, eager to learn, pliable, open to being molded and groomed into seasoned leaders; loaded with potential, gold in the making; can be reckless at times, but these risk takers are important for your future			

Meet them where they are. You will likely find church leaders in your over-sixty group who will share this dream and give some of their time and energy to helping you birth the new while they continue in the existing organization. To accomplish this shared dream effectively, you will need to form a number of lay-led ministry teams to birth the new. *Make clear that everyone is not expected to participate in both structures. The goal is not to add more ministries for the same faithful people. The goal is to begin ministries to attract those under thirty, especially those outside the church.* Handing off tasks to lay-led teams builds ownership, empowers new leaders, and nurtures creativity. (I discuss this in greater detail in *Reframing Spiritual Formation: Discipleship in an Unchurched Culture*.)

Potential Ministries

Many of the ministries you'll consider will target those under thirty; some will focus on those over sixty. But many of the ministries can involve both groups. Watch for ministries that are intergenerational, cross age spans, or involve those over sixty in roles that minister, mentor, or model an example for those under thirty. A great example of this is marriage mentors, in which those who have stable, healthy marriages mentor newlyweds from the younger generation. Another piece of this might be "adopt a grandparent," in which young families who do not have local parents/grandparents might adopt a grandparent for their children. May also make multicultural connections also for mentoring and adopting.

Include ministry to single parents.

Census figures indicate that this is a fast-growing group in most communities, and most would be delighted to have an "adopted grandparent" or mentor. Check out these websites for ideas: www.fatherhood.org and www.focusonthefamily.com.

Plan for ministry for those who are divorced.

Divorce recovery is a significant ministry for most communities. It touches all age groups and can be a great area for persons in stable marriages and those who are retired to develop mentoring relationships and be of service. For more information, go to www.divorcerecovery.org.

Minister to adults in dual-career marriages.

Both the husband and the wife are employed outside the home in most marriages today. Acknowledging their needs—such as stress management, family finances, and personal organizational skills—and planning ministries for them will attract these families to your church.

Look for opportunities to plan ministry that addresses faith and work issues.

This represents a growing concern and movement across the country. Many adults both over and under thirty have a desire for their faith to intersect with their daily lives. For ideas to support this ministry, see my *The Gathered and Scattered Church*, www.faith-at-work.net, and www.marketplaceministries.com.

Build Bible study or discipleship groups around common interests rather than age groups or life stages.

Sociologists are now telling us that a new "family" is emerging in our culture. They associate it with "urban tribes," groups of people who may or may not be biologically connected, who find a common affinity and build their relationships around that commonness. They provide support and companionship for one another much like the traditional family unit.

Common interests often bond people in the church more quickly than being at the same life stage. This is one reason recreation is often a way to get people into the church. Examples of interest groups include motorcycle riders, campers, ball teams, parents who have experienced the death of a child, women business owners, newcomers to the community, or any other interest group in the church. Bridges can be built with common interests. The group ministers to one another and fellowships with one another. Often they are doing this already. Adding appropriate Bible study deepens their bonds. This is also another way to cross age barriers.

Many movie themes address spiritual formation. For example, *Selma, Unbroken, Into the Woods, The Help, Peaceful Warrior,* and *Akeelah and the Bee* are excellent examples that made it to the big screen. These movies can serve as a platform for discussion groups and ongoing dialogue. For additional guidelines for this type of movie dialogue group, contact www.transformingsolutions.org for a free guide sheet of coaching questions. Or use one of the volumes in the Chalice Press Popular Insights series as a starting point for discussion of modern themes and issues.

Build on your strengths rather than your weaknesses.

Most churches can't do everything well. Discern what God has called you and your members to do, and discover how he has gifted you. He never calls unless he has first gifted you to fulfill his calling. Remember that God also calls us to things larger than we are, so we have to depend on God and the miraculous divine power.

Find and follow your focus.

Once you discover God's calling and gifting, follow it. Delete activities, budget items, and leadership positions that do not directly help you in accomplishing your mission. Rethink ongoing activities such as Bible study in light of your new mission focus and retool ongoing activities as needed.

Retool your staffing and leadership core.

As they keep in mind the shifting in culture and demographics, many churches are rethinking their staff positions and organization. For instance, some churches and communities have many Baby Boomers who are readying themselves for early retirement. To meet their needs and also to multiply the church's ministry and expand its leadership base, a church might begin one or more groups for people in midlife such as Halftime groups (www.halftime.org). Or a church in a community with lots of families with young children may choose to redirect funds from student ministry to childhood and family ministry, knowing that they will later expand the ministry to students as children reach that age.

Reinvent the church's organization.

Most churches' organizational structure hasn't changed significantly in the last fifty years. To focus and target your ministry on specific people groups, organization and budgeting must shift. What type of organization is needed now to address the needs of those over sixty as well as those under thirty? What's working now? What's not working that needs to be stopped so you can reallocate time, energy, money, and other resources?

Consider decentralizing your church.

This is a big challenge for most who have understood and valued a church that has always met at one place at the same time. In our culture we may need a decentralized approach, as was true in the Acts of the Apostles in the early days of establishing the New Testament church.

Empower lay leadership teams.

Ministry teams have been mentioned several times in this chapter. Ministry teams involve the people in the pew. These believers in Christ are the real ministers and always have been. All believers are called and gifted. Now the institution must trust the Holy Spirit to guide them to birth the new. Traditional church culture sends everything through committees for approval. Empowering lay teams means cutting through the red tape and trusting lay-led ministry teams to preserve the core values of the church and to find new directions without having to have everything approved.

Move from institutional care to valuing personal call.

Traditional church culture values buildings and programs. Now the church must have both buildings and structures that empower the called and gifted. Instead of filling slots on a program-based chart, build your structure on the needs of those in your church as well as those you seek to reach and find places for people to use the gifts God has given them to serve your church.

Create partnerships and alliances with the community.

Working alongside or in cooperation with local service agencies can help the church in two ways:

1. through such alliances your leaders can find fulfilling ways to minister to others

2. people in your church who may need the help from the community agencies or services can find it.

Work with schools, nursing homes, funeral homes, counselors, social service agencies, county agents, and higher education institutions. Partner with churches from other denominations. Maybe you could create a partnership and add a staff position for several churches that would reach a new people group.

Volunteer work is an excellent way to give the younger generation hands-on experience and to build community and connection. The younger generation will be much more interested in giving their time and feeling involved. They want to be included in making a difference and experiencing its effect. They are much happier giving time and energy to an actual need than simply donating money, walking away, and not really knowing how a donation was really used.

Help the congregation understand the cultural shifts.

Educate your congregation about generational differences, postmodernism, and the cultural and ethnic diversity in your community. Do research to see which groups of people are underserved by churches. This is a critical step and cannot be ignored or minimized.

Create networks that foster intergenerational and lifelong learning.

Differences in generations and cultures separate people. Find ways to build bridges in your church among adults, children, and youth of the church and the community. You will enrich the life of the church as well as the lives of the individuals involved.

Allow time for the transition to take place.

Don't try to do everything at once. Don't expect the church size to double overnight. Don't expect everyone to like everything you're doing. Realize that some people over sixty will leave no matter how hard you work to include them.

Pray constantly. Plan well. Move at a steady pace. Work hard. Expect great things from God.

Love the legitimizers.

Everyone who has power in the church is not necessarily the most visible, the one with the most jobs, the one who gives the most money, or the one who talks the most—though all of those are important and you would do well to get them on board well in advance of any significant changes you make. Sometimes a senior adult woman whose stalwart faithfulness has shaped the culture of the church yields more influence than all the speeches the pastor and deacon chairman can make.

Be careful how you enlist the support of these senior members. Ask their advice. Love them. Don't patronize or try to manipulate them. Be honest. Show them the need, the biblical basis, the desirability—the mandate—for the church to be on mission; and you'll win their support.

Solicit support both publicly and privately. Remember the types of experiences that those over sixty value—public prayer services, commissioning of groups to lead in new approaches, and recognition for leadership and work done.

Affirm all generations and cultures/ethnicities in the process.

Remember that Boomers and Millennials are "Me" generations. They won't like an all-out effort to reach those under thirty without losing those over sixty if they feel their generation is being ignored. Affirm their leadership. Remember to use the tools they like, such as business skills of research and marketing. Let them know the church needs them to take leadership roles in reaching a new generation.

And don't forget the Busters who are already in the church. They like stories. Enlist them to test new ideas. Tell stories of changed lives. Keep the process relational.

Make transformation, not change, the goal.

Change is difficult for many people. Just saying the word *change* may invite opposition. The goal should be finding solutions and trying new methods and approaches so that, with Paul, you might say:

> For though I am free with respect to all, I have made myself a slave to all, so that I might win more of them. To the Jews I became as a Jew, in order to win Jews. To those under the law I became as one under the law (though I myself am not under the law) so that I might win those under the law. To those outside the law I became as one outside the law (though I am not free from God's law but am under Christ's law) so that I might win those outside the law. To the weak I became weak, so that I might win the weak. I have become all things to all people, that I might by all means save some. I do it all for the sake of the gospel, so that I may share in its blessings. (1 Cor. 9:19–23)

10

Win-Win for Your
Forty- or Fifty-Somethings?

Invariably, when leading seminars around the focus of this book, several people ask "What about the forty or fifty crowd?" I'm in that crowd, and Cornell (a contributor to this book) is fast approaching that crowd, so we are concerned too. Cornell will be experiencing his thirties and forties as a postmodern thinker and bridge-builder. We are convinced that those in this age group are important and critical for creating, modeling, and serving as catalysts for reaching people under thirty while keeping people over sixty. Granted, some people in their forties and fifties are postmodern in values and thinking patterns and behaviors. There are also persons in this age group who more resemble persons and values of those who are modern in their values and behaviors. Again, we are talking more in generalities when we talk of age, for the values of postmodernism and modernism can be found in persons of any age. Those of us in this age group (forties to fifties) are transitional leaders in a transitional culture in a transitioning age for the church. We can make it or break it by our attitudes, behaviors, and engagement or apathy. So how do we plug in?

Modeling

Every generation and culture learns much by the modeling of those around them—in families, workplaces, communities, and churches. The forties and fifties crowd are in the prime of their careers, families, finances, and influence. How will you maximize your influence to share your faith with the next generation of leaders and Christians?

Consider being a role model of faith formation in your families, among your children and grandchildren. Spend time in prayer with them. Share your faith journey—both your successes and your struggles. Be open and honest. Look for God at work in your midst and celebrate that with others.

Catalysts

Serving as catalysts for change, transition, and transformation probably best summarizes the impact the forties-fifties crowd can have on the church and faith life in America. The dreams I see make me what I am. This adage calls us to the future. What are your dreams for bridging the generation and diversity gaps in your family, community, workplace, and church? What are your dreams of valuing the diversity of those around you and learning from them?

How can the forties-fifties crowd serve as catalysts for reaching people under thirty while keeping people over sixty? Consider:

- Investing your time, energy, and financial resources in productive efforts discussed in this book.
- Being intentional about creating opportunities for dialogue between generations and cultures in your family, through Bible study groups, in the community, and at the workplace.
- Being intentional about creating multigenerational, multicultural missional experiences in which you work together and debrief together about how you experienced God at work in your lives.
- Serving in places of leadership, within your areas of expertise and calling, that will help set the pace of change and take leaders and organization to the next level.

A special note here regarding the role of this age group in the second generation of various ethnic or international groups. What a great responsibility and opportunity the second-generation leaders have in being church for the younger and the older generations. Their value to the older generation is a strength to build on. Their value as parents of bilingual, multicultural children helps them to see the world of those over sixty *and* the world of the generation under thirty. Leading them, modeling for them, being with them, and guiding them as bridge-builders is a great opportunity for building a church for all generations and cultures.

Thought Leaders/Innovators

Serving as a thought leader and innovator is key and is suited for the forties-fifties crowd. Churches need innovators and thought leaders to help introduce and manage the changes we are discussing in this book. A church I'm coaching in Atlanta is considering creating a ministry to attract and provide launch pads for entrepreneurs who want to make a difference. What a great idea for outreach and deepening impact!

Are you a hunter, gatherer, or stallion? Pastors and staff members need friends and support persons during the days of change and transition—leaders they can dialogue with, trust, empower, and unleash for ministry in the church and the world.

Many persons in their fifties are retiring early with great financial resources, knowledge, expertise, and discretionary time. Use these gifts to help move your church forward, to awaken the church in the community and the world. I predict that as the Boomers retire and move into the role of current seniors, the church and culture will experience another seismic shift. The shifts can be positive and transformational, or the shifts can be detrimental and discouraging. The tipping point is determined by the church's plan and strategy to engage and mobilize retiring Boomers in meaningful and formative ways. If churches ignore or simply try to replicate what is now the "senior adult ministries" model, Boomers will join Millennials in moving away from the church into meaningful nonprofit organizations to exercise their passions. As a retiring Boomer, volunteer your time in faith-based organizations and in the workplace. Maybe you will be a volunteer chaplain for the police department; maybe you will give your time as a volunteer at hospitals or in hospice programs or in boys/girls clubs. The list is endless. Move your life from success to significance by the investments you make and the leaders and shifts you birth. Creating incubators for faith-based entrepreneurs might just be the seedbed for attracting and mobilizing early retirees in 21st-century churches.

Bridge-Builders between Generations

Another great opportunity for the forties-fifties crowd is to be a bridge-builder between the generations and the various philosophies of life and church. Persons in this age group know values of persons under thirty because they have children, grandchildren, or siblings in that age group. They are also in the stage of honoring their parents and grandparents, and some are beginning the challenges of caring for their aging parents/grandparents. This crowd has children and grandchildren in some instances who have a different learning style, value system, and personal preference and learning style when it comes to church.

Relational and Organizational Capital and Skills Investment

What a great opportunity this group has to be the church in the world and not just within the walls of the institutional church. This group is heavily engaged in the workplace, in leisure, and in making decisions about how they invest their relational capital. "Whom do they relate to and with?" and "Why?" are key questions that guide many values and decisions of this age group. Being intentional about this, within the confines of their beliefs about how and where to do church and be church surface regularly and call us to a deeper faithfulness than many have ever known or tried. Building intentional relationships with others that model authenticity, love, appreciation, and encouragement and that give verbal and nonverbal affirmations of one's faith life are critical contributions that move the church forward and engage persons from various generations.

Being open to change and embracing the unknown takes great courage and surrender. What is God calling you to surrender to move your church forward in kingdom business? What are you being called to let go of in order to embrace something new? Lessons in courage and surrender are tough at best.

COACHING QUESTIONS

- So what are your takeaways from this chapter?
- What insights have you had about people in their forties and fifties that you are willing to act on now?
- Who can help you move forward in being church for all generations?

11

Celebrating Church for a Diverse World

God has done and is doing some marvelous things in churches reaching folks the diversity of population under thirty and keeping people over sixty. We have finally decided to believe what we've been taught to say all our lives: the building is not the church; we are church to and for one another. The church is looking to the future instead of the past, and church leaders over sixty are paving the way.

You may feel that what you are doing is so radically different that it is a step of faith unlike any you have ever taken before. You may feel like Peter walking on water and hoping you don't lose your courage and begin to sink. Keep your eyes on Jesus. Continue to listen to what God is saying to you. Acknowledge your fear, at least to yourself, and ask God to give you the courage for the next step. Remember that God called Abraham to leave home without telling him his destination, and Abraham, in faith, obeyed. Enlist one or two trusted peers outside your church to give you support and to whom you can be accountable. Enlisting a Christian coach to walk alongside you and your leaders during this transition offers a confidential, trustworthy relationship to help you face learning curves with courage, confidence, and hope.[1]

An online article discusses the national trend of struggling churches:

The best time to plan perennials is in the fall; plants put energy into their roots during the cold months of winter so that they can gather nutrients to blossom and yet fruit again. Perhaps a similar phenomenon is happening in churches as well.

"Maybe the church is not going to be so much a building as it will be a group of people," said Rev. Sam Hobson. "And that was the early church, too. What we've done to the church is we've institutionalized it, and part of that came about through the whole adoption of the Roman Empire of Christianity—and it was forced on people to be the religion of the stat.... and even the Reformation was followed by its own institutionalization."[2]

Give ministries time to work. If they are not working at all, go in a new direction. You'll learn from every ministry you try. Remember that these missteps are in no way failures to minister to under thirty; they are just efforts in continuing to look for the church's next opportunity and reallocating resources to meet a new need. That's one of the benefits of lay-led ministry teams. They are not like the old list of church committees that last forever with positions that must be filled every year. Lay-led ministry teams may be permanent, but they are more likely set up to meet a particular need. When the need is met, the ministry team ceases to function. Those involved move on to a new mission.

Ultimately this whole book, this entire idea of keeping adults over sixty while reaching those under thirty, is a matter of evangelism. It's finding those who need Jesus Christ in the world and sharing the Good News with them. It's connecting with their needs and making and growing disciples.

Aaron LaFalce, worship leader at Seacoast in Asheville, North Carolina, reflects, "Christianity is at its strongest when it's not on top as far as handing out laws and handing out have-tos, because that's not the way the faith started to begin with. It wasn't something that was legislated. People were held captive by the love that Jesus had."[3]

The church is to be in the world redeeming the world to Christ; it just may not look like it has in the past. God has blessed this age with a deep spiritual thirst and desire to be involved in hands-on missions. What a gift! However, in many situations traditional churches, structures, and traditions are not capturing and channeling this thirst among the younger generation. As the church changes, you may see evidence like the following paradigm shifts Eric Swanson, a leadership community director, has listed.[4] All are worth celebrating!

FROM	TO
Building walls	Building bridges
Measuring attendance	Measuring impact
Encouraging the saints to attend the service	Equipping the saints for the works of service
"Serve us"	Service
Duplication of human services and ministries	Partnering with existing services and ministries
Fellowship	Functional unity
Condemning the city	Blessing the city and praying for it
Being a minister in a congregation	Being a minister in a parish
Anecdote and speculation	Valid information
Teacher	Learner

Certainly, as some will declare, it's a both/and, not an either/or, situation for the church. While this is certainly true about Swanson's research, the reality and challenge for the church of the twenty-first century is the amount of our time, energy, money, personnel, and focus balanced between the two columns. What we say and believe is not always what we actually practice. What about you? Where are the disconnects? What do you need to work on now to bring greater consistency between your talk and your walk? Learning to live a balanced and God-directed life is a challenge at best. Such a challenge is real whether you are modern or postmodern, churched or unchurched. Learning to discover and live into your life calling and vision is a concept we can use to connect with all generations.

Discerning God's Will—Learning to Live into Your Destiny

God created us for a specific purpose—to fellowship with him and to live into our destiny. Our destiny is that for which God created us—finding our mission and purpose in life that brings meaning, a sense of belonging and finding our place. God never calls a person to live outside of that person's calling and gifting. God never calls without also equipping (Eph. 4; 1 Pet. 2:8–10). How do we learn to live into our destiny and God's perfect plan for our lives and churches? Let me share some tips that have been working for me and on me as I stretch to fulfill God's perfect plan for my life. My hope is that these new learnings for me might be transforming solutions for you too.

- Turn prayer time more into listening than talking or asking.
- Follow your heart and passion, not the expectations created by others.
- Trust that with every vision God has a provision.
- Move into events, activities, and relationships that provide energy rather than drain energy.
- If God doesn't provide for something, know that God is likely not interested in it. In other words, don't spend all your time pushing on doors that God has locked; walk through the doors God has ajar.
- There are places in life where we move forward at a rapid pace, when things just seem to come together. At this time understand we need to rest on the step, but the step is not meant to be the destination. Get off the step, and hire a life coach (www.TransformingSolutions.org)!
- God promises to provide all our *needs*, not all our *wants*. God's provisions are often there to help us with other issues.
- It's always dangerous and risky to follow a dream. When Moses sent the spies to scout out the land, to move into their destiny, ten of the twelve were intimidated by what they saw and heard, and claimed that giants were in the land. Giants will always be in front of our dreams.
- We are called to learn to use what we have, not what we don't have.
- It's not what we have in us but what we can get out of us that God has planted in us; that is the key to living into our destiny.
- God calls us to work out our own salvation and dream.

T. D. Jakes makes an analogy between our destiny, calling, and gifting with the diamond mines in Africa—potentially the richest continent on earth. But the diamonds have to be mined. Many believers and churches are like this. What's in your "diamond mine"? How can you move and live into your destiny? What will it take for you and your congregation to discover the "diamonds" God has planted within you? Maybe you can explore the difference between the form and the function of the church.

Cornell is a great illustration of this. I've had the joy of watching the gold and diamonds within him come forth as he has peeled away layers of hurt, pain, bad decisions, and addictions to discover hope, healing, health, faith, and purpose. Truly Cornell, along with many Millennials, are "gold in the making." Just because they cannot or will not find their place in traditional churches does not mean they do not have faith or that they are not "gold in the making." It just means that God is working on them in different ways, through different means and by methods that are often unfamiliar to those of us in an older church culture. While this may be a disappointment for some church culture people, I'm sure it is not a disappointment to God. After all, I think God is more concerned about life and heart transformation than church participation. Sometimes our man-made forms and traditions prevent us from seeing the gold in others or helping their gold to come forth. Think about it. Jesus used some nontraditional means in his ministry. He often went against the grain of the religious establishment to reach the people of his day who were not finding their place in the synagogue, but who were thirsty for wholeness.

The Form and Function of a Church

Form and function are key concepts. The function of the church is unchanging; it is the Great Commission and the Great Commandment. The form is the place we need new organization and reflection. Forms are man-made, functions are God-made.

The writings of Gene Getz have helped me clarify Scripture at this point. Gene explains, "Wherever you have people, you have function. And wherever you have function you have form. Put another way, you cannot have 'organism' without 'organization.'"[5] He further illustrates that the New Testament is more concerned about the function of the church than the forms of the church. In Hebrews 10:25 the church is given a directive and function—simply "to meet together." The passage does not specify when or how often or where they are to meet. Neither does it suggest a specific order of service.

When form and structure are mentioned in Scripture, it is partially described and varies from one New Testament setting to another. Acts 5:42a suggests that the apostles did teach and preach from house to house, but they also went to teach "in the temple." Seems to me that much of the stress and disease found in many churches is because the mission has become dictated more by members than by God, and members often fight to preserve forms/structures/programs rather than to preserve God's mandates and missions for his church. Somewhere we've felt that church was created for believers rather than as a mission point for reaching nonbelievers. If we were doing our jobs according to God's plan, we wouldn't have more than 85 to 90 percent of our churches plateaued or declining in attendance during a population boom, and the unchurched population in America would not have increased 92 percent between 1991 and 2004.[6] Neither would Christianity's focus and revival be shifting from North America to Third World countries.

COACHING QUESTIONS

- How do you respond to this?
- Where does most of your time and energy go—form or function preservation?
- What is valued more by the leadership core of your church—preserving the forms or fulfilling the Great Commission and Great Commandment?

I realize these are tough realities to swallow. I also realize that some will debate them, and that is their privilege. I also realize and deeply feel that many of us will realize we have been part of the problem rather than part of the solution. I want to leave a legacy of being part of the solution. What about you?

Transforming Solutions: Setting New and Clear Standards for Leaders

The church not only has a membership and financial crisis but we have an increasingly threatening leadership deficit. An organization never moves beyond its leadership. Leaders rarely grow forward without clear guidelines, goals, vision, values, and accountability. Rarely can you change a church structure until you first change the values, vision, and investment of leadership. What might this look like? Consider expecting and enlisting key leaders to:

- *Be present.* Attendance, involvement, and consistency of leadership are critical. More of what we learn is caught by being around our leaders and being mentored by leaders than words taught in classes. Leaders need to commit to faith attendance at functions where core values are being lifted up and communicated. Leaders should be present unless providentially hindered, and accountable when absent.
- *Be prepared.* Leaders must be trained and mentored, so they can mentor others as part of their commitment to leadership. They should multiply themselves through at least two other people each year. Leaders should be expected to participate in at least one major training event per year, and that training should be funded by the church.
- *Be disciple-makers.* Leaders need to be disciples of Christ and intentional disciple-makers with others who are ready to learn, grow, and move into leadership. This is where core values and vision of the new are birthed, sustained, and developed. Intentional disciple-making is essential yet rarely practiced. Every thriving church I know of has leaders who are committed

to being present, prepared, and making disciples. Every plateaued, dying church I know avoids these standards.

- *Be engaged in spiritual life disciplines.* Prayer, fasting, a personal ministry, having a strong personal witness, and Bible study are essential lifelines for leaders. Leaders should be asked regularly to share what God is doing in these dimensions of their life.
- *Be accountable to other capable, trusted, and mature spiritual leaders for carrying out their function in the body of Christ.* When leaders begin to relax on these essentials, lay leaders need to hold them accountable in love, helping them to move forward rather than become stuck in complacency. Somehow we have to find ways to strengthen the body of Christ through loving and invited accountability. Biblical accountability is invited, not imposed. Leaders must see the value of accountability in their lives and ministry.

What are the standards for your leaders? What are your standards for being a leader? What will it take for you to be a better leader?

The call of God for his church is to be on mission; to be salt, light, and leaven and to be faithful and fruitful. Unfortunately, in the decades gone by, many Christians and churches were identified more by their doing than by their being. The postmodern world is calling us to *be. Moving a church forward and reaching people under thirty and keeping people over sixty is about relationships, values clarification, renewal of commitment to Christ, and moving the church forward, as well as the power of connection.* To make this shift happen, powerful connection that resides in relationships is essential.

The Power of Connection

Heartfelt connection generates great power, even between different generations, cultures, and ethnicities! Connection clarifies calling, fuels dreams, empowers ministry, and moves one toward fulfilling God's unique mission for each person in the heartfelt connection. The biblical story of Mary and Elizabeth illustrates this principle so clearly.

> In the days of King Herod of Judea, there was a priest named Zechariah, who belonged to the priestly order of Abijah. His wife was a descendant of Aaron, and her name was Elizabeth. Both of them were righteous before God, living blamelessly according to all the commandments and regulations of the Lord. But they had no children, because Elizabeth was barren, and both were getting on in years....
>
> After those day.... Elizabeth conceived, and for five months she remained in seclusion. She said, "This is what the Lord has done for me when he looked favorable on me and took away the disgrace I have endured among my people."
>
> In the sixth month the angel Gabriel was sent by God to a town in Galilee called Nazareth, to a virgin engaged to a man whose name was Joseph, of the house of David. The virgin's name was Mary. And he

came to her and said, "Greetings favored one! The Lord is with you…
And now, your relative Elizabeth in her old age has also conceived a
son; and this is the sixth month for her who was said to be barren. For
nothing will be impossible with God."…

In those days Mary set out and went with haste to a Judean town
in the hill country, where she entered the house of Zechariah and
greeted Elizabeth. When Elizabeth heard Mary's greeting, the child
leaped in her womb. And Elizabeth was filled with the Holy Spirit and
exclaimed with a loud cry, "Blessed are you among women, and blessed
is the fruit of your womb. And why has this happened to me, that the
mother of my Lord comes to me? For as soon as I heard the sound of
your greeting, the child in my womb leaped for joy. And blessed is she
who believed that there would be a fulfillment of what was spoken to
her by the Lord."…

And Mary remained with her about three months and then
returned to her home.

Now the time came for Elizabeth to give birth, and she bore a son.
Her neighbors and relatives heard that the Lord had shown his great
mercy to her, and they rejoiced with her. (Luke 1:5–8, 24–28, 36–37,
39–45, 56–58)

We are not told much about Elizabeth's pregnancy, but we can speculate.
The story seems to imply that she had felt no movement in her womb prior to
her encounter with Mary (her overwhelming excitement at feeling the baby
"leap" in her womb at the arrival of Mary). Elizabeth may have been wondering
if she would have a stillbirth. No movement creates some anxiety for mothers.
No movement within does not always mean death, but often a craving for
connection. Think of this: she had been barren for years, and now she was
pregnant. Wow! Imagine that.

Mary, in her youth and anxiety at the prospect of being a young mother,
comes to visit Elizabeth. The connection between them was powerful. Their
hearts, souls, and callings connected and gave momentum to that which they
were birthing. That which God had planted within them and that they were
carrying was nourished by their connection with each other! I suspect that all
of a sudden things became very clear to these new mothers. I think they saw
into the future—theirs and their children's future. I think their hearts connected
around unanswered questions they were living with, fears about their futures.
(After all, neither of them was supposed to be birthing anything by the average
standard/expectations.) I also think the embarrassment and shame each had
been living with for some time began to disappear because they knew in their
hearts that God was up to something with and through them! God gave divine
blessing and assurance, and their joy was so great that they broke out in song.
Mary's Magnificat is perhaps the most significant song in the New Testament
(Lk. 1:46–55).

When Mary and Elizabeth came together, sparks began to fly in each of their lives and spirits. They realized they were both pregnant with destiny! The future was being birthed in and through them!

Interestingly, God chose to use these two women from two generations, from two walks of life, with two different family structures, with two different visions for their babies' futures. Together they could share their excitement with someone else who shared their passion, calling, and focus in life. It would be reasonable to conclude, then, that if our baby is not leaping within us (that which God is birthing in and through us), then we might be around the wrong people! Hang out with people who cause your dream to jump inside you, to grow, to be nourished! Do not hang around with people who drain your dream or passion. Commit to opening the door only to persons who cause your baby to leap!

COACHING QUESTIONS

- What is God birthing in and through you?
- Who are the people that cause your baby to leap within you?
- Where are the places that fuel your dreams?
- Who are those in other generations that fuel your dreams and cause your baby to leap?
- How can you learn from those others and vice versa?
- What is needed to make this happen now?

Reaching People under 30 While Keeping People over 60: Creating Community across Generations is about building bridges, not barriers, between the various generations, cultures, ethnic groups and between Millennials and church culture as we learn to be faithful to the call of God on our lives. Postmoderns and Millennials seek authenticity, hope, healing, community, redemption, and reconciliation through the relationships they build, through the experiences they engage in individually and with others. Postmoderns and Millennials treasure the rituals and traditions they create and embrace to mark landmarks in their faith journey and life experiences. This is not unlike persons from the modern and church culture, however occasionally distinct and different. Every generation and culture creates their own faith steps and road maps to faith and fulfillment. Moving toward God and a faith community is part of life for moderns and postmoderns. Now that we have five or more generations living at the same time, sometimes in the same family, we are faced with learning to value and share our differences while building on our similarities in the journey of faith and life.

What does it mean to be church in a postmodern world? What does it mean to be true and honest to one's calling and values while at the same time living in and being church amid generational, political, denominational, and spiritual diversity? Such is the challenge of today's church. Such is the scope of this book. We hope that you find some new hope and practical handles for building bridges that nurture the faith of all in your family, congregation, and community. God moves and leads us through fire, famine, family, Scriptures, traditions, rituals, clouds, etc. Let's look to God together and listen carefully, that we not miss the divine presence among us or others.

- What have you read in this book that connects to your church and your situation?
- What insights have you had that you are willing to act on now?
- Who can help you move forward in being church for all generations and cultural groups?

We hope that you've had new insights about your church and the generations of people who make up your church. We pray that you might see the value and strengths of each generation and some pathways of being church for all generations. Remember, you change values before you change structures, and change and transition take time, prayer, patience, and perseverance. Press on.

Conclusion

Coaching Conversation with Paul Anderson

Paul Anderson was a student in a seminary class I was teaching. The focus of the class was "Empowering Laity for Ministry." I loved teaching the class because it was at the heart of my own call and the essence of my local church ministry. Paul captured my attention early. I heard the heart of this young African American pastor for impacting the city, for mobilizing his church, and for making a difference in the world.

After his graduation, we lost touch personally, but I often heard of his ministerial adventures, challenges, and pastoral opportunities. His passions seemed to continue, and his skills continued to be refined.

While he pastored a rapidly growing African American church outside Raleigh, North Carolina, we reconnected, and it was clear to me that his skills and passion were still driving his ministry. Then God called him from that congregation in order to plant a multicultural congregation. I invited Paul to share some of this pastoral journey with us as a way of closing the book on a pastoral, practical, and encouraging note.

Paul pastors Fountain of Raleigh Fellowship in Raleigh, North Carolina.

1. What are the core values of Fountain of Raleigh Fellowship?

MISSION

To be a ministry that fulfills the scripture of Matthew 28:16–20 by sharing the Gospel of Jesus Christ to the local and global communities through all available communication outlets.

PURPOSE and VISION

The purpose of The Fountain of Raleigh is to glorify God through His Son, Jesus Christ, the Head of the Church, empowered by the Holy Spirit. We accomplish this through the biblical means of:

WORSHIP

This is the practice of guiding people to experience the presence of God, which guides to an awareness of His holiness, lordship and grace. We encourage worship through: Personal Worship; Family Worship; Corporate Worship.

This is the practice of guiding people to experience the presence of God, which guides to an awareness of His holiness, lordship, and grace.

We encourage worship through:

Personal Worship
Family Worship
Corporate Worship

Our worship is very diverse. We have a diverse group of persons who have accepted Jesus Christ. They are diverse in that some of them have come from no faith tradition whatsoever and others are genuine converts from Islam and others. We also have people groups who are Native American, African American, Caucasian, and others from Africa, Asia, Native American, Latin America, Central America, Caribbean Islands, Haiti, England, Australia, Netherlands and others. Our size is approximately four hundred persons each Sunday in worship.

Our worship service and style is an integration of traditional Baptist with contemporary flavor of multiple genres of music. We also have a flavor of high church style, with all the functional elements of an ecclesial order of worship with high spiritual emphasis. There is a unique element of interlacing traditional church songs to weave in those over sixty and maintaining the interest of those in much younger age categories. It is our belief that worship is what we were created to do, and this is the way we connect to God and bridge our connection to each other. It is worship that we focus on—glorifying the Father through the Son as the Holy Spirit welcomes us into His presence. It is a sense of forgetting about ourselves that we concentrate on God, thus removing the barriers that hinder worship. It is this context of worship that sees the will and Word of God transforming our lives and perspective of God and each other. It is through this act of worship that we see God's will for true worship as seen in the New Testament Church. It is a group of diverse people coming together for one single purpose: glorifying God Almighty

WITNESSING

This is the presentation of the Good News (Gospel of Jesus Christ) in a clear, uncompromising manner so that our communities, both local and global, may come to a personal acceptance of Jesus Christ as Savior and Lord.

We encourage witnessing through:

Personal Evangelism
Missions (local and global)

We witness through our civic engagement with nonprofits that deliver goods and services to our local county and the world. Since our inception as a congregation, we have donated our time, talent, and treasure to the world in missionary outreach. It is our belief that witness not only occurs with teaching and preaching the Good News of Jesus Christ, but also by His manifested presence in the life of each believer.

We teach personal evangelism to our "ministry partners," the name we use for what is commonly called a church member. It is our belief and core value that each ministry partner should engage in personal discipleship through the sharing of one's faith in Jesus Christ by using scriptural references to demonstrate God's love to all human beings regardless of their past lifestyles or behaviors.

In concert with organizations such as Urban Ministries, Interfaith Food Shuttle, Helen Wright Center for Woman and others, our congregation engages on a monthly basis in delivering food to those who are at or below the poverty level.

We also travel to Africa and down the street to demonstrate "hands on," our feet going where we send financial support. We partner with approximately seven mission organizations to share the gospel with college students, people groups, and targeted populations such as detention centers, correctional institutions both state and federal. We do all of this in harmony with the declaration of Jesus ministry as he quoted Isaiah 61.

EDIFICATION

This is the practice of bringing people up to maturity in Christ. We encourage edification through Prayer, Relationships, Instruction, and Service.

We educate through our worship service, Bible study, small groups, women's ministry, men's, youth adult, youth ministry, children's ministry, senior adult ministry, and hands on engagement of extending "goodwill" to all humanity.

2. What are three key challenges you experience in a multiethnic, multicultural community of faith?

A. Reaching our immediate neighbors has been a major challenge. I am of the opinion that one of the key challenges we have faced is relocating from renting space to purchasing space. The facility that we purchased placed us in a geographical location in the county, and not the city limits; therefore we are bordered by a residential neighborhood. It was our surprise that the neighborhood had reservation about the church being in its backyard. However, there was a church here in the location for several years. We were surprised that the neighbors across the street welcomed us with open arms, (we make our space available for their homeowners association meeting), but the neighborhood adjacent to the property, after two years, has yet to say welcome to the community. I believe they were expecting a congregation that was not African American. Seems their feeling could be "fences make good neighbor.... "

B. The second challenge we face is engaging with other churches in the community. Since our purchase of the property, we have yet to be visited by any of the neighboring churches to say welcome to the community. I am not certain why this the case. Could it be that there is a fear of a perceived competition or whatever? I am puzzled because I attended and graduated from the same seminary or have an affiliation with the same university and religious convention or organization. The church that was in this location had the denominational affiliation.

C. The third challenge that I have observed is that our congregation is very welcoming and accepting of the majority culture; however, our numbers with those guests do not grow at the rate as other ethnic groups. I have observed that most frequently African Americans will integrate into the white congregations, but most whites do not integrate into the predominately African American congregations. The pastors can have comparable training, education, social, and economic equity—and it still does not happen. The teaching ministry of the church can be of equal quality, but it still may not happen.

In light of the most recent political elections within the past ten years, we have a president who is considered as being African American and court cases of white law enforcement officers found innocent of the deaths of African American males. I am not sure of what's going on. I do believe that politics and race is a contributing factor.

The issue of race is real factor. I thought that if I attended the schools and made grades it would be an equalizer; however, skin complexion continues to be an issue as I see it. Our style of worship is Baptist in nature; however, the stereotype of being church in all ways does not apply to us. We are generally in worship for an hour and half. We have advertised using electronic and print media to reach all of the populations.

3. What are three successes of Fountain Fellowship?

We see our first success as being able to defy the odds of surviving and thriving as a congregation for five years. Within our first three years of existence we were able to fund missions and ministry at 10 percent of our income along with the purchase a nearly seventeen-acre campus with a sixteen thousand square foot building. We perceived this as God's approval of this ministry and it's philosophy as we interpret the application of Scripture into our practical method of ministry.

We see our second success as being able to reach people from multiple backgrounds and bring them a place of peace with Jesus Christ as their Savior and Lord. We have been able to bring people to Christ and welcome them into fellowship with them having a sense of calling on their lives. As people unite with our fellowship, they have the opportunity to attend an instructional class series to help them identify with their calling and purpose for living. In this series they receive the opportunity to explore and discover God's purpose for them living on the planet. Thus, they are identifying with the purpose and the will of God for their life.

We see our third success as being the ordination of women into the deacon ministry. This was our very first ordination service for deacons, and we made it an intentional decision to select women and men deacons with equality in functionality. This was a milestone for us. This has not only been a statement of the equality of genders, but it also means our fellowship is growing, and we share in the group of individuals and teach others how to duplicate what they have been taught.

4. What are lessons in leading a multicultural church you would share with others on or facing a similar journey?

A. Please be intentional and transparent with the congregation on what are the targeted groups. Make sure you share the realistic expectations of how difficult and frustrating the work can be. It is frustrating because some people think their current fellowship should be the ones they remember or the one they are used to being a part of.

B. Walk your congregation through a process of uncovering and discovering their biases as they relate to diverse people groups.

C. Also walk them through a process of determining how they perceive leadership shared with men and women within the fellowship.

D. Make certain that your congregation polity is shared with existing and new members. Within that documentation have your plans of leadership succession clearly stated.

E. Have clarity on your process of leadership selection and clearly defined term limits.

5. What have you learned from me that has helped or inspired your leadership/pastoral journey?

I have learned numerous nuggets of truth from you. One thing that stands out the most is your belief of passing the torch to the next runner with the greatest amount of accuracy and preciseness. You were taught Christian education by one of, if not the greatest Christian educators of all times, Dr. Findley Edge. You have always impressed upon me the importance of getting it right the first time! This kind of committed approach of transferring information that is practical and helpful is not just for the moment, but for all times. I believe this transferring of data is not just data transferred, but it data transferred with care and compassion. This is what stands out for me and places you head and shoulders above the rest. You care! The relational aspect of being called to this work by God and endorsed by the people is a divine intersection. Your intersection with God causes you to be able to find common ground with other individuals.

You share knowledge and information in a manner that you desire to be helpful to both the facilitator and receiver of that knowledge/information. This explains how and why God deposits you into the lives of churches, denominations, and individuals that seek you. I am of the opinion that you are God's voice for such a time as this. You are a voice heard in a loving and a compassionate tone that welcomes the listeners to what is being communicated without unnecessary interference. There are many voices in our contemporary world; however, your voice has compassion and clarity.

I have learned the method of not shouting the message, but rather sharing the message as a pastor who sincerely believes what he says. I understand that the message of Jesus Christ must be shared with a coaching team. A team in a relay race has to have someone on the sidelines encouraging the racers to move forward while staying in their lanes. I have a deeper understanding of why it is important to respect boundaries and starting blocks. It is so important for the lead runner to realize he or she has to make a good hand off to the next runner. You have instilled within me the importance of a good hand off. Your contemporary friends Dr. Bruce Powers and Dr. William Clemmons helped me hear you and your instructions so much clearer.

6. What's your dream for this book?

My dream is that this book will be a guide for congregations to fully understand that God's team has more inclusion than exclusion. It is a team of multigenerational, multicultural, and multiracial individuals, each needed in order for us all to win the race.

For our readers, we hope the manuscript brings you hope, healing, and moves you forward in *Reaching People under 30 while Keeping People over 60!* Let us hear from you through our websites.

Notes

Chapter 1: Pastors Burn Out

[1]Edward H. Hammett, *Spiritual Leadership in a Secular Age: Building Bridges instead of Barriers* (St. Louis: Lake Hickory Resources, 2005; repr., St. Louis: TCP Books, 2006); *Making the* Church Work: Converting the Church for the 21st Century, 2nd ed. (Macon, GA.: Smith & Helwys, 2000).

[2]John Bingham, "Churches Are Best Social Melting Pots in Modern Britain," *The Telegraph*, December 7, 2014, accessed January 11, 2015, http://www.telegraph.co.uk/news/religion/11276878/Churches-are-best-social-melting-pots-in-modern-Britain.html.

[3]Carey Nieuwhof, "12 Cultural Trends Church Leaders Can't Ignore (But Might)," June 7, 2013, accessed January 11, 2015, http://careynieuwhof.com/2013/06/12-cultural-trends-church-leaders-cant-ignore-but-might/?utm_content=buffer87665&utm_medium=social&utm_source=facebook.com&utm_campaign=buffer.

[4]I share a proven and practical process of recovery and revitalization in *Recovering Hope for Your Church: Moving Beyond Maintenance & Missional to Incarnational Engagement* (St. Louis: Chalice Press, 2014). This forms the framework for the contextualized congregational coaching we do and for the Congregational Coach Certification program we lead throughout the year and across the country.

[5]I discuss this at length *in Spiritual Leadership in a Secular Age* (St. Louis: Lake Hickory Resources, 2005; repr., St. Louis: Chalice Press, 2006) and two articles on "Alternative Careers for Today's Distressed Clergy" for *Rev! Magazine*, August 2003.

[6]"Eugene Peterson: 'Pastoring Is Not a Very Glamorous Job,'" *Leadership Journal*, October 18, 2013, accessed January 11, 2015, http://www.christianitytoday.com/le/trendwatch/2013/10-18/eugene-peterson-pastoring-is-not-very-glamorous-job.html.

[7]David Olsen, "Clergy Sometimes Neglect their own Needs While Helping Others," *The Press Enterprise*, September 27, 2010, accessed January 11, 2015, http://www.pe.com/articles/clergy-607370-health-time.html.

[8]Travis Loller, "Southern Baptist Convention Membership Declined for Seventh Year," *Huffington Post*, December 13, 2014, accessed January 11, 2015, http://www.huffingtonpost.com/2014/05/29/southern-baptist-convention-membership-decline_n_5411695.html.

[9]Ibid.

[10]"10 Facts about America's Churchless," Barna Group, December 10, 2014, accessed January 11, 2015, https://www.barna.org/barna-update/culture/698-10-facts-about-america-s-churchless#.VLMVY1o7b8s.

[11]Josh Packard and Ashleigh Hope, Church Refugees: Sociologists Reveals Why People are DONE with Church but Not Their Faith (Loveland, Colo.: Group Publishing, 2015).

[12]"Five Trends among the Unchurched," Barna Group, accessed January 11, 2015, https://www.barna.org/barna-update/culture/685-five-trends-among-the-unchurched#.VLMX5Vo7b8u.

[13]"More Than 100 Million Unchurched in the United States?" Leadership Network, based on Tom Clegg and Warren Bird, *Missing in America: Making an Eternal Difference in the World Next Door* (Loveland, CO: Group Publishing, 2007); and Mark Chavez, American Religion: *Contemporary Trends* (Princeton, NJ: Princeton University Press, 2011), accessed January 11, 2015, http://leadnet.org/more_than_100_million_unchurched_in_the_united_states.

[14]Ibid., Chavez, *American Religion*, 2.

[15]Ibid., 45, 55.

[16]Ibid., 47, 49.

[17]Ibid., 46, 48.

[18]Ibid., 17–24.

[19]Statistics taken from "Trends among Christians in the U.S.," *Religious Tolerance*, accessed January 11, 2015, http://www.religioustolerance.org/chr_tren.htm. Religioustolerance.org is a website of the Ontario Consultants on Religious Tolerance.

[20]Ibid.

[21]Ibid.

[22]Ibid.

[23]Ibid.

[24]Ibid.

[25]From   http://www.barna.org/FlexPage.aspx?Page=BarnaUpdate&BarnaUpdateID= 149. The Barna Group provides primary research, communications tools, printed resources, leadership development for young people, and church facilitation and enhancement.

[26]Ibid.

[27]Ibid.

[28]Ibid.

[29]Ibid.

[30]Ibid.

[31]Ibid.

[32]See http://www.barna.org/FlexPage.aspx?Page=BarnaUpdate&BarnaUpdateID=163.

[33]Ed Stetzer, "The State of the Church in America: Hint: It's Not Dying" *Christianity Today*, October, 1, 2013, www.ChristianityToday.com/edstetzer/2013/october.

[34]See http://www.barna.org/FlexPage.aspx?Page=BarnaUpdate&BarnaUpdateID=163.

[35]Ibid.

[36]"Churches in the Fall: Local Churches Get Back to Their Roots in a Rapidly Changing Millennial Culture," *Mountain Xpress*, December 24, 2014, accessed January 11, 2015, http://mountainx.com/news/churches-in-the-fall.

[37]See more at https://baptistnews.com/opinion/columns/item/29999-a-new-church-is-coming#sthash.9sw6kvhW.pdf.

[38]Ibid.

[39]Ed Stetzer, "Too Many So-Called Christians Merely Giving Lip Service to Jesus," *Charisma News*, March, 28, 2014, accessed January 12, 2015, http://www.charismanews.com/opinion/43298-christian-it-s-more-than-just-a-label.

[40]"Churches in the Fall," http://mountainx.com/news/churches-in-the-fall.

Chapter 2: Hotel or Hospital?

[1]Carey Nieuwolf, "Why We Need for Entrepreneurial Church Leaders, Not Shepherds," March, 24, 2014, accessed January 12, 2014, http://careynieuwhof.com/2014/03/why-we-need-more-entrepreneurial-church-leaders-not-more-shepherds.

[2]http://nextchurch.net/next-resources/bill-habicht-chicago-2015/#.VXSDtep_lhg

[3]Quoted in Jordan Foltz, "Churches in the Fall: Local Churches Get Back to Their Roots in a Rapidly Changing Millennial Culture http://mountainx.com/news/churches-in-the-fall.

[4]Ibid.

[5]Jolene Cassellius Erlacher, "3 Keys to Engaging Millennials on Your Ministry Team, *Ministry Matters*, September 2, 2014, accessed January 12, 2014, http://www.ministrymatters.com/all/entry/5388/3-keys-to-engaging-millennials-on-your-ministry-team.

Chapter 3: When Generations Collide

[1]George Bullard, "Are Millennials Different than Baby Boomers 40 Years Ago?," *George Bullard's Journey*, September 1, 2014, accessed January 12, 2015, http://bullardjournal.blogs.com/bullardjournal/2014/09/are-millennials-different-than-baby-boomers-40-years-ago.html#sthash.zycxlrif.dpuf.

[2]Richard Eisenberg, "A Guide to the New Retirement Communities,"Next Avenue, , April 2, 2014, accessed January 12, 2015, http://www.nextavenue.org/blog/guide-new-retirement-communities.

[3]Paul Taylor and George Gao, "Generation X: America's Neglected Middle Child," Fact Tank, June 5, 2014, accessed January 12, 2015, http://www.pewresearch.org/fact-tank/2014/06/05/generation-x-americas-neglected-middle-child.

[4]Christopher Ingraham, "Americans Lie about How Much They Go to Church, even if They Don't Belong to One," *Washington Post*, May 19, 2014, accessed January 12, 2015, http://www.washingtonpost.com/blogs/wonkblog/wp/2014/05/19/americans-lie-about-how-much-they-go-to-church-even-if-they-dont-belong-to-one. Also Josh Packard and Ashleigh Hope, Church Refugees: Sociologists Reveals Why People are DONE with Church but Not Their Faith (Loveland, Colo.: Group Publishing, 2015).

[5]Bruce Gourley, "Baptist Identity and Millennials: Re-imagining Church," June 19, 2014, accessed January 15, 2014, http://baptistnews.com/opinion/commentaries/item/28839-baptist-identity-and-millennials-re-imagining-church.

[6]Judi Slayden Hayes, "The Generations of a Postmodern World" in Chris Adams, *Women Reaching Women: Beginning and Building a Growing Women's Ministry* (Nashville: LifeWay Press, 2005), 28–47.

[7]"Fragmented Populations Require Diverse Means of Connection," June 23, 2003, from https://www.barna.org/index.php?option=com_content&view=article&id=123:fragmented-populations-require-diverse-means-of-connection&catid=5:barna-update&Itemid=134#.VZqKKUVqCag.

[8]George Barna, "Gracefully Passing the Baton," April 26, 2004, from http://fourpercent.blogspot.com/2009/12/gracefully-passing-baton-by-george.html.

[9]Ibid.

[10]Ibid.

[11]Ibid.

[12]George Bullard, "Many Congregations Are Stuck in an Overly Churched Culture," George Bullard's Journey, August 7, 2014, accessed January 12, 2014, http://bullardjournal.blogs.com/bullardjournal/2014/08/many-congregations-are-stuck-in-an-overly-churched-culture.html.

[13]Carol Howard Merritt, "What the Retirement of Baby Boomers Could Mean for the Church," *Christian Century*, May 8, 2014, accessed January 12, 2015, http://www.christiancentury.org/blogs/archive/2014-05/what-retirement-baby-boomers-could-mean-church.

[14]See Amy Hanson, "Creating a New Story for the New Old" blog, http://amyhanson.org.

[15]Vicki Brown, "Churches Need to Rethink Service Options for Retiring Baby Boomers," *Baptist Standard*, September 5, 2014, accessed January 12, 2015, https://www.baptiststandard.com/news/faith-culture/16910-churches-need-to-rethink-service-options-for-aging-boomers.

[16]Jeff Strickler, "Baby Boomers Are Flocking to Church Ministry, *Minneapolis Star Tribune*, October 4, 2013, accessed January 12, 2015, http://www.startribune.com/lifestyle/226387701.html?page=all&prepage=1&c=y#continue.

[17]Thom S. Rainer, "The Buster Generation," *Leading Adults* (Winter 2003–2004): 26–27.

[18]Ibid.

[19]Ibid.

[20]Ibid.

[21]Victoria Stunt, "Generation Y and Religion: As Church Attendance Falls, Young Believers Ponder the Future of Faith," *Huffington Post*, December 10, 2012, accessed January 12, 2015, http://www.huffingtonpost.ca/2012/12/10/generation-y-religion-canada-millennials-faith_n_2244548.html.

[22]Frank Powell, "10 Reasons Churches Are Not Reaching Millennials," Restoring Culture through Christ, June 25, 2014, accessed January 13, 2015, full text at http://frankpowell.me/ten-reasons-church-absent-millennials.

[23]Molly Worthern, "Did the Southern Baptist 'Conservative Resurgence' Fail?" The Daily Beast, June 1, 2014, http://www.thedailybeast.com/articles/2014/06/01/did-the-southern-baptist-conservative-resurgence-fail.html.

Chapter 4: Mission vs. Personal Preferences

[1]C. Peter Wagner, *The Church in the Workplace: How God's People Can Transform Society* (Ventura, CA.: Regal Books, 2006), 6.

[2]"Amazing Grace: A Church for Men," http://vimeopro.com/churchformen/church-for-men.

Chapter 5: Cultural Realities

[1]Bruce Gourley, "Baptist Identity and Millennials: Re-imagining Church," *Baptist News Global*, June 19, 2014, accessed January 13, 2015, http://baptistnews.com/opinion/commentaries/item/28839-baptist-identity-and-millennials-re-imagining-church.

[2]Ed Stetzer, "The State of the Church in America: Hint: It's Not Dying," *Christianity Today*, October 1, 2013, www.christianitytoday.com/edstetzer/2013/october/state-of-american-church.html.

[3]Ed Stetzer, "The State of the Church in America: Hint: It's Not Dying," *Christianity Today*,

October 1, 2013, www.christianitytoday.com/edstetzer/2013/october/state-of-american-church.html.

⁴Ibid.

⁵Ibid.

⁶Ed Stetzer, "Creating an Assessment Culture By Being of Berea and Issachar," *Christianity Today*, October 22, 2013, www.christianitytoday.com/edstetzer/2013/october/what-are-two-factors-that-churches-should-consider-in-creat.html.

⁷"4 Trends in Christianity That Could Scare You, According to Ed Stetzer," *Charisma News*, June 4, 2014, accessed January 13, 2015, http://www.charismanews.com/culture/44114-4-trends-in-christianity-that-could-scare-you-according-to-ed-stetzer.

⁸Thom Schultz, "The Rise of the Dones," Holy Soup, November 12, 2014, accessed January 13, 2015, http://holysoup.com/2014/11/12/the-rise-of-the-dones.

⁹See Peter Wagner's materials in *The Church in the Workplace: How God's People Can Transform Society* (Ventura, CA: Regal, 2006.)

¹⁰Barna Group, "Twentysomethings Struggle to Find Their Place in Christian Churches," September 24, 2003, accessed June 27, 2015, www.barna.org.

¹¹Ibid.

¹²Ibid.

¹³David Kinnaman, *You Lost Me* (Grand Rapids: Baker, 2011).

¹⁴Gary Kinnaman, quoted in *You Lost Me*, 232.

¹⁵Josh Gregoire, "Millennials Don't Have to Be a Lost Generation: Three Ideas," *Church Leaders*, accessed January 13, 2015, http://www.churchleaders.com/pastors/pastor-how-to/170815-josh-gregoire-millennials-don-t-have-to-be-a-lost-generation-three-ideas.html.

¹⁶The historical overview depends heavily on Dan Kimball, *The Emerging Church* (Grand Rapids: Zondervan, 2003).

¹⁷Graham Johnston, *Preaching to a Postmodern World* (Grand Rapids: Baker, 2001), 25.

¹⁸Adapted from Len Hjalmarson, "A New Way of Leading," http://www.reality.org.nz/article.php?ID=302&x=2154.

¹⁹Chris Altrock, *Preaching to Pluralists: How to Proclaim Christ in a Postmodern Age* (St. Louis: Chalice Press, 2004), 8, quoting Leonard Sweet, *Soul Tsunami* (Grand Rapids: Zondervan, 1999) and Jimmy Long, *Generating Hope* (Downers Grove, Ill.: IVP, 1997).

²⁰Altrock, *Preaching to Pluralists*, 9–10.

²¹Leonard Sweet, *Postmodern Pilgrims: First Century Passion for 21st Century World* (Nashville: Broadman & Holman, 2000).

²²Leonard Sweet with Edward Hammett, *The Gospel According to Starbucks: Living with a Grande Passion* (Colorado Springs: Waterbrook Press, 2007).

²³Patricia Corrigan, "Worship Includes 'All Ages and All Stages' at a San Mateo Church," *Faith & Leadership*, October 21, 2014, accessed January 13, 2005, http://www.faithandleadership.com/features/articles/worship-includes-all-ages-and-all-stages-san-mateo-church.

²⁴Edward Hammett, "Why Some Believers Are Leaving the Church, " The Columbia Partnership, December 10, 2013, accessed January 14, 2015, http://columbiapartnership.typepad.com/the_columbia_partnership/2013/12/why-believers-are-losing-interest-in-church.html#more.

²⁵Christopher Ingraham, "Americans Lie about How Much They Go to Church, even if They Don't Belong to One," *Washington Post*, May 19, 2014, accessed January 14, 2015, http://www.washingtonpost.com/blogs/wonkblog/wp/2014/05/19/americans-lie-about-how-much-they-go-to-church-even-if-they-dont-belong-to-one.

²⁶Perry Chang, "Best Practices for Reaching Young Adults," *Leading Ideas*, May 7, 2014, accessed January 14, 2015, http://www.churchleadership.com/leadingideas/leaddocs/2014/140507_article2.html.

²⁷Tobin Grant, "Why 1940s America Wasn't as Religious as You Think—the Rise and Fall of American Religion," Religion News Service, December 11, 2014, accessed January 14, 2015, http://tobingrant.religionnews.com/2014/12/11/1940s-america-wasnt-religious-think-rise-fall-american-religion/#sthash.IMXoQYkj.dpuf.

²⁸From http://www.americanmissionary.org.

²⁹Thom Rainer, "Eleven of the Most Common Mistakes Churches Make," Church Central, accessed January 14, 2015, http://www.churchcentral.com/blogs/eleven-of-the-most-common-mistakes-churches-make/?style=print.

[30]Eric Swanson and Rick Rusaw, *The Externally Focused Church* (Loveland,CO: Group, 2004).

[31]"50 Ways to Take Church to the Community," Lewis Center for Church Leadership, accessed January 14, 2014, http://www.churchleadership.com/50Ways/CommunityChurch.html.

Chapter 6: Creating Community

[1]Zak Cheney-Rice, "National Geographic Determined What Americans Will Look Like in 2050, and It's Beautiful, April 10, 2014, accessed June 27, 2015, http://mic.com/articles/87359/national-geographic-determined-what-americans-will-look-like-in-2050-and-it-s-beautiful

Chapter 7: Win-Win for Your Church?

[1]Patricia Corrigan, "Worship Includes 'All Ages and All States' at a San Mateo Church," *Faith & Leadership*, October 21, 2014, accessed January 14, 2015, http://www.faithandleadership.com/features/articles/worship-includes-all-ages-and-all-stages-san-mateo-church.

[2]Ronny Russell, *Can a Church Live Again? The Revitalization of a 21st-Century Church* (Macon, GA: Smith & Helwys, 2003), 44.

[3]Thom Rainer and Eric Geiger, *Simple Church: Returning to God's Process for Making Disciples* (Nashville: Broadman Press, 2006).

[4]Gene Wilkes, *Paul on Leadership: Servant Leadership in a Ministry of Transition* (Nashville: Lifeway, 2004), 43–50.

[5]Adapted from Tom McGehee, *Whoosh: Business in the Fast Lane* (New York: Perseus Books, 2001).

[6]Dave Travis, *Church Champion Update*, November 12, 2001, available through www.leadnet.org. For more research and information on multicampus churches, go to www.leadnet.org and Dave Ferguson, "The Multi-site Church: Some of the Strengths of this New Life Form," *Leadership Journal* (Spring 2003): 81–85.

[7]Carey Nieuwhof, "6 Reasons You're Losing High Capacity Volunteers, March 28, 2014, accessed January 14, 2015, http://careynieuwhof.com/2014/03/6-reasons-youre-losing-high-capacity-volunteers/?utm_content=bufferfc71d&utm_medium=social&utm_source=facebook.com&utm_campaign=buffer.

[8]For more information see Ron Martoia, *Morph: The Texture of Leadership for Tomorrow's Church* (Loveland, CO: Group, 2002) and William M. Easum, *Unfreezing Moves: Following Jesus into the Mission Field* (Nashville: Abingdon Press, 2002).

[9]Explore various models. See these websites for suggestions for models:, www.rotation.org, www.logosdor.com, www.churchcentral.com, www.companionsinchrist.org, www.ethicsdaily.com.,

[10]Loren Mead, *Financial Meltdown in the Mainline* (Bethesda, MD: Alban Institute, 1998).

[11]See www.emptytomb.org and www.barna.org for statistical data.

[12]Will McRaney, "Sharing Christ with the Confused," www.lifeway.com.

Chapter 8: Bible Study?

[1]Edward H. Hammett, *Spiritual Leadership for a Secular Age: Building Bridges instead of Barriers* (St. Louis: Lake Hickory Resources, 2005; repr., St. Louis: Chalice Press, 2006); Jane Creswell, *Christ-Centered Coaching: 7 Benefits for Ministry Leaders* (St. Louis: Lake Hickory Resources, 2006; repr., St. Louis: Chalice Press, 2007); Linda J. Miller and Chad W. Hall, *Coaching for Christian Leaders: A Practical Guide* (St. Louis: Chalice Press, 2007).

[2]Andrea Bailey, "A Pastor's Guide to Digital Outreach," *Outreach* (Jan/Feb. 2007): 101–04.

[3]Read more about the ministry to the disconnected at http://www.lifeway.com/lwc/article_main_page/0%2C1703%2CA%3D165392%26M%3D201113%2C00.html.

[4]"Discipleship for Busy Adults" is an article I wrote several years ago, which first appeared in Lifeway Press's *Leading Adults* magazine in August, 2004. You can find an expansion of it in *Spiritual Leadership in a Secular Age*.

Chapter 9: Multicultural Ministry

[1]Tom Bandy, online forum at www.easumbandy.org May 29, 2002.

Chapter 11: Celebrating Church for a Diverse World

[1]Coaching and consulting services can be obtained by contacting www.thecolumbiapartnership. org or www.transformingsolutions.org.

[2]Jordan Foltz, "Churches in the Fall: Local Churches Get Back to Their Roots in a Rapidly Changing Millennial Culture," *Mountain Xpress*, December 24, 2014, accessed January 15, 2015, http://mountainx.com/news/churches-in-the-fall.

[3]Ibid.

[4]Eric Swanson, "Ten Paradigm Shifts Toward Community Transformation," www. intheworkplace.com/articles_view.asp?articleid=12856&columnid=1935.

[5]Gene Getz, *Sharpening the Focus of the Church* (Wheaton, IL: Victor Books, 1984), 33–36.

[6]Statistics obtained at americanmissionary.org in 2004 (now infaith.org).

Bibliography and Online Resources

Books

Bahme, Eric. The MBE (Mission-Based Entrepreneur Revolution): *Developing Economic Engines That Drive Mission-Based Movements*. Portland, OR: Kingdom Point, 2009.

Bandy, Thomas G. *Coaching Change: Breaking Down Resistance, Building Up Hope*. Nashville: Abingdon Press, 2000.

Barna, George. *Rechurching the Unchurched*. Ventura, CA: Barna Research Group, 2000.

Barton, Ruth Haley. *Pursuing God's Will Together: A Discernment Practice for Leadership Groups*. Downers Grove, IL, IVP, 2012.

Bullard, George. *Pursuing the Full Kingdom Potential of Your Congregation*. St. Louis: Lake Hickory Resources, 2006.

Chands, Samuel R., and Cecil B. Murphy. *Futuring: Leading Your Church into Tomorrow*. Grand Rapids: Baker Books, 2002.

Chevez, Mark. *American Religion: Contemporary Trends*. Princeton, NJ: Princeton Press, 2011.

Cloud, Henry. *Necessary Endings: The Employees, Businesses, and Relationships That All of Us Have to Give Up in Order to Move Forward*. New York: Harper Collins, 2010.

DeYamaz, Mark and Harry Li. *Leading a Healthy Multi-ethnic Church*. Grand Rapids: Zondervan, 2013

Everts, Don. *Jesus with Dirty Feet: A Down-to-Earth Look at Christianity*. Downers Grove, IL: InterVarsity Press, 2003.

Garrison, David. Truth, *Understanding, Purpose & Five Living Generations*. New York: Dog Fish Jones, 2013.

Gibbs, Eddie, and Ryan Bolger. *Emerging Churches: Creating Christian Community in Post Modern Cultures*. Grand Rapids: Baker Books, 2006.

Goleman, Daniel. *Focus: The Hidden Driver of Excellence*. New York: Harper Collins, 2013.

Green, Michael. *Sharing Your Faith with Friends and Family: Talking about Jesus without Offending*. Grand Rapids: Baker Books, 2005.

Griffiths, Michael C. *Encouraging New Christians*. Downers Grove, IL: InterVarsity Press, 1964.

Hammett, Edward H. *The Gathered and the Scattered Church*. Macon, GA: Smyth & Helwys, 2d ed., 2005.

_____. *Making the Church Work*. Macon, Ga.: Smyth & Helwys, 2000.

_____. *Recovering Hope for Your Church: Moving Beyond Maintenance & Missional to Incarnational Engagement*. TCP Leadership Series. St. Louis: Chalice, 2014.

_____. *Reframing Spiritual Formation: Discipleship in an Unchurched Culture*. Macon, Ga.: Smyth & Helwys, 2002.

_____. *Spiritual Leadership in a Secular Age: Building Bridges instead of Barriers*. St. Louis: Lake Hickory Resources, 2005.

Hunter, George. *Celtic Evangelism*. Nashville: Abingdon Press, 2002.

_____. *Church for the Unchurched*. Nashville: Abingdon Press, 2000.

_____. *Should We Change Our Game Plan*. Nashville: Abingdon Press, 2013.

Jakes, T. D. Instinct: *The Power to Unleash Your Unborn Drive*. Nashville: Faith Words, 2014.

McIntosh, Gary L. *Being Church in a Multi-ethnic Community*. Indianapolis: Weslyan Publishing House, 2013.

_____. *One Church, Four Generations: Understanding and Reaching All Ages in Your Church*. Grand Rapids: Baker Books, 2002.

_____. *Staffing Your Church for Growth*. Grand Rapids: Baker Books, 2001.

McLaren, Brian. *Finding Faith*. Grand Rapids: Zondervan, 2002.

Mead, Loren B. *Financial Meltdown in the Mainline?* New York: Alban Institute, 1998.

Merritt, Carol Howard. *Tribal Church: Ministering to the Missing Generation*. Durham, NC: Alban Institute, 2007.

Moore, Frank. *Coffee Shop Theology*. Boston: Beacon Press, 1999.

Powers, John. *The BodyLife Journey*. Nashville: LifeWay, 2001.

_____. *Redefining Church Membership*. Nashville: LifeWay Press, 2001.

Rainer, Thom. *Surprising Insights from the Unchurched*. Grand Rapids: Zondervan, 2001.

_____. *The Unchurched Next Door: Understanding Faith Stages as Keys to Sharing Your Faith*. Grand Rapids: Zondervan, 2003.

Regele, Mike, and Mark Schulz. *Death of the Church*. Grand Rapids: Zondervan, 1996.

Richardson, Rick. *Circles of Belonging*. Downers Grove, IL: InterVarsity Press, 1999.

_____. *Evangelism Outside the Box*. Downers Grove, IL: InterVarsity Press, 2001.

Rusaw, Rick, and Eric Swanson. *The Externally Focused Church*. Loveland, CO: Group, 2004.

Sanders, Alvin. *Bridging the Diversity Gap: Leading Toward God's Multi-Ethnic Kingdom*. Indianapolis: Wesleyan Publishing, 2013.

Schultz, Thom. *Why Nobody Wants to Go to Church Anymore*. Loveland, CO: Group Publishing, 2013.

Shaw, Hayden. *Sticking Points: How to Get Four Generations Working Together in the 12 Places They Come Apart*. New York: Tyndale House, 2013.

Smith, Efrin. *The Post-Black and Post-White Church: Becoming a Loving Community in a Multi-Ethnic World*. Dallas: Leadership Network, 2012.

Southerland, Dan. *Transitioning*. Grand Rapids: Zondervan, 2002.

Stiller, Brian C. *Preaching Parables to Postmoderns*. Minneapolis: Augsburg, 2005.

Strauss, William, and Neil Howe. *Generations: The History of America's Future, 1584 to 2069.* New York: William Morrow, 1991.

Sweet, Leonard. *Post-Modern Pilgrims: First-Century Passion for the 21st-Century Church.* Nashville: Broadman & Holman, 2000.

_____. *The Three Hardest Words in the World to Get Right.* Colorado Springs: Waterbrook Press, 2006.

Sweet, Leonard. *The Gospel According to Starbucks: Living with a Grande Passion. With Questions for Coaching and Conversation* by Edward Hammett. Colorado Springs: Waterbrook Press, 2007.

Taylor, Paul. *The Next America: Boomers , Millennials and the Looming Generational Showdown.* New York: Public Affairs, 2014.

White, James Emery. *Embracing the Mysterious God.* Downers Grove, IL: InterVarsity Press, 2003

_____. *A Search for the Spiritual: Exploring Real Christianity.* Grand Rapids, Mich.: Baker Books, 1998.

Periodicals and Online

Foltz, Jordan. "Churches in the Fall." *Mountain Xpress*, AshevilleNC, December 24–30, 2014, 8–14, www.mountainx.com.

Hsu, Albert. "Suburban Spirituality." *Christianity Today* July 2003: 30–34.

NetResults Magazine. Published by Tom Bandy and Bill Easum.

Rainer, Thom S. "The Builder Generation." *Leading Adults,* Summer 2004: 26–27.

Online Resources

www.easumbandy.com (Resources from Bill Easum, Tom Bandy, and others.)

Rainer, Thom R. "The Bridger Generation, the Family, and the Church." http://www.rainergroup.com/rainergroup/bridger_generation.asp

www.broadwaychurchchicago.org

www.bullardjournal.org. (Great articles, book reviews from business and church world, online coaching and leadership training)

www.christianethicstoday.com

www.churchstaffing.org

www.21stcenturystrategies.com

www.fellowshiponline.org (church in Little Rock, Arkansas)

www.pghopendoor.org

www.hopechurchalive.org

www.wooddale.org

www.reallifeministries.com

www.pghopendoor.org (church in Pittsburgh)

www.hopecommunitychurchtr.org (church in Manitowoc, Wisconsin)

www.wooddale.org (church in Eden Prairie, Minnesota)

www.reallifeministries.com (church in Post Falls, Idaho)

www.missionalusa.com

www.leadnet.org

www.master-planning.com (Bobb Biehl's life planning, strategy planning, and team building resources)

www.netresults.org (Tom Bandy and Bill Easum's website/journal)

www.enewhope.org (New Hope Fellowship in Hawaii—team-based philosophy)

www.perimeter.org (church in Atlanta)

www.preachhim.org/BAPTIZE.htm (To Baptize or Not Baptize?)

www.religioustolerance.org/chr_divi2.htm

www.loveoutloudws.com

www.thecolumbiapartnership.org (Coaching and consulting services)

www.transformingsolutions.org